To,

Michael & Carol,

In appreciation.
Hope you'll be able to see these places in real life soon!

With best regards,
Hock Seng & Wendy.

1993.

Wild Places of Australia

*View through Ellery Gorge,
Ellery Creek Park, Northern
Territory*

WILD PLACES OF AUSTRALIA

LEE PEARCE
Special Photography

LAWRENCE DURRANT AND VALERIE PARV
Descriptive Text and Directory

BAY BOOKS   SYDNEY   LONDON

Text © Bay Books
Photographs © Lee Pearce, Wild Images of Australia
Published by Bay Books
Suite 501, Henry Lawson Business Centre,
Birkenhead Point, Drummoyne NSW 2047
Reprinted 1991
National Library of Australia
Card No and ISBN 0 85835 539 6
Printed in Hong Kong
by Toppan Printing Company

PHOTOGRAPHIC CONTRIBUTIONS

Bay Picture Library
Hanlon, T.M.S: page 159
National Parks Authority of Western Australia: pages 58, 59, 117, 148 (Photo by A. Start)
National Parks Service, Victoria: pages 105, 106, 143
Queensland National Parks and Wildlife Service: page 133
National Parks and Wildlife Service Staff, Hunter District, New South Wales: pages 71, 92

CONTENTS

PREFACE

This book consists of two parts: a descriptive text and a directory.

The first part of the book describes Australian national parks according to types of environment. This means you can turn directly to a section which provides information about the kind of terrain which appeals to you and which offers parks with opportunities for your preferred recreational activities.

In each of the first three chapters of this section, the descriptions of national parks are arranged in a sequence which starts with those in the Cape York region and progresses clockwise around the country.

The chapter entitled 'The Outback' describes those parks in hard-to-reach places, mostly in the dry inland (though some touch the coast), where you can still find the traditional Australia of the pioneer squatters, the historical Australia of the explorers, and the pre-historical Australia of the Aborigines.

The Centre is given a chapter to itself, this being a part of our country with a special character, distant from the places where most of us live, and yet no longer, in these days of the package tour, off the beaten track.

The second part of the book is a directory of the national parks of Australia, arranged according to state. It gives detailed information about each park — where it is, how to get there, and what you can see once you are there.

Exclusions

Although national parks administrations in all Australian states have agreed on a common definition (on paper, at least) of what a national park is, interpretations vary in practice. Legislation which more precisely defines these publicly owned lands differs from state to state. To confuse matters further, each state has reserves in various other categories. What could be classed as a national park in one state may be called a nature reserve or a conservation park (or something else — there are twenty-three different possibilities) in another state. As a rule, we have included every area in Australia designated 'national park'. Other areas have also been included, where warranted for reasons such as size, conservation value or uniqueness. In some cases these areas are quite small, such as Mon Repos, but size alone is not an indication of an area's value. Except in a very few special cases, all state parks, state reserves, recreation areas, game reserves, historical sites and Aboriginal sites have been excluded.

Nambung National Park,
Western Australia

INTRODUCTION

When Judge Cornelius Hedges of Montana suggested in 1870, that a scenically splendid region of the Rocky Mountains in northwest Wyoming should be 'set apart as a great national park', he coined a phrase — and initiated a concept — which has since been adopted by the whole world. The portion of country he referred to became the Yellowstone National Park in 1872. This was the world's first national park.

The new phrase was imported into Australia in 1879, when the colonial government of New South Wales declared an area of 18 000 acres (7290 hectares) beside Port Hacking, near Sydney, to be 'The National Park'. This was the world's second national park. (It later became the Royal National Park.)

It is questionable whether the Australian politicians had precisely the same concept in mind as had Judge Hedges. In a memorable statement to the United States Congress, the good Judge had expounded his view of what a national park should be. 'This great wilderness does not belong to us,' he said. 'It belongs to the nation.' And he went on to urge that the tract of land he was talking about should be set aside as a public park '. . . never to be changed but to be kept sacred always.'

The National Park at Port Hacking, just beyond the southern suburbs of Sydney, had a very different character and would offer different attractions from the remote and rugged Wyoming park's. The Australian administrators saw their park as a conveniently located recreation ground for the people of the expanding city. Another of its purposes, it appears, was to assist the newly formed New South Wales Zoological Society in its plans to introduce animals from overseas — as game and for their scientific and aesthetic interest — in a process then much advocated by the educated and the wealthy, known as 'acclimatisation'.

Seven years after its creation, Australia's first national park got its own railway station. By that time it already had a network of roads, a causeway across the river, a boathouse, stables, a smithy, an orchard and a deerpark. The trustees were empowered to set aside portions of the park as ornamental gardens and lawns, as racecourses, cricket grounds or bathing places, or for 'the exercise or encampment of naval and military forces'. Clearly, this was something very different from Cornelius Hedges' notion of a place 'never to be changed but to be kept sacred always'.

This difference in attitudes about just what purpose national parks should serve has persisted to the present day — if not throughout the world then certainly here in Australia. The two conflicting (or, at least, divergent) attitudes may be represented as the conservationist and the recreational viewpoints. The basic question is: should a national park be an area of absolute wilderness or may it be modified to meet human recreational needs? Assent to the latter half of the question raises two further questions: what forms of recreation are permissible and what kind of degree of modification are acceptable?

As readers of this book will quickly discover, national parks authorities in all Australian states are still wrestling with these unresolved questions. The parks and reserves reviewed in the following pages represent a variety of answers to the century-old quandary, ranging from remote desert areas lacking even an access road, to parks which contain extensive tourist resort development with accommodation buildings, shops and, in one case, a cinema. This variety is indeed a significant feature of our present-day national parks scene, and it may astound you. Our country, you will be bound to agree, has national parks to satisfy the most diverse tastes.

Despite many conflicts and difficulties, the cause which a century ago sprang

The Breadknife, a large volcanic core from an ancient volcano in the Warrumbungle National Park, central New South Wales (Lee Pearce)

9

from one American citizen's concern to preserve a particular tract of country in its pristine state, has made enormous advances. It has grown into a worldwide movement. Few countries remain without their own systems of national parks.

In this country, after a long period of painfully slow, spasmodic progress, the national parks movement has at last, in very recent years, gained popular acceptance and a firm place among the community's institutions. Right up to the 1960s, the effort to arouse public and government awareness of the need for national parks was maintained by a forward-looking minority in each state. These zealous idealists were responsible for saving many areas now prized as essential parts of the national estate from the grasp of those who would have put the land to more 'productive' uses.

Not until 1967 was an Act passed by an Australian state legislature establishing a National Parks and Wildlife Service. New South Wales led the field. By 1977, every state had set up its own authority to administer national parks, as also had the Northern Territory and the Commonwealth.

Naturally enough, this radical change in the status of national parks and their administration, occurring at a time of burgeoning community consciousness of conservation issues, has stirred public interest in the parks themselves to an unprecedented degree. Greater numbers of people than ever before are now visiting national parks. The increase in the area of land given over to national parks has been explosive in recent times. For example, in the last decade of the hundred years since declaration of that first national park near Sydney, the total area devoted to national parks in New South Wales more than doubled, increasing from 820 000 hectares in March 1969 to 1 906 000 hectares in March 1979.

The directory at the back of this book lists almost three hundred Australian national parks. No doubt, by the time you find yourself reading these words, the number will have risen even further and numerous changes will have occurred to outdate our text in other particulars. Developments are moving too fast in this field for it to be otherwise.

This is as it should be. We Australians have almost left it too late. You might imagine that Australia, of all countries, must have huge areas of open space still untainted by the influence of modern man. (Is ours not the emptiest continent after Antarctica?) The truth is that only a few pockets of this vast land of ours have remained untouched by the effects of European occupation. In just 200 years, through a vigorous program of tree-felling, hunting, pastoralism, agriculture, urbanisation and pollution, we Australians have succeeded in changing the face of the whole country and exterminating a number of species of its endemic fauna. We have also introduced other species (rabbits, pigs, goats and water buffaloes are some of the more obvious examples) which have proliferated to become pests, competing with indigenous species for food resources and causing havoc to the environment.

Belatedly we are trying to make amends. National parks will not restore the country to its former condition. Nothing can do that. But they, together with the other categories of reserves set aside for conservation purposes, give us a fighting chance of preserving what is left of our natural heritage.

Does it matter? Opinions inevitably differ on this fundamental question. Your answer depends upon your feeling about man's place in the natural order. In these closing years of the twentieth century, however, it is no longer fashionable to start from the assumption that man is the Lord of Creation, with an unquestionable right to plunder the resources of the world for his own comfort or profit without concern for other species or for future generations. Led by the ecologists, popular thinking seems to be swinging round to the view that man is simply part of a total system of interdependent life forms. Interestingly, ecology, the branch of biology which deals with the interrelationships between organisms and their environment, made its appearance about the same time as the emergence of the national parks movement.

For most of us, the philosophy behind national parks is of only passing interest, something we have little time to dwell upon. What is important is the opportunity the parks give us for getting out there where the air is fresh and the countryside is untrammelled. Our need for recreation — re-creating ourselves — draws us to

Spectacular sunset over Ayers Rock, Uluru National Park, Northern Territory (Lee Pearce)

national parks. They are places where we can temporarily escape from the hassles of our daily lives, from our largely man-made environments, into a natural environment where we rediscover our sense of oneness with the real world and of wonder at its marvels. We thus restore our humanity and revive our too much neglected relationship with our planet, earth, and with the other living things that share it with us.

Judge Cornelius Hedges spoke of wilderness as something sacred, something worth preserving. Only a few years earlier, Sir William Denison, Governor of New South Wales, had used the word differently when he wrote: 'Of this great continent, more than three-fourths is absolute howling wilderness.' European Australians carried this attitude towards the natural Australian environment — that it was hostile and must be tamed before they could live comfortably with it — right into the twentieth century.

We feel differently about wilderness now. Suddenly, what was formerly feared is valued. Now that man has almost eliminated wilderness from his world, he realises his need of it. As his technology, with all its unanticipated side-effects, becomes ever more pervasive and threatening, those shrinking areas of our world that retain their primeval character become ever more precious.

The national parks of Australia represent an attempt to hold on to the last vestiges of our vanishing wilderness, so that we, and generations of Australians yet unborn, may have the chance to see it, smell it, touch it, take a walk in it. The wilderness, we are learning, is not a place of desolation but a living community to which we are related. Here, thousands of species have their natural and rightful dwelling places. They are our fellow passengers on this planet, travelling with us through space and time. Many of them are unique to our corner of the planet. And it falls to us to serve as their protectors.

The wilderness is our common inheritance from the past. We must strive to preserve it so that it may be passed on undiminished to those who will come after us. Meanwhile, we may enjoy its beauty, its immense variety, its fascination, its power to teach and its power to soothe. But we should never lose sight of how fragile it is. The wilderness will disappear under our feet unless we remember that it can survive only if it remains a place where man himself is just a well-mannered visitor. Keep this in mind when you visit a national park. Try to be a good conservator. Leave nothing but footprints; take nothing but photographs — and memories.

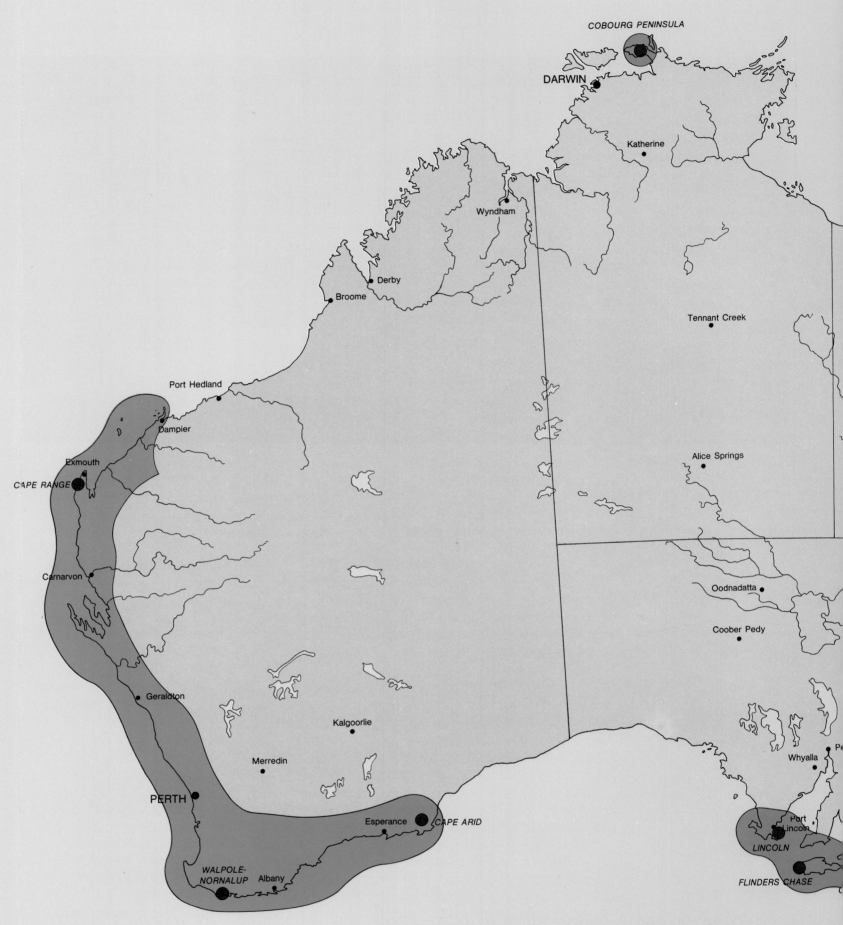

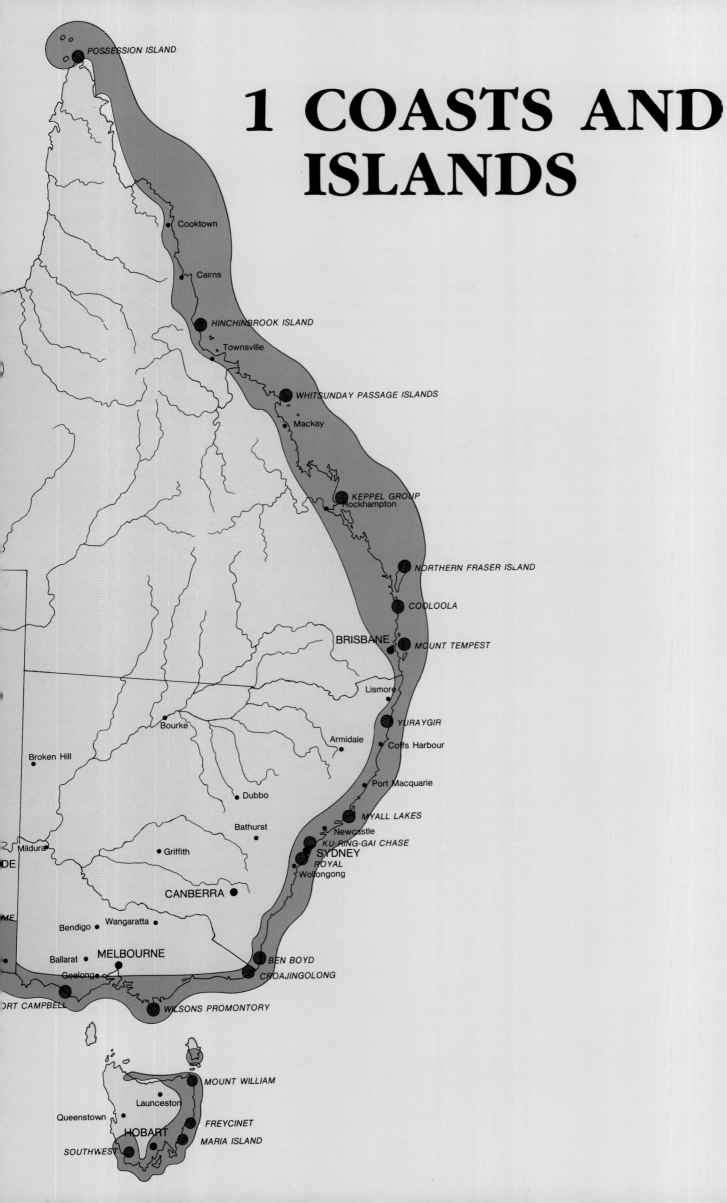

1 COASTS AND ISLANDS

POSSESSION ISLAND

Cooktown

Cairns

HINCHINBROOK ISLAND

Townsville

WHITSUNDAY PASSAGE ISLANDS

Mackay

KEPPEL GROUP

Rockhampton

NORTHERN FRASER ISLAND

COOLOOLA

BRISBANE

MOUNT TEMPEST

Lismore

YURAYGIR

Armidale

Coffs Harbour

Bourke

Port Macquarie

Dubbo

MYALL LAKES

Broken Hill

Bathurst

Newcastle

KU-RING-GAI CHASE

SYDNEY

Griffith

ROYAL

Wollongong

Mildura

CANBERRA

Bendigo   Wangaratta

Ballarat

MELBOURNE

BEN BOYD

Geelong

CROAJINGOLONG

PORT CAMPBELL

WILSONS PROMONTORY

MOUNT WILLIAM

Launceston

Queenstown

FREYCINET

HOBART

MARIA ISLAND

SOUTHWEST

Australia has a coastline more than 20 000 kilometres long — which happens to be equivalent to almost half the circumference of the Earth. The locations of Australia's coastal national parks, distributed around this long continental perimeter, range through thirty-three degrees of latitude, from the tropics to the cold Southern Ocean, and forty degrees of longitude, from the eastern edge of the Indian Ocean to the Western Pacific. This geographical range is reflected in the wide diversity of scenery and of natural habitats to be found in the very large number of coastal parks.

QUEENSLAND — INCLUDING THE GREAT BARRIER REEF

Northern Queensland's major coastal feature, the Great Barrier Reef, extends 2000 kilometres from Torres Strait to the Tropic of Capricorn. Although not a continuous single reef but, rather, a complex system comprising thousands of separate reefs and hundreds of coral islands, or cays, this is nevertheless the world's largest coral reef system.

A coral reef consists of a mound of the limestone skeletons of coral polyps, which may have accumulated over thousands or even millions of years, topped by a veneer of living coral. Most corals live in colonies. Each polyp individually secretes a cup-shaped external limestone skeleton for protection. All the polyps in a colony are connected together by extensions of their body tissues outside the skeleton. As successive generations die, the limestone consolidates into the structure we call a coral reef.

Each clump of living coral is made up of thousands of individuals joined together in this way. Within a small area, you may find hundreds of different species forming colonies which differ in shape and colour. The colours are in the living tissues of the polyps, as well as in countless numbers of the single-celled marine plants called algae, which live within the corals. Some of the formations most often seen are given such popular descriptive names as staghorns, brain corals, table corals and boulder corals. The varied shapes and colours create the garden-like beauty that attracts legions of visitors year after year to North Queensland islands.

The reef has been built along the edge of the continental shelf. Corals require very specific environmental conditions. Generally, water temperature must be in the 20° C to 30° C range and water must be shallow, admitting sunlight. Most colonies are formed between mid-tide levels and down to depths of about fifty metres. The surface of a living reef is never above high-tide level, for the polyps would not survive long exposure to air.

These shallow tropical waters also suit a wide range of other sea creatures. The vast lagoon enclosed by the outer reef teems with marine life, most of it as colourful as the coral. Of the estimated 2000 species of fish found here many are magnificently arrayed, such as the harlequin tusk fish, with its stripes of brilliant red, green, pale blue and black. Some, like the moorish idol, are popular aquarium fish. Giant clams as big as one metre across are quite common. Various univalve molluscs live in the sandy seabed, including cowries and helmet shells, and many more. The beautifully tinted, shell-less nudibranches (sea-slugs) also inhabit these waters.

There are two distinctly different kinds of islands inside the reef: continental islands and coral cays. Those immediately fringing the mainland shore are continental islands — the summits of submerged mountains isolated from the mainland thousands of years ago by a rise in sea-level. Most consist of steep-sided peaks. Some have high, craggy cliffs. They are of the same substance as the adjacent mainland and usually carry similar vegetation, some having populations of mammals such as possums, dingoes and fruit bats. Many offer good anchorages in secluded bays with sandy beaches, whilst elsewhere there may be tidal flats with mangrove communities. A number possess fringing coral reefs.

Coral cays, by contrast, are invariably flat and low-lying. Each was formed by an accumulation of sand and reef debris, brought by winds and tides, atop a platform reef. Grasses and trees have grown from wind-blown or bird-borne seeds. Bird droppings and rotting vegetation have provided nourishment, enriching the sandy ground, and the cover of vegetation, in turn, has protected such islands from wind and tide erosion. The larger cays are ringed by beaches of white coral sand. Behind this grows a belt of shrubs, usually including casuarinas, pandanus and tournefortia. The interior is often thickly forested, the types of trees varying throughout the region.

This region has a varied and fascinating wildlife, outside the water as well as in it. Turtles are numerous. The dugong or sea cow — the docile grey mammal thought to have given rise to the myth of the mermaid — is also to be seen in these waters, though it is much less common than formerly. Most in evidence most of the time are the birds. Many different species of seabirds nest on the islands. The greater frigate bird, famous for the huge, bright-red throat pouch which the male inflates like a balloon, in display, breeds on northern barrier reef islands. A sharp-eyed observer may also recognise the red-tailed tropic bird. Of the several pigeon species to be seen, the sleek white Torres Strait pigeon, with dark grey tail, is perhaps the one most closely associated with this region.

All Queensland's coastal islands are wildlife sanctuaries. Many of them, individually or in groups, have been declared national parks, making a list of some forty separate parks. They include both coral cays and continental islands. And they range from well-known tourist resorts to uninhabited islets accessible only to those with their own yachts. Camping is permitted on several but campers are advised to take their own fresh water. Any further tourist development on the islands must await new solutions to the problems of providing a water supply and disposing of sewage and wastes.

Beautiful coral formations in the waters around Lizard Island, North Queensland (Lee Pearce)

*(Opposite page) Butterfly cod
Butterfly fish among the coral*

Our most northerly national park is tiny Possession Island (not in fact part of the Barrier Reef system), which lies close to the northwest corner of Cape York Peninsula. Consisting of a low ridge thinly covered with scrubby vegetation, it is fringed by sandflats and mangroves. Gold-miners visited the island around the end of the nineteenth century. Otherwise it has attracted little attention since Lieutenant James Cook landed here in 1770 to hoist the English flag and formally lay claim to the whole of the east coast of Australia on behalf of his king. Possession Island has little to merit attention other than its association with our national history.

The east coast of Cape York Peninsula has long stretches of white sand beaches, in many places backed by extensive dune systems. Swampy hollows between dunes support a mixed low coastal scrub ('wallum' scrub) made up largely of banksia, grevillea and melaleuca species. Some inter-tidal areas support mangroves. Where mountain slopes rise close to the shore, and on many of the hilly islands, there are areas of dense tropical rainforest.

Granite or sandstone headlands shelter many bays from the southeast trade winds, which blow off the Coral Sea from May to September. That is the dry season, the best time to visit this part of the country. In the wet summer season, cyclones often bring violent storms, rivers flood the plains, and roads become impassable. During the months of the Dry, however, the weather is generally warm and sunny. The shallow lagoon waters gently lap against the white beaches, the ocean swell having spent its force against the outer reef, creating ideal conditions for the enjoyment of all the pleasures of this popular holiday province.

On the mainland, the rainforests provide a rich habitat for flora and fauna,

*The clear waters of Sandy Bay,
Lizard Island* (Lee Pearce)

supporting a multitude of life forms. The largest creature of these mainland rainforests (described more fully in Chapter 2, Highlands and Forests) is the cassowary. On the forest fringes you may also encounter the scrub fowl or the larger and more colourful brush turkey; both are mound builders. Agile (or sandy) wallabies are the marsupials most often seen, though several types of kangaroos occur throughout the region. The small, shy, reddish-brown creature that hops swiftly away into the scrub as you approach is probably a pademelon.

The most northerly national park embracing a segment of the mainland coast is Jardine River National Park. This is described in Chapter 3, The Outback.

Cape Melville

At Bathurst Bay, reached by boat, a long sweep of sandy beach is backed by low melaleuca and eucalypt woodland, with patches of swamp, palms and coastal heath. Behind rises the minor tableland of the Melville Range, mostly bare granite, covered in jumbled boulders, with some vine scrub. Much of this remarkable coastal scenery is enclosed within the Cape Melville National Park, which also includes the five rugged islands of the Flinders Group, with their high cliffs, eucalypt forests and mangrove forests. Some of the islands have small galleries of Aboriginal rock art.

Lizard Island

Lizard Island, northeast of Cape Flattery, is a granite island surrounded by coral reefs. It is also a national park. Although relatively small, this island has varied habitats: grassland, swamp, rainforest, heath, mangroves and open forest. Cook came ashore here in 1770 and climbed to the island's highest point (360 metres above sea-level, now known as Cook's Look) to search the horizon for a way through the coral barrier to the open sea. The island's name was inspired by the profusion of lizards seen by Cook and his party. The lizards, including sand goannas which grow to one and a half metres, still live here, together with flying foxes (fruit bats), olive-backed sunbirds, ospreys, and many seabirds.

A tourist resort on Lizard Island offers accommodation and facilities for water-skiing, snorkelling and inspecting the coral reefs. Camping is permitted. Boating trips to uninhabited islands nearby extend the attractions of a holiday here, providing opportunities for looking at more coral formations and for observing turtles, reef herons, Torres Strait pigeons, pelicans and colonies of seabirds such as white-capped noddies and wedge-tailed shearwaters.

Cedar Bay

Small parks along the North Queensland coast include one at the mouth of the Endeavour River, near Cooktown (where Cook careened his ship, *Endeavour*, in 1770 after being grounded on a coral reef), and a portion of the mountainous, densely vegetated country south of Cooktown, at Cedar Bay. A number of the smaller islands in the area also have national park status.

Green Island

Green Island, a large coral cay close to Cairns, has a long-established tourist resort. The rest of the island and the whole of the surrounding reef are a national park. The island is flat and barely above high tide level. But it has beautiful white beaches, dense rainforest and stands of other vegetation types, with an abundant bird life. The crown-of-thorns starfish, which feeds upon coral polyps, has had a severe effect upon the coral growth here in recent years.

Dunk Island

Numerous small islands and strips of coast between Cairns and Ingham form national parks. Of these, Dunk Island is perhaps the most renowned for its tourist resort. Dunk has an interesting history, a rugged terrain and a network of walking tracks leading through rainforest to a high central ridge. Camping is permitted.

Hinchinbrook Island

North Queensland's biggest island is Hinchinbrook Island. Essentially a high ridge of granite with several mountain peaks, it is separated from the mainland by a maze of narrow winding channels which cut through a forest of mangroves. Hinchinbrook remains largely untouched by civilisation, too rugged to have been tamed. Its thickly forested peaks rise to more than 1000 metres. Together with the channel and a segment of mainland coast beside the southern half of the island, it forms the largest national park within the Barrier Reef.

This is a park for those who seek the solitude of wild places. A small tourist resort has been developed at the northern end of the island. A camping area, with tank water, is also located at this end but well away from the tourist resort. The interior

Green turtle on the sands of Heron Island

of the island remains a wilderness, the vegetation consisting predominantly of eucalypts, with tropical rainforest in the south and west. The fascinating world of the mangroves may be explored by boat or by using a boardwalk constructed to facilitate scientific observation. Three short walking tracks lead to ocean beaches.

Magnetic Island	Magnetic Island, a short ferry trip from Townsville, has a permanent population, hotels and several tourist resorts in the pretty bays along its coast. The greater part of this rugged island is, however, national park. If your taste in holidays is to divide your time between lazing on a beach and hiking strenuously through rocky hills, returning each evening to hotel-style comfort and a three-course dinner, Magnetic Island could be just the right place. You will find suburban gardens resplendent with showy bougainvillea. In the hills, the bare branches of the kapok trees flourish their big, bright yellow flowers. You can watch the rock wallabies — mysteriously invisible during the day — hopping past the windows of your dining room after dark. You can take a walk along the coast, pausing to swim at several beaches, and catch a bus back to your holiday home. You may hire a small car or a bicycle. You may explore offshore reefs with your snorkel and goggles, or explore right around the island by boat.
Cape Cleveland *Cape Upstart*	Cape Cleveland, just south of Townsville, is a granite outcrop. The Cape Cleveland National Park has mangrove forests, salt pans and marine plains, with many creeks and swamps which attract water birds. Cape Upstart National Park, a little further south and across Upstart Bay from the great Burdekin River delta, is yet another granite outcrop. Best reached by boat, its beaches and rocks are popular fishing locations.
Whitsunday Passage	The Whitsunday Passage, near Proserpine, is surely one of the most beautiful places in Australia for a holiday on water. Fifty-five islands of the Whitsunday Group are wholly or largely dedicated as national parks. Many have fringing coral reefs. They range in size from the large and mountainous Whitsunday and Hook Islands to tiny rock islets. The larger islands consist of green jungle-covered peaks, their slopes cut by gorges, with white beaches where they meet the sea. Seen from the mainland, they spread across the whole horizon. Hayman Island, at the northern end of Whitsunday Passage, is a well-known tourist resort but is not a national park. Lindeman and Long Islands, both in the Whitsunday Group, combine holiday resorts with national parks. These islands are some distance from the Barrier Reef, but it is possible to take a trip in a seaplane to the outer reef and there transfer to a glass-bottomed boat. Or you may visit a specially constructed underwater observatory on Hook Island.
Conway Range	On the mainland side of the Whitsunday Passage, the steep slopes of the Conway Range plunge into the water like a reflection of the island peaks to the east. This coastal range is also a national park, incorporating Cape Conway, which separates Whitsunday Passage from Repulse Bay. It is forested country, undeveloped except where the road to Shute Harbour passes through its northern end. Here there are camping and picnic facilities and some walking tracks. Shute Harbour is the departure point for launches servicing the islands.
Brampton Island *Newry Group*	Reaching southward from Cape Conway are more chains of islands, the largest of which form the Cumberland Group. Best known of these is Brampton Island, which offers tourist accommodation. Constructed walking tracks lead through woods of stunted brush box (*Tristania conferta*) to casuarina-fringed beaches. The nearest mainland centre for launch or aircraft transport is Mackay. The islands of the Newry Group, closer inshore, have eucalypt forests and some good sandy beaches. Camping is permitted on Rabbit Island.
Guardfish Cluster	Most of the dozens of islands within easy reach, by boat, of Mackay are rocky and offer poor anchorages. Curlew, largest island of the Guardfish Cluster, eighty kilometres to the southeast of the port, has especially fine beaches.
Cape Hillsborough *Cape Palmerston* *West Hill Island* *Crested terns in flight*	To the north of Mackay, Cape Hillsborough National Park, together with nearby Wedge Island, contains mangroves, eucalypt forest and hoop pine rainforest, with a rocky and sandy shoreline. There are picnic facilities in the park, and caravan and tent camping sites close by. South of Sarina, the larger Cape Palmerston National Park has a long sandy beach, a large area of mangrove forest and melaleuca scrub. The ground rises rapidly inland, eucalypts covering the mountain slopes, with

23

patches of palm forest. From the heights of Mount Funnel, you look down upon a sea jewelled with islands. A little further south is another small national park, embracing West Hill Island and a portion of coast. To reach this retreat you must go by boat, or walk from Carmila.

Keppel Group

Eleven islands of the Keppel Group, off Yeppoon, are reserved as national parks. These are small continental islands whose chief attraction is simply as landing places when boating.

Capricorn Group
Bunker Group

At its southern extremity, the Great Barrier Reef curves shoreward in the shape of the tail of a question mark, pointing towards Sandy Cape, the northern tip of Fraser Island. As the scatter of islands crosses the Tropic of Capricorn they become the Capricorn Group, with the Bunker Group to the south. All these are coral islands. In the Capricorn Group, the greater part of Heron Island is a national park, as are the three islands of the Bunker Group.

Heron is a flat coral cay, densely forested with pisonias, with a skirt of pandanus and casuarinas close to the beaches. Hundreds of female green turtles visit these beaches each September to deposit their eggs in the sand. After laying the eggs, usually at night, the turtles cover them over and return to the sea. Like the white-capped noddies which nest between August and January in the pisonia trees, they are apparently undisturbed by the presence of humans. Wedge-tailed shearwaters (alternatively known as little muttonbirds or wedge-tailed petrels) also nest on this island, in burrows or simply under the vegetation canopy

Small though it is, Heron Island is an invaluable national park, providing a wonderful opportunity for human visitors to observe the reef wildlife at close quarters. The University of Queensland has a research station here. The island also has a well-known tourist resort. It is reached by boat or helicopter from Gladstone. No camping is allowed.

The three islands of the Bunker Group are undeveloped coral cays with vegetation similar to that of Heron Island. All are important seabird nesting sites. Permits to visit these islands are not issued between September and February, which is the gannet nesting season.

Eurimbula
Woodgate
Burrum River

Eurimbula National Park, on the coast south of Gladstone, preserves an area of sandy coastal lowland which carries patches of hoop pine forest. Woodgate National Park, which includes Woodgate Head, is between Bundaberg and Maryborough. Wallum heath behind the sand dunes is full of interest for lovers of wildflowers. Burrum River National Park, on the south side of the river mouth near Burrum Heads (opposite Woodgate), offers similar scenery and vegetation.

Pied cormorants inhabit Queensland's coast and islands (Lee Pearce)

*Great Sandy Island
(Fraser Island)*

The world's biggest sand island lies just off the Queensland coast at the point where the outline of the continent takes a turn towards the southwest. This is Fraser Island, celebrated environmental rarity recently rescued from possible destruction by the ending of sand-mining operations. The national park which occupies the northern part of the island uses the island's original name: Great Sandy Island. The later name commemorates the captain of the *Stirling Castle*, who, with his wife, was a castaway on this island and was killed here by Aborigines in 1836.

This is a very different environment from those of the islands to the north. Yet here, also, you will find eucalypt forests, rainforest containing hoop pine and kauri, as well as heath and swamp. The sand dunes are piled up to 200 metres high. Freshwater lakes lie in hollows in the dunes, well above sea-level, their beds cemented by the chemical interaction of minerals in the sand with organic material. Larger lakes have developed their own white sand beaches.

Smooth, beautiful, ocean beaches stretch all the way along the mainland coast from Noosa and continue for the whole length of Fraser Island. Interest is added to the scene here and there by lofty dunes of multi-hued sands and by the grounded hulks of wrecked ships which have become bizarre landmarks

*Noosa
Cooloola*

Fraser Island can be reached only by boat, vehicular barge or aircraft. If staying at Noosa Heads, you could easily arrange to take excursions through the three national parks in the locality (the others being Noosa and Cooloola). Noosa National Park, though quite small, offers an extensive system of walking tracks and picnic facilities in a setting of lovely coastal scenery. The bigger Cooloola National Park comprises a sand-dune habitat with both heath and rainforest vegetation. A camping area is accessible via a sand road through state forest. A delightful alternative way to see this park is to take a boat trip up the Noosa River and across the placid Lake Cootharaba.

*Mount Tempest
Blue Lake*

Small national parks are located on two more of Southern Queensland's sand islands. On Moreton Island, Mount Tempest is the central feature of a park which carries its name. Reaching 285 metres above sea-level, it is reputed to be the world's highest coastal sand dune. Ferry services from several places around Brisbane and regular flights from Brisbane airport provide access to the island, which has no roads but has a tourist resort, at Tangalooma, opposite Redcliffe. Blue Lake National Park on North Stradbroke Island comprises a freshwater lake surrounded by eucalypt woodland. Road access is difficult but there are daily vehicular barge services to the island.

NEW SOUTH WALES

The long, beautiful beaches of smooth sand for which Southern Queensland is famous continue along much of the coast of New South Wales. Except in the Sydney metropolitan region, nowhere in this state has beach-front commercial development taken place on the same scale as that seen in Queensland's Gold Coast. In fact, a very high proportion of the New South Wales coastline is reserved — and protected from development — in national parks.

Unlike the calcareous (limestone) sands which form the great beach-dune systems of South Australia, the sands of the east coast beaches are siliceous. Inner dunes, thousands of years old, contain rich deposits of rutile, zircon and ilmenite. Consequently many miles of these dunes have been mined at various places along the coast. Some beach-sand mining is still going on. Controversy surrounds this activity. Those who wish to see the natural environment remain unspoilt argue against allowing any further mining. Those who see the minerals as a resource to be exploited argue that mining is good for the nation's economy and creates employment. They also claim that they take care to restore the dune vegetation which their activities destroy, though their critics claim that such efforts are ineffective.

The argument has actually provoked public interest in, and support for, the cause of preserving the beach environment. The upshot is that extensive additions have been made to New South Wales's string of coastal national parks in very recent years, many new parks having been established in areas that were formerly subjected to sand mining. In an ironical turnabout, this means that the nature-lover can now reach many formerly inaccessible coastal areas by using roads built by the mining companies. However, there are still some areas owned by the companies from which the public is excluded. And there are still scars across the sand dunes in some parks where regeneration is proving to be a slow and difficult process.

The beaches of northern New South Wales are backed by massive dune systems and divided by spectacular rocky headlands. Behind the dunes there are usually broad stretches of sandy heath or swamp and frequently also lakes. These varied environments carry a diverse vegetation with an abundance of flowering shrubs. They are also rich in animal life.

Broadwater

Between Ballina and Coffs Harbour, huge segments of the coast to north and south of the complex estuary of the Clarence River have been incorporated into national parks. Broadwater National Park, which occupies a strip of coastal sandplain between the Pacific Highway and the sea, just outside the resort town of Evans Head, at first sight appears most unpromising. Apart from its eight kilometre long unbroken sweep of superb beach free of human intrusions, you may wonder what was worth protecting in this patch of swamp and scrubby heath. If you see it in the spring, when Christmas bells, golden bush pea, swamp lilies, sun orchids and heath plants paint it with brilliant colours, you will have your answer. The park attracts a wide range of birds, from seabirds to honeyeaters, including ibis, herons and brolgas. Emus are occasionally seen here, as is Australia's representative of the stork family, the black-and-white jabiru.

Bundjalung

South of Evans Head, thirty-eight kilometres of coastline are included in Bundjalung National Park, which reaches to Iluka, at the mouth of the Clarence River. It features the tranquil beauty of the Esk River, freshwater lakes, mangrove mudflats and estuarine sandbars. Enjoy a peaceful picnic or barbecue, or camp in the bush and spend a few days walking, boating, fishing or surfing.

Yuraygir

To the south of Yamba, just past the village of Angourie, is the northern boundary of Yuraygir National Park. The northern section, formerly Angourie National Park, extends to Red Cliff (near Brooms Head), where there are picnicking and car-camping areas. As in several of the national parks along this coast, here you can camp beside a lake, listening to the rhythmic grumbling of the surf and yet be completely sheltered from the ocean winds by sand dunes and banksia thickets. You have a choice between beachwalks and bushwalks, between surfing and freshwater swimming. You will be entertained by sights such as a flotilla of black swans gliding over the lake, or a party of red-necked stints, those remarkable little migratory waders that come each year all the way from Siberia, trotting along the sand at the edge of the water. A local magpie will come around to share your breakfast.

Yuraygir extends as far south as Red Rock, just up the coast from Woolgoolga, taking in the former Red Rock National Park. Here, the campsite at Station Creek is reached by roads through state forests. The creek, with its swampy perimeter, provides an ideal habitat for many water birds, ranging from black ducks to the graceful large egret. This is one of the few known refuges on the mainland of the rare swamp parrot (also known as the ground parrot), which is unlikely to be seen by the casual observer since it is both nocturnal and extremely shy. By contrast, wallabies may be seen unconcernedly hopping through the camping area in the middle of the day.

Bushcamping is permitted. There are good walks along the series of beaches — smaller here, each with its own character, between rocky headlands — or through the bush, either south to Saltwater Creek and Red Rock or north to Wooli. And there are several good places for swimming.

Hat Head

Like many of the rivers along this coast, the Macleay River, which flows through Kempsey, curves northward as it meanders across the coastal plain on its way to the sea. The floodplain below Kempsey has long ago been turned into pastureland. Here,

Brilliant purple pig-face

Golden glory pea

cattle egrets and little egrets wander among the cows, searching the grass for insects. In low-lying places the land becomes swamp. Where it rises, it carries eucalypt forest. Along the seaward perimeter of this corridor, extending from just south of Smoky Cape to the southern side of Hat Head village, is Hat Head National Park.

This park is mainly for birds and beach-lovers. It provides a habitat for the many nomadic species which move north or south with the changing seasons. It also provides for human travellers. Car-camping sites are located at Hungry Head, just beyond the southern boundary, behind massive sand dunes laced together by coast banksias, pig-face (*Carpobrotus* spp.) and spinifex, and at South Smoky Beach, near Smoky Cape, where you camp in a grove of paperbarks behind the dune ridge, close to the lighthouse-topped headland. Here you will usually have miles of open beach to yourself. You may visit the lighthouse. And you are only a few minutes' drive from South West Rocks, the sheltered sandy crescent of Trial Bay and the superbly situated Trial Bay goal.

Crowdy Bay

Crowdy Bay National Park reaches from Diamond Head, just south of Laurieton, almost to Crowdy Head. Car-camp at Diamond Head and walk over the headland to enjoy views of coastline, lakes and wooded hills, and to discover an environment which contrasts sharply with the dense coastal heath down below, with its masses of flowering tea-trees and banksias. Up on the steep, exposed, moorland slopes you will find coast banksias stunted to knee-height by the sea winds. You will also find flannel flowers, both golden and white paper daisies (*Helichrysum* spp.), rice flowers (*Pimelia* spp.), pink-flowered boronias, and lots more.

Myall Lakes

Largest of the New South Wales coastal parks is Myall Lakes National Park, midway between Taree and Newcastle. This park's principal feature is a series of interconnecting lakes separated from the sea by high dunes and a wooded sandplain. A good sand-and-gravel road, built by sand-miners, traverses the park from north to south along the strip between lakes and sea. Mungo Brush, at the southern end, is the site of a delightfully situated camping ground beside a lake called the Broadwater. A second campsite, complete with showers and other facilities, is on the other side of the lake, reached by road and ferry from Mungo Brush or by road from Bulahdelah. Bushcamping is permitted elsewhere in the park.

Looking downstream from Mungo Brush in the Myall Lakes National Park

This is easy walking country, with tracks winding through open woods of banksias, eucalypts and red gums (*Angophora costata*). Spring brings a profusion of wildflowers, with masses of shoulder-high flannel flowers. Also prominent are the huge golden flowers of the wedge pea (*Gompholobium latifolium*) and the bright pinks of wax flowers (*Eriostemon australis*), *Boronia mollis* and *Melaleuca thymifolia*, and there are scores of other flowering shrubs of many colours.

The lakes provide a perfect environment for aquatic sports, including swimming. One popular way of seeing the park is to hire a houseboat at Tea Gardens and cruise up the Myall River into the chain of lakes. This way you get to meet many of the water birds at close quarters, especially the bold pelicans. And you see the lake-frontage forests of paperbarks and gums, and the narrow beaches of silver sand from a fresh angle as you glide across the Broadwater, pass through the narrow connecting channel into Boolambayte Lake and from there into Myall Lake, an impressive stretch of water with several islands, many bays, and a background of steep, forested hills.

The Hawkesbury River rises in high country to the south of Sydney, flows north along the edge of the Blue Mountains, takes an abrupt turn to the southeast at Wiseman's Ferry and joins the sea close to the city's northern suburbs. The river has cut its wide channel through an eastern extension of the sandstone plateau which forms the major ridges of the Blue Mountains, here called the Hornsby Plateau. Its estuary, Broken Bay, is another of the many places along Australia's east coast whose name is a legacy of James Cook's 1770 visit. The headlands guarding Broken Bay are Barranjoey to the south, topped by a lighthouse and connected to the Palm Beach peninsula by a sand spit, and Box Head on the northern side.

Bouddi

Box Head and a segment of the nearby coast fall within the Bouddi National Park. This relatively small but scenically beautiful park encloses the eastern side of a minor coastal range which forms the peninsula between the ocean and Brisbane Water. Its highest point is Mount Bouddi (152 metres). The park's general features are typical of the terrain around the lower Hawkesbury and the Sydney coast: hills cut by many streams, some deep gullies, open heathland, dramatic rock cliffs and sandy beaches. Vegetation, if not luxuriant, is rich in variety. Bouddi offers fascinating walks — through temperate rainforest, along clifftops, along wave-eroded rock platforms — spectacular coastal views, and a series of secluded beaches, some accessible only to walkers. White-breasted sea-eagles nest around the cliffs. In more secluded parts, you may come across bower birds or lyre birds. This is a good place for camping — beside a beach, if you wish — for swimming, or for lazing in the sun. A 283 hectare extension to seaward from the central portion of the park represents New South Wales's first marine park. Fishing is not permitted within the bounds of the marine extension.

Brisbane Water
Ku-ring-gai Chase

Brisbane Water National Park and Ku-ring-gai Chase National Park also embrace areas of this sandstone country around the Hawkesbury estuary, lying respectively on the northern and southern shores of the river. The Brisbane Water National Park, despite being sandwiched between the river and the Sydney-Newcastle freeway and despite the electrified Sydney-Gosford railway line intruding into it, consists of rugged, wild country. Several well-constructed walking tracks lead through different sections of the park, giving a choice of half-day walks or an extended walk of about thirty kilometres through the full length of the park, camping along the way if you wish. Habitats include open woodland, swamp, mangrove mudflats and deep gorges containing subtropical rainforest with tree ferns, cabbage-tree palms, elkhorns and rock and tree orchids.

The drowned valleys of the lower Hawkesbury and its host of tributary creeks form a complex of fiord-like waterways that is one of the great scenic glories of the Sydney region. Ku-ring-gai Chase National Park, reached through the city's northern suburbs, encloses an area of bushland that is extensively dissected by several of these water-filled valleys. Roads lead through the park to popular picnic grounds close to commercial marinas at Bobbin Head and Coal and Candle Creek, to the small settlement at Cottage Point on Cowan Creek, and to a scenic lookout at Commodore Heights, West Head, which rises high above the estuary. The West Head road follows the spine of the Lambert Peninsula, which divides Cowan Creek from the lake-like inlet called Pittwater. From this spine many walking tracks radiate east and west, crossing the heath-covered plateau, climbing hills and descending through wooded valleys to beaches and bays, or winding out to clifftop viewing points. Any of these walks can easily be accomplished in half a day. Some terminate at ferry wharves.

Frequent glimpses of blue waterways separating dark-green hills add to the delights of walking in these Hawkesbury parks. The vegetation changes in character continually as you progress: first an expanse of low heath and sparse grasses on white sand, then a dense screen of head-high shrubs; now you pass beneath tall eucalypts, now smaller banksias. You find sandstone crags that have weathered into fantastic shapes. On rock platforms and under rock overhangs, you can find examples of Aboriginal art. In winter and spring, the varieties of wildflowers run into hundreds, some of the more apparent being the blooms of waratah, wattles, tea-trees, lambertia, golden guinea flowers, geebung, grevilleas, hakeas, banksias, boronias, heaths and many pea flowers. Tread softly and you will sometimes see a handsome tree goanna or a swamp wallaby, or a group of strutting lyre birds.

Not surprisingly, boating is enormously popular on these waterways. There are many charming bays and beaches to be reached by boat. What is more, from the water you get the most splendid views of the tumbling green hillsides with their dense cover of twisted Sydney red gums — often astonishingly firmly rooted in the narrowest of crevices, and growing almost to the waterline — and their honey-coloured, weather-sculptured rocks. Launches and houseboats may be hired. Camping is permitted at the Basin on Pittwater, which may be reached via a walking track or by ferry from Palm Beach.

America Bay, one of many peaceful inlets in Ku-ring-gai Chase National Park

Sydney Harbour National Park, covering a total of 388 hectares in separate groups, is set on the foreshores of one of the world's most beautiful harbours. These isolated patches of greenery, set aside in the past for defence and other reasons, now provide a welcome relief from the rows of red brick houses and asphalt. Included in the park are South Head, Nielsen Park, Hermitage Foreshores and North Head. Islands include Shark, Rodd and Clark. Favourite stopping points for visitors are the Quarantine Station and Dobroyd Head. The latter commands impressive views of the harbour, as do most other parts of the park.

Although only small in total area, this park has significant scenic recreational value for the inhabitants of our largest city and their visitors. From the headlands you get the most exciting panoramic views of the city and its labyrinth of waterways. A visit to North Head, preferably in Spring, is a must for visitors: the variety of wildflowers is really quite amazing. Some areas of the park contain relics of old Sydney, and examples of Aboriginal rock carvings. Night-time views from the park are not to be missed, especially from South Head.

Royal

Australia's first (and the world's second) national park was proclaimed in April 1879. Originally called simply The National Park but known as the Royal National Park since a visit by Queen Elizabeth in 1955, it now covers 15 000 hectares, taking in twenty-one kilometres of coastline south of Port Hacking. The main entrance is just thirty kilometres from Sydney along the Princes Highway.

The terrain within the Royal consists of a ramp-like plateau which slopes gently from south to north. The Port Hacking River, which rises outside the southern boundary, flows northward through the full length of the park. There are similarities with the other Sydney coastal parks but everything here is on a grander scale, from the miles of towering, horizontally layered sandstone cliffs and the rock platforms with surf breaking over them, to the dense rainforest, with its tall turpentine trees, palms, figs, lianas and epiphytic ferns. Grasses, low shrubs and scattered, stunted mallee cover the high sandstone plateau. There are also open forests of blackbutt and Sydney bluegum with an understorey of flowering shrubs, including noble Gymea lilies (*Doryanthes excelsa*), which hold up their deep-red flowers, like huge Olympic torches, on straight green stems that reach more than twice the height of a man.

Big Marley and Little Marley beaches (above) and Big Marley beach (below) show the opportunities for surfing, walking and exploring rock pools in the Royal National Park

Roads traverse the park, leading to the several small suburban settlements on the southern shore of Port Hacking and to two ocean surfing beaches. Other beaches are accessible only to walkers. The Royal offers more scope for bushwalking and camping than any other coastal park close to Sydney. A complex of walking tracks includes the popular coast walk, which follows the shoreline for almost the whole length of the park. At Audley, the park centre, lawns and fireplaces provide for family sport and picnics. Here you may hire a boat and row up-river into the heart of the rainforest. This may give you your best chance of seeing some of the wild inhabitants, including swamp wallabies, brushtail and ringtail possums, lyrebirds, satin bower birds, wonga pigeons and others of the 200 bird species known to frequent the Royal. Among the animals you may see in more open areas are the small herds of Javanese rusa deer and fallow deer, descendants of those introduced towards the end of the nineteenth century.

The south coast of New South Wales, beyond the industrial complex of Wollongong, is a rural region famed for its cheeses, with scattered fishing settlements and small holiday towns situated on many bays or at river mouths. There are five national parks along this stretch of coast, each unique in character, as well as a number of nature reserves.

Seven Mile Beach

(Over pages) Brush-tailed possum
In Ben Boyd National Park, The Pinnacles, near Eden

Seven Mile Beach National Park occupies a narrow strip of shoreline between Gerroa, south of Kiama, and Shoalhaven Heads, comprising eight kilometres of beautiful beaches backed by dunes. Dunes near the sea have a cover of spinifex and coast wattle with stands of tea-tree and coast banksia. Further inland they carry a woodland of bangalay (*Eucalyptus botryoides*) and blackbutt (*E. pilularis*).

Murramarang	Murramarang National Park on the coast between Ulladulla and Batemans Bay, although barely two kilometres across at its widest point, offers a much more varied landscape. The park consists of three sections, with a total length of twenty-seven kilometres of coastline, occupying the seaward side of the Murramarang Range and Durras Lake. The coastline is scalloped with bays and beaches, some of which are deeply set between headlands. Vegetation is dominated by wet eucalypt forest, largely of spotted gum (*Eucalyptus maculata*) with an understorey of burrawangs (*Macrozamia* spp.), slow-growing cycads with dark-green, palm-like leaves. Some sheltered gullies have rainforest remnants. Woodland gives way to casuarina and banksia heath on windswept headlands. Wildlife includes kangaroos, wallabies, parrots and honeyeaters. Among many types of seabirds you may see are muttonbirds (shearwaters) and the sooty oystercatcher. Campsites are located within and near the park. Bushcamping is permitted, under certain conditions, 500 metres away from roads.
Wallaga Lake	The coastal lakes of this region provide habitats for a varied population of water birds, most conspicuously black swans, black ducks and the handsome blue-breasted swamp hen. Wallaga Lake National Park, near Bermagui, takes in most of the western shore of one such lake. Eucalypt-covered ridges slope steeply on the water's edge, where they form a series of secluded bays. This is good bushwalking country offering the additional delights of fishing and swimming. To enjoy it to the full, bring your own small boat or hire a runabout at Regatta Point. Camping is not permitted within the park, which has no roads and no developed amenities, but you will find motels and caravan parks at Regatta Point and Beauty Point on the eastern shore of the lake. Beautiful ocean beaches add to the district's attractions.
Mimosa Rocks	Mimosa Rocks National Park, south of Bermagui, consists of five sections embracing twelve kilometres of heavily timbered coastline with cliffs, beaches, caves, headlands, offshore islands, and considerable lengths of lake or lagoon shoreline. Just off Aragunnu Beach in the northern section, the Mimosa Rocks, like nearby Bunga Head, are relics of past volcanic activity. Roads give access to several parts of the park, including Aragunnu Beach, the eastern shore of Wapengo Lake, Picnic Point and Middle Beach. You may camp at these places, after notifying the Narooma District Office of the NPWS. This is wonderful country for short coastal bushwalks, offering interestingly varied views and perhaps the chance to have a whole beach or a whole lake all to yourself.
Ben Boyd	Eden, the major fishing port in the south of New South Wales, occupies a peninsula which juts into Twofold Bay. In the 1840s, the banker Ben Boyd developed a whaling station on the southern shore of this bay and nursed a dream of a great future for the town he began to build, which he called Boydtown. Little is left of Boydtown today. The whales have also gone. But the biggest New South Wales coastal park south of the Royal embraces two segments of this coast, to north and south of Twofold Bay. This is Ben Boyd National Park.
	The northern section of the park, bounded on its inland side by the Princes Highway, reaches to the shore of Pambula Lake and the mouth of the Pambula River. It features long beaches, fascinating rock formations and colourful cliffs of red and brown shales, sandstones and conglomerates. The southern section, which extends to Green Cape and the shore of Disaster Bay, sits between the sea and a belt of state forest, with the relics of Boydtown to its north and the Nadgee Nature Reserve to the south. Thus insulated, it has remained largely unspoilt country supporting a wealth of native wildlife. Coastal heathland with a dense cover of flowering shrubs merges into tall eucalypt woodland. Grey kangaroos, swamp wallabies, red-necked wallabies and goannas are all quite common. Campers may also see yellow-bellied gliders, wombats and marsupial mice. Conspicuous among the many bird species are lyrebirds, yellow-tailed black cockatoos and white-breasted sea-eagles. This park also serves as a haven for the ground parrot.
	Boyd's Tower, built by Ben Boyd as a lighthouse and used as a lookout tower for spotting whales, offers impressive coastal views. Basic camping facilities are provided at two locations.

VICTORIA

At the state border, outlying hills of the Great Dividing Range reach almost to the sea. This is the southeast corner of the continent. From here, the coastline begins to incline westward, running due west from Point Hicks (Cape Everard) to the bend at Lakes Entrance, from where it heads southwest, thrusting a broad wedge of land into the shallow waters of Bass Strait. Here, the coastal plain and the adjacent foothills present the rural landscapes of the Gippsland region. Long sections of this coast have been reserved in national parks.

Croajingolong

Croajingolong National Park extends for nearly 100 kilometres from the border to Sydenham Inlet, where the Bemm River joins the sea. Covering an area of 86 000 hectares, this is a far bigger park than any of those on the coasts of Queensland or New South Wales. Declared a national park in 1979, Croajingolong absorbs the previously existing smaller parks of Mallacoota Inlet, Wingan Inlet and Captain James Cook (near Point Hicks), taking in all the coastline between, with

(Top) Grey kangaroos can often be seen grazing in Croajingolong National Park

(Bottom) The beautiful rainbow lorikeet (Lee Pearce)

extensive additions.

Not surprisingly, the animals which inhabit the southern section of Ben Boyd National Park are also present in this area. This corner of Australia is a crossroads for flora and fauna species. Here, where the rainforests and sclerophyll forests reach their southern mainland limit, east coast plant and animal species overlap with those of the south. The distribution range of many birds of the east coast forests extends no further south or west. The scarlet honeyeater and the wonga pigeon are examples. On the other hand, the range of the blue-winged parrot of Tasmania and southern Victoria does not extend to the east coast. Some of the birds of the seashore commonly seen on east coast beaches, including several of the migratory waders, come no further south, whilst the native hooded dotterel and the black-faced cormorant, both familiar on Bass Strait shores, move no further north. Offshore, seals breed on some of the islands around this underside of the continent.

Croajingolong has enough space and a varied enough range of scenery and habitats to satisfy many recreational needs. Families can enjoy a holiday boating, fishing, swimming and relaxing on beaches, perhaps picnicking at a different beauty spot each day. Even car trips can be exciting in this world of forests and water. You may encounter a goanna crossing the road, glimpse a wallaby or a snake as it retreats into the bush, watch herds of kangaroos grazing, pass beneath treetops alive with the movement, the colour and the chatter of rainbow lorikeets. You will see cockatoos and king parrots, eastern and crimson rosellas, high-soaring sea-eagles, and scores of other birds which you may compete to put names to. You may camp. Or you may enjoy hotel comfort at Mallacoota township. Or drive to secluded Wingan Inlet and make your camp there. Or, for an adventure, take your own water supply and camp overnight at Thurra River.

Others may prefer to seek the peace of the wild bushland, taking a walk to some point on the coast not reached by roads, perhaps following the course of one of the many streams. The park contains whole stream systems untouched by man's activities. Some of these waterways could be explored by canoe. You will pass through eucalypt forests, grass-tree plains, rainforest, heathlands and swampy wetland. Around springtime, the heaths in particular are daubed with the colours of many wildflowers.

The coastal inlets of Croajingolong are drowned valleys, their wide waterways resulting from the rise in sea-level after the last Ice Age. The landscape is hilly, with several granite promontories, including historic Point Hicks (Cape Everard), the first point on Australia's coast to have been seen by James Cook, in 1770. By contrast, the Gippsland Lakes further east sit above a submerged plain. Over the centuries since the sea inundated the plain, the perpetual action of the southwest swell in Bass Strait, aided by the prevailing westerly winds, has deposited long barriers of material washed from the seabed, creating a series of lagoons. Alluvial deposits from many rivers, trapped in the still waters behind the sand barriers, have extended the dryland areas. The outermost (and most recently formed) barrier is the sandspit known as Ninety Mile Beach. Its dunes are partially fixed by spinifex, with tea-trees, coast banksias and manna gums (*Eucalyptus viminalis*) on the inland side. Behind it lies the narrow Lake Reeve, more than sixty kilometres long, separated by an older barrier from Lakes Victoria, King and Wellington. At the eastern end of this complex of lakes, a channel was cut through to the sea in 1889. The fishing port of Lakes Entrance stands on the eastern side of the channel.

The Lakes

The long peninsula of the inner dune barrier, which has Lake Reeve on its seaward side and Lake Victoria on the inland side, comprises the Lakes National Park. Lake Reeve itself, together with most of Ninety Mile Beach, forms the Gippsland Coastal Park. Roads lead into both parks at the southwestern end. Otherwise, access is by boat. The national park contains an extremely diverse flora and fauna, with habitats ranging from saltmarsh and paperbark shrublands to woodlands of eucalypts, banksias and acacias. Aquatic birdlife is prolific as you would expect. Eastern grey kangaroos are also abundant, and wallabies, possums and emus may also be observed. The coastal park provides one of the longest unbroken stretches of beach in the whole continent.

(Opposite page) Ninety-mile Beach at Lakes Entrance

At the southernmost tip of the mainland — the point of the wedge — stands Wilsons Promontory. This massive granite outcrop has been a national park since 1905. The 'Prom' and the islands of the Furneaux Group are the highest peaks of a mountain range which formerly linked Tasmania to the mainland. They all became islands some 10 000 years ago, during the same rise in sea-level that flooded many river valleys further north. The same wave action which built the long dunes that hold back the Gippsland lakes also built up a sandspit, tying the hump of Wilsons Promontory to the nearby coast. This is the Yanakie Isthmus. The resulting bay, formerly a channel, is Corner Inlet.

The Prom provides a varied environment of rugged hills and valleys, sheltered sandy beaches, and weatherbeaten cliffs and rocks. The range rises to 754 metres at Mount Latrobe. Eucalypt forests on the slopes contrast with the coastal heath found on the sandy isthmus, where the tallest trees are *Banksia serrata* and the swamp she-oak (*Casuarina paludosa*). Patches of rainforest occur in high gullies, showing an overlap of mainland and Tasmanian species. In Lilly Pilly Gully, the lilly pilly (*Acmena smithii*, formerly designated *Eugenia smithii*) is found in company with the Tasmanian blue gum (*Eucalyptus globulus*). At higher elevations, some gully habitats have stands of the Tasmanian myrtle or Antarctic beech (*Nothofagus cunninghamii*).

A road allows the visitor to drive thirty-two kilometres into the park to Tidal River, where a camping ground with 500 sites offers most of the amenities that civilised man requires — except electricity. There is even a general store, a post office, an open-air cinema and a summer-resident doctor. Fireplaces are few and fires are not permitted from November to May, so a portable stove is necessary if you plan an extended stay. Advance bookings are essential in holiday periods. Lodge accommodation is also available. Walking tracks from Tidal River and from points along the road lead to bays, beaches and other places of interest, including Lilly Pilly Gully and the summit of Mount Bishop. The park has more than eighty kilometres of walking tracks. You could explore a different part of this fascinating coastal range every day for a week, if you wished. Wildlife is surprisingly abundant, with koalas, wombats, possums, wallabies, kangaroos and emus, and a wealth of birdlife. The beautiful firetail, a grass-finch rarely seen on the mainland though plentiful in Tasmania, is fairly common and has become quite tame.

Occupying what is arguably the most scenically dramatic segment of the entire Australian coastline is Port Campbell National Park, 240 kilometres by road southwest of Melbourne. Here, the character of the coastal landscape differs markedly from anything to be seen anywhere else in this country. The rock beneath the coastal plain of Victoria's western district south of Warrnambool consists of limestone, laid down as marine deposits ten to twenty million years ago. At Port Campbell, the limestone bedrock meets the sea in a line of cliffs. In the unending battle between the Southern Ocean and the land, these cliffs have been cut and drilled into a fantastic natural sculpture, a series of headlands and deep indentations, exhibiting a splendid variety of forms.

The national park embraces all the best-known features of this coast in a thirty-two kilometre strip. The Twelve Apostles, at the eastern end, are stacks of a resistant limestone left standing after the sea eroded away all the surrounding rock. Some still support vegetation. Like all the other formations at Port Campbell, they are still being chiselled away by the pounding waves and will eventually disappear. Here you can see the forces that shape landscape actually at work, a reminder that the world we live in and look upon is a dynamic environment. Towards the Peterborough end you will find the Arch and the double-arched London Bridge, where the sea has bitten through narrow rock promontories.

These are treacherous seas with a changing pattern of currents and strong onshore tides that produce high and powerful waves. Many ships were driven on to this unforgiving shore in earlier days. Most celebrated of these incidents was the wreck of the three-masted iron clipper, *Loch Ard*, in 1878, in which fifty-two lives were lost. The tragedy is commemorated in the name of the Loch Ard Gorge.

The rocks, cliff ledges and stacks provide nesting sites for many seabirds. One stack is called Muttonbird Island, since it houses a breeding colony of short-tailed shearwaters. Thousands of these plump, brownish-black birds rear their chicks here in the summer months, returning to the nesting sites in dense flocks at dusk each day. At the London Bridge beach lives a colony of fairy penguins. In the narrow strip of coastal heath on the clifftops you may come across blue-winged parrots or tawny-crowned honeyeaters. Birds of prey are often seen wheeling overhead, usually kestrels, swamp harriers or brown goshawks. Further back from the cliff edge, casuarinas and banksias give way to stunted messmate stringbarks (*Eucalyptus obliqua*). This wooded habitat shelters wallabies, ringtail possums and echidnas.

Tourist roads and walking tracks lead to lookout points. A two and a half kilometre walking track from a parking area near Port Campbell has been specially designed to introduce the visitor to the historic and natural features of the park. The National Parks Service operates a camping area in Port Campbell which has powered and unpowered sites, hot showers and laundry facilities.

Towering multicoloured stacks of limestone stand along the coastline of Port Campbell National Park (Lee Pearce)

Majestic limestone cliffs, spires and islands at Port Campbell are the result of millions of years of erosion (Lee Pearce)

TASMANIA

Strzelecki

The string of islands across the eastern end of Bass Strait marks the line of the land bridge that formerly joined Tasmania and the mainland. These islands are the granite peaks of a long ridge which reaches its highest points at Wilsons Promontory in Victoria, and the Strzelecki Range, on Flinders Island. Strzelecki National Park, in the southwest corner of the island, embraces several precipitous granite peaks Dense, closed forest covers much of the park, with exposed rock on higher slopes, but there are also patches of heath and coastal scrub. The eastern grey kangaroo, formerly an inhabitant, has now disappeared from the island. Two species of marsupial mammals which have survived here are the red-necked wallaby and the little Tasmanian pademelon. Two creatures which survive in great numbers, despite strenuous past eradication efforts, are the copperhead and the tiger snake.

Flinders, the largest island of the Furneaux Group, has a scattered human population which depends mainly upon farming and fishing, with some tourist business. Exports are sheep, cattle, wool, crayfish, abalone, scallops and muttonbirds. Visitor accommodation is provided by a hotel, two guest houses, private farms and holiday cottages. Cars, campervans and caravans may be hired. Daily passenger flights

from Melbourne and Launceston serve the major centre, Whitemark. Lady Barron, in the south, is the island's major trading and crayfishing port.

The first Europeans to live on the Bass Strait islands were the sealers. Cape Barren Island, to the south of Flinders, was the site of a settlement established as a base for sealing operations late in the eighteenth century. Matthew Flinders reported an abundance of seals in 1798. By 1803, some 200 men were working on and around the islands, clubbing the seals to death. The valuable skins were shipped to Sydney. Originally, three seal species inhabited these waters: the elephant seal, the hair seal and the fur seal. The first two types have long ago vanished. Only a small population of fur seals survives.

The Cape Barren goose has fared rather better. This handsome, pale-grey bird (the young are attractively piebald) occurs nowhere else in the world but around the southern shores of Australia, nesting on islands from the Recherche Archipelago to the Furneaux Group. From the days of the sealers, both the birds and their eggs were eaten. The flesh is said to taste delicious. Naturalist John Gould reported in 1839 that the race was 'almost extirpated'. Now fully protected, the Cape Barren goose population today numbers upward of 9000 and is thought to be increasing. The main Bass Strait nesting sites are now on small islands off the west coast of Flinders Island. The birds visit the larger islands during summer to forage on the pastures.

Most of the outer islands are conservation reserves. Several of them are nesting sites for the muttonbird (the short-tailed shearwater). Despite the fact that it has been harvested for commercial purposes for many years, this species is also increasing. Fat nestlings are taken during the short annual muttonbird season, from late March to the end of April. After spending the summer months in and around their Australian rookeries, the muttonbirds migrate in large flocks across the Pacific to spend the northern summer in Japan or Alaska, returning to southern Australia in time for the next breeding season, in September.

Many of the seabirds to be seen around Tasmania's coasts are visitors from Antarctica, including several petrel species. Two of the smallest petrels breed at sites off southern Australia, including islands in Bass Strait. Of the giants among seabirds, the albatrosses, only one species is known to have nesting sites in Australian waters, the shy or white-capped albatross. Breeding colonies are found on Albatross Island in Bass Strait and on two islands off southern Tasmania. The biggest member of the race, the wandering albatross, breeds on subantarctic islands, including Macquarie Island (which is a Tasmanian Nature Reserve). The Australasian gannet, often seen around Tasmania's coasts, has a few nesting sites on small rocky islands in these waters but the majority of the population is of New Zealand origin. Penguins seen around Tasmania include the fairy (or little) penguin, which is the only type to breed in Australia, the rockhopper penguin, recognisable by the small yellow tufts which stick out behind its ears like straws, and the larger (but less frequently encountered) fiordland penguin, a visitor from New Zealand, identified by its huge red bill and yellow eyebrows.

Mount William

The granite 'stepping stones' across eastern Bass Strait lead to the northeast corner of Tasmania. Here, the Mount William National Park encloses a segment of coastline where the same ancient granite occurs. Mount William itself, which rises to 216 metres, is outside the park. Within the park is a large area of coastal dry sclerophyll forest, extensive coastal heath, and an animal population which includes over half the species of Tasmania's native vertebrates. The shore has long beaches of white sand.

Asbestos Range

Asbestos Range National Park, on the north coast, also has attractive beaches. Situated at the northern end of Asbestos Range, named for the asbestos which was mined at the southern end of the range in the 1890s, it takes in Badger Head, with wide beaches on either side, and West Head, at the mouth of the River Tamar. The low, forested hills provide an ideal habitat for the Tasmanian forester kangaroo, once hunted to the verge of extinction but now fully protected throughout the state. Essentially the same species as the great grey kangaroo of mainland Australia, the Tasmanian forester has the heavier build characteristic of insular species and its fur is usually more reddish-brown in tone.

(Opposite page) The white-capped albatross of Tasmania's rocky coast

45

White-capped albatross

Fledgling Tasmanian mutton-bird or short-tailed shearwater

Rocky Cape

Rocky Cape National Park, west of Wynyard, is renowned for its wildflowers. Although only small in area, it is also a place packed with interest for students of geology and archaeology. The hard quartzite foundation of Rocky Cape has been shaped by 700 million years of geological events. These have included many changes in sea-level, periods of volcanic lava flow, and the movement of material from inland mountains by glaciers. Remnants of shellfish and bones of animals, birds and fish found in caves on this rocky shore have provided many clues to the story of the now extinct Tasmanian Aborigines.

Several different plant communities occur within the park, corresponding with the differing soil types, which range through a basalt-based soil, sands and gravels, peat, and sandstone and quartzite rock. Some 275 species have been identified. They include boronias, eriostemons, correas, pink heath, fringe myrtle, guinea flowers, many pea flowers, Christmas bells, native rose (*Bauera rubioides*), orchids, tea-trees, grass-trees, wattles — including the sunshine wattle (*Acacia botrycephala*), which flowers after autumn rains — paperbarks and banksias. This is the only place in Tasmania where the *Banksia serrata* grows.

In this natural garden, the birds are as varied and as colourful as the flowers. In addition to the birds of the seashore, you are likely to see yellow-tailed black cockatoos feeding amongst the banksias. Among the nine species of honeyeaters to be found here are two strictly Tasmanian types: the yellow-throated honeyeater and the strong-billed honeyeater. Parrots include the green rosella — also a Tasmanian native — which is more colourful than its name suggests, having a yellow underside, cobalt-blue cheeks and flashes of blue in its wings. Ground animals include wombats, bandicoots, echidnas, and snakes and lizards, the latter group containing some endemic Tasmanian species. Beachcombers will find a remarkable variety of seashells and other marine fauna to attract their interest. Sea stars are especially abundant. And you cannot fail to notice the bands of bright orange lichen, like stripes of gaudy paint, splashed along the rocks above the high-tide mark. Vividly coloured lichens occur in many places along the Tasmanian coastline.

The east coast of the island state has several fishing towns, many miles of beautiful sandy beaches, and two more national parks, each unique in character: Freycinet and Maria Island.

The rugged coast of Rocky Cape is fascinating to the naturalist and anyone who enjoys observing its wide variety of plant and animal life.

Cooks Beach, Freycinet
National Park

Freycinet

Just south of Bicheno, a range of granite mountains forms the Freycinet Peninsula. The road along the first part of the peninsula skirts Moulting Lagoon, a breeding ground for the black swan and a haven for many other water birds. The village of Coles Bay at the end of the road has a motel, shops, holiday cottages, a caravan park and a youth hostel. This is where the Freycinet National Park begins. To enter it, you must walk or take to the water.

The craggy hills of Freycinet look down upon the still blue expanse of Great Oyster Bay. Mount Dove, in the pink-granite Hazards at the northern end, rises to 485 metres. The peak of Mount Freycinet, in the southern part, reaches 614 metres above sea-level. There are walking tracks to suit all comers and views to soothe all dispositions. In spring, the coastal heathlands are resplendent with flowers and busy with birds. You may laze on a secluded beach or set to and scale the peaks. You may follow a twenty-five kilometre circuit which takes in something of everything, including rocky clifftops and eucalypt forests. You may camp and perhaps dangle a line to catch your breakfast. Alternatively, you may explore the bays and beaches by boat, taking a side trip to nearby Schouten Island, which is included in the national park.

Maria Island

A little further south, Maria Island lies five kilometres off the coast. Named by Tasman in 1642, this island has served many purposes since the Aborigines abandoned it after the coming of the white man: as a penal settlement in the early nineteenth century, as a place for grazing stock, as the location for various industrial enterprises from the 1880s until 1930. A nature reserve since 1965, it is now a national park.

At the northern end of the island, the historic settlement of Darlington, which once had a population of 260, is a ghost town. Only the ranger and his family live there now. Many of the old buildings have been restored, so that the visitor walking amongst them may gain some feeling of the island's past. At the same time, efforts have been made to re-establish the native fauna. Forester kangaroos, Bennett's wallabies, wombats, potoroos, bettongs and bandicoots have all been introduced. Emus may be seen wandering among the buildings. The once abundant Tasmanian emu, a short-legged subspecies, had become extinct by the mid-1800s. It is hoped that here, in an environment protected from urbanisation, with no motor cars except the ranger's work vehicles, these native animals will flourish.

To reach Maria Island you must charter a boat from Orford or Triabunna. You must bring all your camping gear and food with you. Once you step ashore, you must walk. The island is some twenty kilometres long by thirteen kilometres at its maximum width. Along the eastern side, hills rise steeply above great cliffs, the highest point being the summit of Mount Maria (710 metres). The ground inclines more gently towards the western shore, where there are good beaches, with some swamps and lagoons. About half the island has a cover of open eucalypt forest, with a thicker growth in wet gullies on the mountain slopes. The bird life is richly varied. Birds characteristic of virtually all the typical Tasmanian habitats may be observed in a morning's walk. In addition to the many birds of the seashore, several duck species are commonly observed around the lagoons, while many parrots, honeyeaters and robins occur throughout the island. Green rosellas are quite common. The ground parrot may also be seen. One of Australia's rarest subspecies, the forty-spotted pardalote, is surviving in Maria's eucalypt forests.

Maria Island is a breeding ground for wildlife. There are huge nesting grounds of seabirds on the ocean bluffs (Lee Pearce)

49

Southwest National Park, which occupies a vast area of Tasmania's southwestern corner, is best known for its mountainous inland (described in Chapter 2, Highlands and Forests) and Lake Pedder, which lies at its northern edge. This huge park, covering some of Australia's wildest, toughest country, is a daunting place to all but the hardiest bushwalkers. Since it takes in a long segment of coastline, it merits inclusion here. This is the coast that deterred Abel Tasman from attempting a landing in 1642. Not until 1815 was it charted, when Captain James Kelly of Hobart discovered and named its major features. It is a bleak, weatherbeaten coast, notched with a multitude of bays guarded by jagged headlands, where powerful seas crash continuously against unyielding mountains. It is a coast littered with rocky islands. And beneath its hungry waters lie the rotting hulks of many lost ships.

The venturesome yachtsman may be attracted by the complex of landlocked waterways that extends deep inland from Port Davey. If you could overcome the problem of keeping yourself supplied with food, you might happily spend a boating holiday probing all the bays and estuaries of this fascinating harbour system. Remember, though, that since the departure of the whalers and the timber-cutters of the late 1800s, no-one other than the tin-mining King family of Melaleuca has chosen to settle in this region. You could be very lonely. And you should be prepared for all kinds of weather. This corner of Tasmania is exposed to the full force of the winds sailors call 'the roaring forties'. Also, it receives frequent icy gales from the Antarctic. At worst, you could experience severe and violent weather. At best, in summer, you might expect calm, mild, sunny days interspersed with days of rain.

Two walking tracks penetrate this wilderness to reach the northern and southern shores of Bathurst Passage, inside Port Davey. The northern track climbs through the valley of the Huon River from Judbury, crossing Arthur Plains, curving around the end of Arthur Range and following the line of the Spring River to its estuary in Joe Page Bay. The southern route is the South Coast Track, which starts south of Catamaran, close to Recherche Bay, and follows the southern coastline from South Cape Bay to Cox Bight before veering northward to Melaleuca Lagoon. It takes you along cliffs and beaches, across the Ironbound Range, and includes a number of river crossings. To attempt either of these walks requires careful planning, adequate equipment, top physical condition, and the company of walkers who know the country.

Partly submerged huon pines dot the bleak surface of Lake Pedder

SOUTH AUSTRALIA

The southeast corner of South Australia has a landscape like no other part of the country. Behind the long sweep of straight shoreline that runs northwestward from Port MacDonnell to Encounter Bay, and extending far inland, lies a region of swamps, sandy flats and sand ridges. The ridges, locally called 'ranges', run parallel to the present shoreline and mark the positions of previous shorelines left high and dry by a receding sea during the early part of the most recent ice age. They are calcareous sand dunes overlying limestone. The highest are those nearest the sea. Along the southern section, the outermost dunes lie between a chain of lakes and the sea. In the north, the outer dunes form the long spit of the Younghusband Peninsula, which encloses the whole 130 kilometre length of the Coorong, a shallow lagoon with an average width of only two kilometres, which forms part of the complex of waterways at the mouth of the Murray River.

The inland part of this region has been extensively modified by a series of large-scale drainage schemes which started in the 1860s and continued through to the 1960s. Former swamplands have been turned into pastoral country. The impoverished soils have been improved by the application of fertilisers and trace elements. Cattle and sheep are fattened on the rich pastures reclaimed from this former wasteland. The widespread winter floods that used to disrupt communication have now been eliminated and the chaotic pattern of creeks and lakes has been tidied up. Only along the coastal fringe are there areas which remain largely untouched by the hand of man. Two sections of the coastal dune systems have been reserved in national parks: Canunda National Park, in the south, from the southern end of Lake Bonney to the township of Southend and Cape Buffon, and Coorong National Park, which embraces the long lagoon south from Murray Mouth.

Canunda

Apart from high cliffs at Cape Buffon, Canunda consists almost entirely of sand dunes, some densely vegetated and stable, others live, drifting dunes. The shifting sands have uncovered Aboriginal camp sites, revealing fireplaces, shell middens and artefacts. Emus are plentiful here. Grey kangaroos, ring-tailed possums, wombats and smaller marsupials dwell here also. Fur seals, leopard seals and sea-lions may occasionally be seen on the beaches. Notable among the many species of birds recorded is the orange-bellied parrot, found only along the western seaboard of Tasmania and the mainland coast from west of Port Phillip to the Coorong This beautiful bird, formerly common throughout southeast Australia, is thought to be declining in numbers. If it is to survive, its remaining habitats must be preserved.

Inland from Canunda, just twenty-four kilometres south of Naracoorte, is one of the best places in Australia to observe ibises and a whole range of other waders and waterfowl. Bool Lagoon, although not classified as a national park, is a game reserve and conservation park under the control of the South Australian National Parks and Wildlife Service. It is really a system of connected lagoons, one of which forms the Hacks Lagoon Conservation Park, which is a wildlife refuge, while the rest is a game reserve in which hunting of certain duck species is permitted on selected open days. Control of the flow of water through the lagoons prevents winter flooding of the surrounding countryside and through the summer creates an almost permanent expanse of water just a metre deep.

With its stands of flooded paperbarks and reeds, Bool Lagoon provides an ideal habitat for a diversity of water birds. In summer it becomes the home of thousands of ibises, principally the straw-necked species but also white and glossy ibises, with spoonbills as neighbours. Earlier in the year, these waterways are busy with black swans and numerous species of ducks, whose breeding season is generally during winter or spring, depending on rainfall and water levels. Perhaps most fascinating of all the birds which visit this refuge are those long-legged dancers, the brolgas, sometimes seen here in flocks numbering hundreds.

(Over page) Ibis sanctuary in South Australia

Coorong

Coorong National Park embraces the long, slender waterway from which it takes its name, together with its inland shore and the dune barrier known as the Younghusband Peninsula. A slice of it is set aside as a game reserve in which rabbits and foxes may be hunted at all times and certain species of ducks may be hunted during the South Australian duck season.

The best way to explore this park is by boat. In any case you cannot drive along the Younghusband Peninsula, though off-road vehicles may be driven on the ocean beach. In a boat, however, the whole length of the Coorong is available to you, from the salty shallows of the southern end to where it joins the ocean at Murray Mouth. Six islands in the Coorong are bird sanctuaries where you may not land without special permission. These islands support breeding colonies of seabirds. One is a pelican rookery. With the aid of binoculars you can enjoy the droll spectacle of pelican family life as these great birds with long necks and enormous pouched bills feed their young.

The pelicans are attracted to the Coorong by the abundance of fish. Mullet, bream and the big, meaty mulloway (also known as jewfish, kingfish or butterfish) are caught here by local fishermen.

Much of this park can be seen from the Princes Highway, which marks the inland boundary for much of the length of the Coorong. There are caravan parks and camp sites along the way. Camping is possible inside the park. An overnight stay gives you the chance to observe kangaroos and wallabies as they venture out to graze on the grasslands at dusk.

Flinders Chase

Australia's third-largest offshore island, Kangaroo Island, lies some twelve kilometres off the tip of the Fleurieu Peninsula, across the waters of Backstairs Passage. Flinders Chase National Park occupies the island's western end, forming a large wedge between the Playford and West End Highways. It contains harsh but varied country and a prolific wildlife. The climate is mediterranean, with hot, dry summers and wet, stormy winters.

In this naturally isolated environment there has been little disturbance to the native flora and fauna, apart from deliberate efforts over the past sixty years to assist their increase. Koalas, ringtail possums, platypuses, wombats, emus, Cape Barren geese and scrub turkeys have all been introduced from the mainland and have become well established. The Kangaroo Island grey kangaroo, with darker fur than its mainland cousins, survives here in considerable numbers. The tammar (or dama) wallaby thrives here though it is now rare on the mainland. What is more, since the establishment of the national park in 1919, most of these animals have become relatively tame. Kangaroos and emus wander happily among visitors in the picnic area at Rocky River, hoping to share a meal.

The higher plateau region in the north of the park has a cover of mallee and stringybark, while taller forests line the streams. In the south, dense mallee scrub clothes an undulating terrain of limestone dunes, and heathlands lie close to the coast. Limestone cliffs add to the park's scenic interest. At Cape Couedic, the island's southwest corner, wave action has cut a tunnel through the rock, a feature known as Admiral's Arch. Here you will often see fur seals and sea-lions swimming and diving for food in the turbulent seas.

Roads cross the park, giving access by car to the principal coastal features. Bushwalkers have the choice of many tracks. You may bushcamp with permission. A campsite with showers and toilets is provided at Rocky River and there are houses for rent.

Further east along the south coast of the island, Cape Gantheaume Conservation Park, which encloses another part of the undulating limestone plateau, offers wilderness walking country with similar vegetation and a population of native marsupials. At the adjacent Seal Bay Conservation Park you may walk among Australian sea-lions: the beach is the home of about 10 per cent of the entire race — and the one place where they have learnt to tolerate the presence of humans.

(Opposite page) Kangaroos in Flinders Chase, Kangaroo Island

Remarkable Rocks, Flinders Chase

Seal at Seal Bay, Kangaroo Island

Innes

On a clear day, you can see Kangaroo Island from Innes National Park, on the southern tip of Yorke Peninsula. Its principal attraction is its varied coastal scenery. An unsealed road makes a circuit of the park, with side roads and walking tracks leading to beaches and headlands. The interior is an area of saltlakes and marshes, with mallee woodland and patches of casuarinas and pines, a zone of coastal heathland and some cleared grassland. The western grey kangaroo is abundant here, though rarely seen in daylight. The discovery of the western whipbird in 1965 was the prime reason for the establishment of the park. The mound-building mallee fowl is also an inhabitant.

Lincoln

Lincoln National Park, on the opposite side of the entrance to Spencer Gulf, takes its name from nearby Port Lincoln. The park occupies the hammerhead-shaped headland which protects Boston Bay and so makes Port Lincoln South Australia's premier natural harbour and the home port of the state's tuna fleet. Its towering limestone cliffs provide nesting sites for the osprey and the white-breasted sea-eagle. Mallee scrub covers the ground away from the clifftops, providing a habitat rich in bird species.

Nullarbor

Further west, Nullarbor National Park encloses much of the former Nullarbor sheep station on the southern edge of the Nullarbor Plain and just west of Head of Bight. The park is bisected by the Eyre Highway. Vegetation consists mainly of saltbush and bluebush, with some mallee scrub close to the coast. This is a characteristic segment of the flat, almost treeless plain that forms the 'arch' of the continent, the arid, empty corridor between east and west. The limestone plain meets the Southern Ocean at this point in a continuous line of precipitous cliffs. For more information about this national park, consult Chapter 3, The Outback.

Pounding seas have created precipitous cliffs which dominate the coastline of Nullarbor National Park

WESTERN AUSTRALIA

The limestone cliffs which mark the southern limit of the Nullarbor Plain come to an end at Israelite Bay. Westward from here, the flat-topped cliffline is replaced by a shore of alternating headlands and beaches, much indented where the sea has gnawed bays between outcrops of resistant granite or metamorphic rocks, and where rivers from the southern edges of the Western Plateau reach the sea. By contrast with the Nullarbor and the deserts beyond it, this is a region which enjoys regular rains. Mainly occurring in winter, rainfall increases markedly from east to west, the annual average ranging from 680 millimetres at Esperance to about 1300 millimetres at Walpole, where the coastline begins to turn northwestward. Coastal mountain ranges make for a landscape full of interest. Outlying peaks thrust up through the sea in several places, notably in the islands of the Recherche Archipelago between Cape Arid and Cape Le Grand.

A string of national parks extends along this southern coast, providing good walking country combined with dramatic coastal scenery and peaceful sandy beaches. Many people come to these parks for camping and fishing holidays. Others come for the beauty to be found in the multitude of wildflowers which bloom on the coastal heathlands and for the fascination of observing the wildlife.

Cape Arid
Cape Le Grand
Stokes Inlet

The national parks at Cape Arid, Cape Le Grand and Stokes Inlet have all these elements. Cape Arid, by far the largest of the three, contains much of the Russell Range, including the sharp quartzite peak of Mount Ragged. This, the most out-of-the-way of these southern parks, can be reached only via rough tracks. Cape Le Grand, closer to Esperance, also has mountains within its boundaries, though these are neither as high nor as extensive as those of the Russell Range. The Western Australian Christmas tree (*Nuytsia floribunda*) lights up the summer scene with its mass of glowing orange-yellow flowers.

The animals of this region include rock wallabies of a species similar to those found on the islands of the Recherche. The parks on this coast also shelter the declining population of one of our smallest marsupials, the honey possum (or noolbenger). This long-snouted mouselike creature climbs acrobatically around banksias and other flowering shrubs, scooping up nectar with its brush-tipped tongue. Strictly nocturnal in habit, it is unlikely to be seen by most visitors.

View from Mount Arid over Ferret Bay in the Cape Arid National Park

58

Natural Bridge, Albany

The gorge, Albany National Park

59

Fitzgerald River

Fitzgerald River National Park occupies a long segment of coast between Hopetoun and Bremer Bay, encompassing the several isolated peaks of the Mount Barren Range. This is a park of great scenic beauty and variety which has become famous for its wildflowers. Here you can see, in abundance, most of the unique plants of the southwest. Much of the park consists of undulating sandplain, which is covered by a richly varied heath vegetation, including many banksias, grevilleas, melaleucas, wattles and pea flowers, with patches of mallee. On the mountain slopes, the bell-fruited mallee and the oak-leaved dryandra are common. River banks and floodplains carry tall eucalypt woodland. Among the many startlingly lovely plants you may see here are the scarlet banksia, the pincushion hakea, and the royal hakea, whose spectacular foliage outshines its inconspicuous flowers.

Several rivers and smaller streams reach the sea within the park, though with some reluctance: all form lagoons behind sand barriers. The principal rivers, the Phillips, Hamersley, Fitzgerald and Gairdner, have carved wide valleys across the sandplain, their terraces now filled by dense scrub. In places, the rivers pass through narrow gorges. The student of geology will find much of interest here. The mountains are massive outcrops of metamorphics, containing quartzites, phyllites, schists and gneisses. Rivers have cut deeply through sedimentary deposits, revealing a number of distinct beds. The exposures include spongolite cliffs and a narrow seam of lignite.

Camping is permitted. Tracks suitable for four-wheel-drive vehicles in dry weather criss-cross the park, though much of it is trackless. School parties have pioneered a coastal walk which takes in beaches and clifftops. Other suggested hikes follow river valleys. Bushwalkers are likely to see western grey kangaroos, emus, and many smaller animals. Bird life is diverse and one interesting inhabitant to look out for is the mallee fowl. Australian sea-lions may sometimes be seen on the shore.

Torndirrup

The promontory south of Albany which encloses Princess Royal Harbour possesses some striking features which attract visitors. One is an arch of granite, known as the Natural Bridge, where the sea pounds over smooth, sloping rock shelves. Nearby is another scenic marvel wrought by the force of the waves: the Gap. These popular features and much of the clifftop area, with its memorable views, are contained within the Torndirrup National Park.

William Bay

The small William Bay National Park, west of Denmark, has a landscape of high sand dunes with stands of Western Australian peppermint (*Agonis flexuosa*), together with hakea and daisy bush (*Olearia*) species. Granite outcrops protrude through the dunes. Shelves of granite slope into the water from the beaches.

Walpole-Nornalup

The majestic karri (*Eucalyptus diversicolor*), Western Australia's tallest tree, grows only in a small area in the southwest where annual rainfall exceeds 1000 millimetres. One of the best places to see karri forest is Walpole-Nornalup National Park, where you can walk through stands of trees several hundred years old. This park encompasses the waterways of Nornalup Inlet and Walpole Inlet and surrounds the small town of Walpole. The South Coast Highway cuts through the park on its way to Walpole from the east. Scenic drives near the township wind through the forests and take you to points overlooking the channel which links the two inlets. A campsite and caravan park at Coalmine Beach, within the park, make an ideal base for a holiday — which could combine car tours, bushwalking, boating, swimming and fishing. Boats may be hired.

In some parts of the park, the karri forests come right to the water's edge; in others, undulating sand dunes are thickly covered with coastal scrub. The multi-coloured display of wildflowers throughout spring and summer, and the abundant birdlife, help to make a stay here an enchanting experience. Beneath the canopy of leaves of the towering karris you will find a fascinating world of colour and bustling life. Stands of the red-flowering gum (*Eucalyptus ficifolia*), one of the world's favourite ornamental garden trees but now rare in the wild, can be seen growing on sand ridges. Elsewhere you will find tall red tingle (*E. jacksonii*) growing among the karris or dominating an understorey of karri oak (*Casuarina decussata*). Many gorgeous parrots, including the western rosella and the purple-crowned lorikeet, brighten the scene as they flash between the trees. At ground level, orchids bloom.

Galahs present a most striking spectacle of colour

(Opposite page) Murchison Gorge near Kalbarri National Park

The southwest thrusts a broad, blunt nose into the Indian Ocean between Cape Leeuwin and Cape Naturaliste. This stretch of coastline is a hard ridge of granite and gneiss overlaid by limestone. In many places, the chemical action of rainwater penetrating the limestone rock has hollowed out caves, creating exquisite drip formations in underground chambers. About 120 caves have been discovered, among the best known being the Jewel and Moondyne Caves, near Augusta, the Mammoth and Lake Caves, south of Margaret River, and Ngilgi Cave, near Yallingup. Those with particularly beautiful stalactite and shawl formations are lit and open to the public. Remains of extinct marsupials, including the thylacine (better known as the Tasmanian tiger), have been found in some caves. The Leeuwin-Naturaliste National Park, a series of reserves, takes in many of the caves together with segments of rocky coastline backed by sandhills and forests of jarrah (*Eucalyptus marginata*), marri (*E. calophylla*), the smaller red-flowering gum and Swan River blackbutt (*E. patens*).

Yalgorup
Yanchep

Calcified root systems of plants have formed into columns of limestone known as The Pinnacles in Nambung National Park

Yalgorup and Yanchep national parks, respectively south and north of Perth, are not strictly coastal in their locations but both enclose areas of coastal plain quite close to beaches. Yalgorup contains a system of parallel lakes noted for their birdlife, as well as coastal heath and woodland. Yanchep, in yet another limestone belt, is renowned for its caves and its wildflowers, especially kangaroo paws (*Anigozanthos* spp.). An area near the park entrance is given over to tourist facilities but otherwise the park is largely in its natural state. Loch McNess attracts large flocks of waterfowl.

Nambung

Among the sand dunes of Nambung National Park, about 250 kilometres north of Perth, you can see the extraordinary Pinnacles Desert. Just a short distance in from the beach, in a landscape of shifting, coloured sands, you will find the petrified 'forest' called The Pinnacles. Thousands of columns of limestone up to five metres tall rise from the sand. Formed over tens of thousands of years, they are calcified root systems of plants which formerly grew in the sand dunes. The result is one of the strangest scenes in nature.

The park area is not in fact a desert. The foredunes support communities of flowering shrubs and sand-binding creepers such as pig-face (*Carprobrotus australis*) and the blue-flowered *Scaevola crassifolia*. Further from the shore, *Acacia* species form dense thickets, while still further in are forests of tuart (*Eucalyptus gomphocephala*) mixed with patches of heath and low woodlands of banksias and casuarinas. Here you will see the striking orange flowers of *Banksia prionotes*. As in all these western parks, emus and western grey kangaroos are the most commonly observed animals, together with a wide variety of birds and reptiles. No camping is permitted within the park. Roads are unsealed and can be very hard on the conventional car. Some tracks to beaches are strictly for four-wheel-drive vehicles only.

Kalbarri

Kalbarri National Park, north of Geraldton, is a large area of sandplain country through which the Murchison River curves and meanders to reach the sea. When the sandstone bedrock was uplifted some two million years ago, the river wore its way down through the rock, creating a scenically magnificent gorge about eighty kilometres long. Roads and hiking trails within the park lead to viewing points and picnic sites and include the sealed main road to Kalbarri township. In some places, short walks lead down to the base of the red sandstone cliffs, where river red gums grow beside the river pools. The sea-cliffs are almost equally fascinating and provide splendid views. Supplies, accommodation, camping and caravan sites are available in the town. This crayfishing port on the estuary of the Murchison is also a popular resort, offering swimming, boating and fishing.

Cape Range

Our final look at the coastal parks of Western Australia takes us up to North West Cape, where an elongated triangle of land juts into the sea at the continent's northwest shoulder. This peninsula has a spine of hills along its centre. Encompassing a large part of the western side is the Cape Range National Park. To reach it, you drive along the Exmouth Gulf side of the peninsula to the tip of the cape, where you pass the massive aerial towers of the US-Australian communications station, and then about twenty kilometres down the Indian Ocean side. You can drive about two-thirds of the length of the park. Good campsites will be found at intervals along the beach.

The hills of the Cape Range reach no more than 315 metres above sea-level but they offer the visitor some impressive scenery and some interesting wildlife. The range consists of layers of sedimentary sandstones and limestones originally laid down horizontally but subsequently uplifted into a dome. Erosion has worn down the dome to form a plateau and has carved deep gorges along the plateau edges, where sheer cliffs of pale yellow rock loom above steep slopes of eroded material.

Within the gorges, permanent pools of fresh water support a mixed population of ground animals and birds. Grey kangaroos and wallabies descend to the narrow coastal plain at dusk to graze. In the rocky ravines, a colony of yellow-footed rock wallabies survives and appears to be untroubled by the comings and goings of humans.

NORTHERN TERRITORY

Cobourg Peninsula

Northeast of Darwin across Van Diemen Gulf, attached to the continent by a narrow isthmus, is the Cobourg Peninsula, which contains Gurig National Park. Remote, tropical, low-lying and deeply indented by the sea, this part of Australia has not attracted Europeans since the abandonment, in 1849, of a colonial outpost proudly named Victoria, on the shore of the long inlet called Port Essington. This had in fact been the second attempt to establish a settlement on the peninsula. Its founders hoped it would become a second Singapore. But Englishmen found the climate and the isolation intolerable.

Cobourg is really an extension of the flat coastal plain on the Top End west of the Arnhem Land escarpment. Its highest point is Mount Roe, a blister on the southern shore, which rises to a mere 160 metres above sea-level. Vegetation cover consists largely of monsoon forest, predominantly tall eucalypts such as the Darwin stringybark (*Eucalyptus tetrodonta*) and the woollybutt (*E. miniata*). The lower storeys include bloodwood (*E. foelscheana*) and ghost gums (*E. papuana*), with pandanus, cycads and tall grasses. There are also stands of white cypress pine (*Callitris columellaris*). Mangrove forests occur on the south coast. The bays along the north coast, by contrast, provide good clear-water anchorages.

Malay fishermen frequented these harbours in their praus on expeditions to catch trepang (the edible sea-slug), long before the arrival of the British. Port Essington was described by its discoverer, Captain Phillip Parker King RN, as being '. . . equal to any harbour I have seen' and by Captain J. J. Bremer, first commandant of the settlement, as '. . . one of the most noble and beautiful harbours that can be imagined.' Only scattered remnants of the town, including chimneys, a kiln and graveyard, remain today.

The military commanders of the early settlements were responsible for the introduction of various exotic animals, which were brought in from Timor and Bali to provide food supplies. Left behind after the settlers departed, these animals became feral and multiplied. Among them were water buffaloes, which found their way to swamp country further south and have since spread far and wide across the floodplains. Banteng cattle and deer remain restricted to the Cobourg Peninsula.

Cobourg Peninsula has been a flora and fauna reserve since 1924 and is now Gurig National Park. With an area of 191 600 hectares, it is the largest national park managed by the Conservation Commission of the Northern Territory (though ownership is vested in the traditional Aboriginal owners). The national park incorporates the Fort Wellington and Victoria Settlement historical reserves, sites of the two nineteenth-century military settlements.

Resident rangers are responsible for wildlife protection, feral animal control, coastal surveillance, supervision of the fishing boats operating around the peninsula's coasts, and management of the historical reserves. In addition, of course, they must keep a watchful eye on the activities of the increasing numbers of visitors arriving by boat, plane and four-wheel drive vehicle.

Hunters should note that shooting is not permitted within the park. Also, crocodiles — both the saltwater and freshwater types — are totally protected. A permit is required to enter the park. Visitors arriving by boat can obtain this from the rangers. Other visitors should obtain a permit from the CC of NT before entering.

The waters off Gurig National Park contain the 229 000 hectare Cobourg Marine Park. This park contains dugong, turtles and a wide variety of fish. The spectacular reefs provide excellent sport for fishing people.

(Over page) View through Glen Helen Gorge, Northern Territory

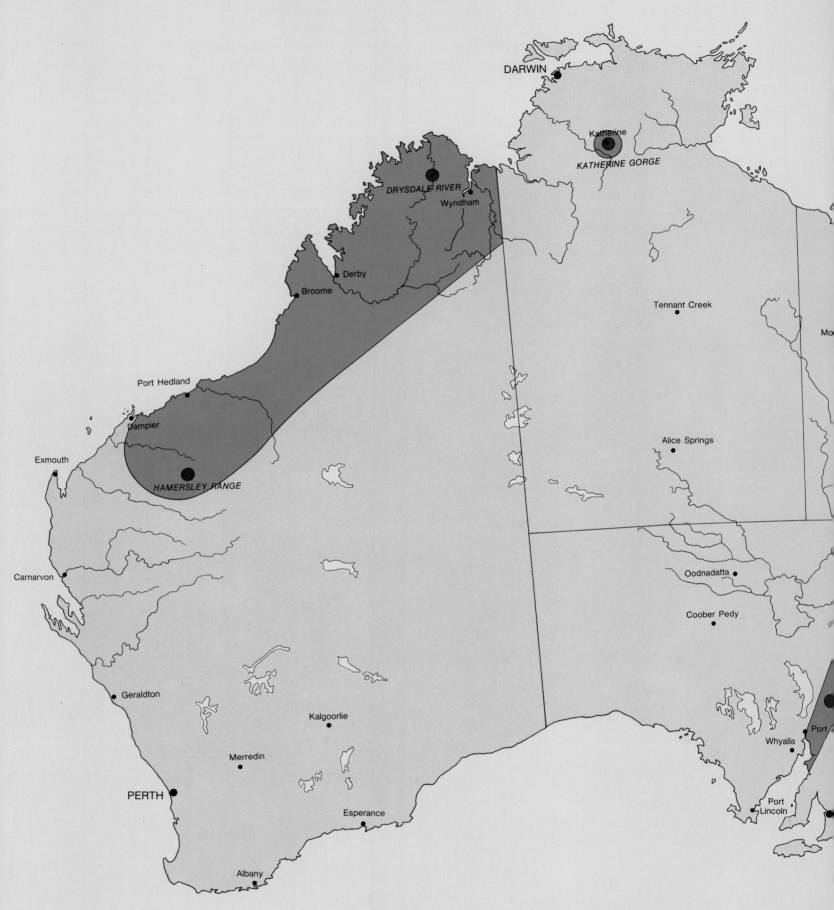

DARWIN

Katherine
KATHERINE GORGE

DRYSDALE RIVER
Wyndham

Derby

Broome

Tennant Creek

Mo

Port Hedland

Dampier

Alice Springs

Exmouth

HAMERSLEY RANGE

Carnarvon

Oodnadatta

Coober Pedy

Geraldton

Kalgoorlie

Merredin

Whyalla

Port

PERTH

Esperance

Port
Lincoln

Albany

Mount

2 HIGHLANDS AND FORESTS

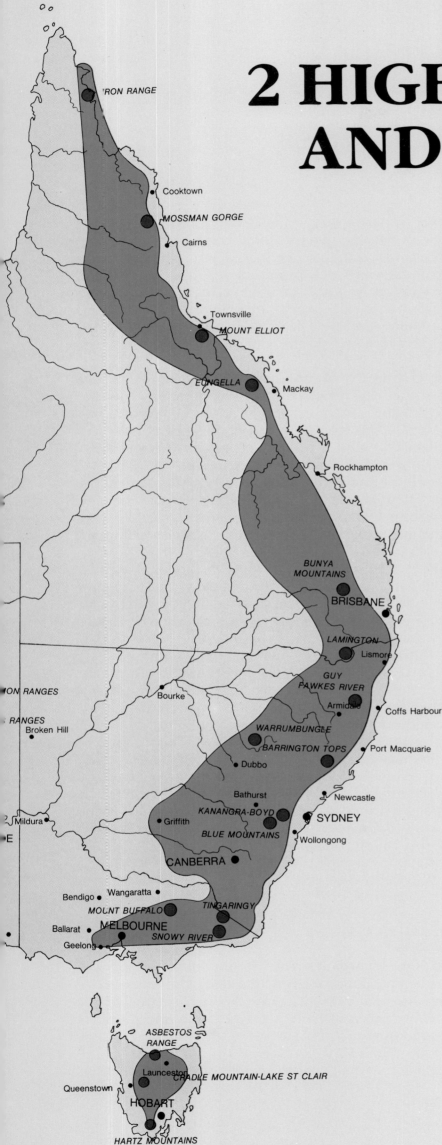

IRON RANGE

Cooktown

MOSSMAN GORGE

Cairns

Townsville

MOUNT ELLIOT

EUNGELLA

Mackay

Rockhampton

BUNYA MOUNTAINS

BRISBANE

LAMINGTON

Lismore

GUY FAWKES RIVER

ON RANGES

Bourke

Armidale

Coffs Harbour

RANGES

Broken Hill

WARRUMBUNGLE

BARRINGTON TOPS

Port Macquarie

Dubbo

Bathurst

Newcastle

Mildura

Griffith

KANANGRA-BOYD

SYDNEY

BLUE MOUNTAINS

Wollongong

CANBERRA

Bendigo

Wangaratta

MOUNT BUFFALO

TINGARINGY

Ballarat

MELBOURNE

SNOWY RIVER

Geelong

ASBESTOS RANGE

Launceston

CRADLE MOUNTAIN-LAKE ST CLAIR

Queenstown

HOBART

HARTZ MOUNTAINS

This ancient land of ours has been planed down by the elements over millions of years to become the flattest of all the continents. Our highest mountains are found in the Eastern Highlands, a discontinuous series of ranges spread along the eastern seaboard and geologically the youngest part of Australia. Even here, the land does not rise to great heights. Our tallest peaks are dwarves by comparison with those of our neighbours, Papua New Guinea and New Zealand. The highest parts of our ranges would form mere foothills if tacked on to the Himalayas of Asia or the Andes of South America.

Nevertheless, our highlands have their own considerable and diverse scenic charms and, in many places, a ruggedness which has defied modern man's drive to dominate and exploit the land, leaving areas of wilderness untouched by the axe, the plough or the motor car. Much of this wilderness country has been conserved in national parks. Some of these parks embrace unique and spectacular landforms — deep gorges, towering cliffs, high waterfalls, bare volcanic plugs, broad valleys, strangely formed rocks — all fascinating and awesome to the human observer. Most also offer a wealth of life-forms. Our highland national parks range from those in the tropical monsoon zone through temperate and alpine environments to those in the arid areas of South Australia and the northwest. The diversity of fauna and flora is correspondingly broad.

The richest habitats of all, the rainforests, are found within the mountain ranges and coastal hills of the east. Although vast areas of lowland rainforest fell to the axes of the timber-cutters in the nineteenth century, to be replaced in the north by crops such as sugar cane, and further south by grazing properties, significantly large pockets of rainforest still stand on many hillsides and in many wet mountain gullies. Some of these are within scheduled state forests and are still under threat. Others — usually those located in terrain too steep for motorised access — have been absorbed into national parks. In all probability, these will quite soon be the last remaining examples of earth's most prolific ecosystem still to be seen in Australia.

The most complex plant community of all, the tropical rainforest, occurs on eastern slopes of the coastal ranges of Queensland up to about 800 metres above sea-level. These luxuriant forests are nature's greenhouses, producing a multi-layered universe of plant life from great red cedars and hoop pines down to ground orchids, ground ferns, mosses, lichens and fungi. Between the leaf canopy and the forest floor the space is filled with an immensely varied and abundant vegetation which includes palms, vines, epiphytic ferns and orchids, and the massive root-curtains of strangler figs. Further from the equator, the rainforests grade through subtropical communities, less dense than the tropical rainforests, to temperate rainforests, which lack the diversity of the tropical communities, generally having a single dominant tree species such as one of the Antarctic beeches, with a shrub or fern understorey.

The fauna of the rainforests is comparable in its variety with the vegetation, being especially abundant in colourful bird species. Ground animals, although not always so readily seen, are nevertheless prolific.

Eucalypts dominate the rest of the highland forests over most of the country. This most essentially Australian tree genus is found everywhere across the continent except in the rainforests (with minor exceptions) and the deserts, occurring in many different forms to suit different environments. Some 600 species have been recorded. The tallest and densest eucalypt forests are found in regions with rainfall above 1000 millimetres, with the Sydney blue gum (*Eucalyptus saligna*) prominent in Queensland and New South Wales, the mountain ash (*E. regnans*), our tallest tree,

forming enormous forests in Tasmania and Victoria, and the handsome karri
(*E. diversicolor*) lording it over a confined area in the southwest corner of Western
Australia. The only tree growing at altitudes above 1300 metres, in the alpine areas
of Victoria and New South Wales, is the snow gum (*E. pauciflora*), which puts on
a fine display of white blossom between December and February.

With the important exception of the isolated ranges of the Centre, Australia's
highlands are almost entirely disposed around the perimeter of the continent. Since
the vast majority of Australians live in cities near the coasts, this means that most
of us have mountainous country at our doorsteps. As by far the largest proportion
of the country's national parks lie in the highland areas, most of us have highland
national parks close at hand — places where we can enjoy vistas of exhilarating
grandeur and experience contact with the living wilderness.

QUEENSLAND

NORTH

Relief maps show a narrow finger of the Eastern Highlands (also known as the Great Dividing Range) reaching along the eastern side of Cape York Peninsula to within 200 kilometres of the tip. Monsoonal rains between December and March bring enough precipitation to this region to keep many rivers flowing throughout the year. In addition, where the hills rise close to the ocean, the winter trade winds spill their moisture. This regular rainfall supports a varied tropical vegetation. Rainforests occur widely on the eastern slopes and lowlands, sustaining an extremely diverse wildlife. In this triangle of territory, where Australia comes closest to Papua New Guinea, species representative of the flora and fauna of countries to our north share the scene with species that are endemic to our own country.

The largest avian inhabitant of the North Queensland rainforests is the cassowary, a flightless bird about the size of the emu, found also in New Guinea and Indonesia. The cassowary is distinguished by its glossy black hair-like plumage, the cobalt blue skin of the neck, and orange-red wattles which hang from the front of the neck. A high ridge of horn on its head apparently serves as a 'crash helmet', protecting the bird as it plunges through thick jungle. Shy, solitary and well camouflaged, the cassowary is not easily seen in the dim light of the rainforest. Individuals can be aggressive, especially when protecting chicks. Cassowaries fight by jumping up and kicking, each powerful foot being equipped with a very sharp, long claw on the inner toe. The rumbling and booming of the cassowary's voice can be heard over considerable distances.

Around the fringes of the rainforests you may see, by contrast, pairs of tiny, brilliantly coloured, olive-backed sunbirds hovering in front of flowers whilst extracting nectar, or plucking spiders from their webs. These bold little birds, well-known visitors to suburban gardens in Cairns and other coastal towns of northeastern Queensland, also live in many parts of Southeast Asia and Papua New Guinea.

Many rare and beautiful birds are found in these northern rainforests: fruit-eaters, such as the spotted catbird and Victoria's riflebird, seed-eaters, such as the blue-faced finch, and several honeyeaters.

Some of the North Queensland parrots are found nowhere else in Australia. These include Australia's largest parrot, the palm cockatoo, and the smallest, the fig parrot. Both these species have family ties with Papua New Guinea. The palm cockatoo's Australian range is confined to the Cape York Peninsula north of Princess Charlotte Bay, especially around the edges of the rainforest, where the jungle meets eucalypt woodland. It is differentiated from the commoner red-tailed black cockatoo (also found in this area) by its lack of red tail feathers and its featherless crimson cheeks. Its powerful bill enables it to open the tough casing of the pandanus palm fruit to eat the kernel.

The prettily coloured fig parrots are more often heard than seen as they flock above the jungle canopy. One subspecies, Marshall's fig parrot, is confined to a few particular patches of rainforest on the eastern side of the peninsula. A second subspecies, the red-browed (or blue-faced) fig parrot, is found only in the rainforests on the eastern edge of the Atherton Tableland between Tully and Cairns. You may be lucky enough to see some of these attractive little birds as they clamber around branches of wild figs, pecking the fruit to obtain the seeds. Flocks occasionally venture into more open woodland.

Two more parrot species, the eclectus (red-sided) parrot and the red-cheeked parrot, both of which range widely through New Guinea, are also found in rainforests of the McIlwraith and Iron Ranges. Birds of the more open woodlands include such well-known species as the gregarious rainbow lorikeet, the sulphur-crested cockatoo, the laughing kookaburra and the blue-winged kookaburra, which prefers wetter paperbark woodlands. A summer migrant from Papua New Guinea is the superbly plumed white-tailed kingfisher (once featured on Australia's 22 cent postage stamp), which nests in termite mounds, usually returning north before May.

Notable among the species of snakes of this region are the deadly taipan, generally active in daylight in open country, and the amethystine python, the largest Australian snake, which grows to seven metres or more. The amethystine python lives in tropical rainforest, where it may be found in caves, under rock slabs or simply lying on the ground in the sun, showing off its handsome tile-patterned markings of dark and light browns.

Two species of tree-kangaroos are known in Australia, one being found only in a small area in the ranges close to Cooktown, the other in high country near Cairns. Related species occur in Papua New Guinea. Another tree-dwelling marsupial of the region whose closest relatives are found in the islands to our north is the cuscus, a short-eared possum. The peninsula has two types, the grey and the spotted. These thickly furred animals spend the day sleeping in forks of trees, usually well concealed by foliage, becoming active at night.

Several other possums have been found in the rainforests of the North Queensland ranges, some of these as yet little studied. Among them are the neatly marked black-and-white striped possum and the green possum (or striped ringtail). Being nocturnal in habit, these gentle and appealing creatures are rarely seen.

These northern mountains also provide habitats for the rare musky rat-kangaroo and two species of small scrub wallabies, the red-legged (or Cape York) pademelon and the red-necked pademelon. The name 'pademelon' is a corruption of an Aboriginal word first adopted by early settlers in the Sydney area. Although these creatures were once quite common along the whole eastern seaboard, the race has shrunk in numbers as suitable habitats have been progressively destroyed. The natural haunt of the pademelon is thick forest undergrowth or long grass, ferns and bushes in swampy country. These timid creatures graze in the early morning and at dusk, eating grass, leaves and young shoots. At the slightest disturbance, they hop swiftly away and are quickly lost to sight.

Spotted Cuscus

The copious plant life of the rainforests abounds in palms, pines, vines, ferns and

Mossman Gorge wilderness area covers some of the most mountainous rainforest in the country and has spectacular scenery along the gorges (Lee Pearce)

Adeline Creek, part of Mossman Gorge (Lee Pearce)

(Opposite page) Mossman Gorge

figs. Giant of the rainforest trees is the red cedar (*Toona australis*), a deciduous tree which bears pink or white flowers in late spring. Once common all along the east coast but extensively exploited for its timber from the middle years of last century, the red cedar is now rare. Much less attractive, from the human point of view, are the stinging trees (*Dendrocnide* spp.). One type grows more than thirty metres tall. Stinging hairs on the round leaves, if touched, cause severe pain which may persist for weeks. There are, however, many plants of exquisite beauty, especially the numerous orchids, which add splashes of glowing colour to the dark glades of the jungle. Perhaps most celebrated of them all is the pink or purple Cooktown Orchid, which has been adopted as Queensland's floral emblem.

The character of the vegetation changes with altitude and exposure to rain-bearing winds. The western slopes of the McIlwraith Range have monsoonal forests which consist largely of deciduous trees. On the eastern side, rainforests occur near the coast. The noble hoop pine (*Araucaria cunninghamii*) is prominent as an emergent, rising through the canopy of the higher forests. On the highest mountain ridges, the rhododendron (*Rhododendron lochae*), another migrant from the north, grows as a low, spreading shrub, sporting brilliant red trumpet flowers in spring and summer. Heath and shrublands cover the sandstone plateaux, and here you will find flowering grevilleas and banksias. Elsewhere, eucalypt forests alternate with open paperbark woodlands.

The Cape York Peninsula is sparsely populated and has few roads. Whilst these circumstances are favourable to the conservation of wilderness and the diverse wildlife, they present problems to the traveller. The rains of the wet season leave most roads impassable until at least May. Driving north of Coen is not considered advisable before August. The recommended way to travel, even then, is by four-wheel-drive vehicle, preferably two parties travelling together in two such vehicles. Supplies of petrol, spare parts, food and water should be carried, as well as equipment for emergencies. River crossings can be difficult and sometimes hazardous, even in the Dry, and the difficulties increase the further north you go.

If you decide, notwithstanding the difficulties, to explore this part of the country, plan your trip carefully, seek informed advice, and make certain your vehicle is absolutely reliable. Also, it would be wise to consult the Queensland National Parks and Wildlife Service before you head north.

Iron Range

Iron Range National Park, on the east coast of the peninsula, is of particular significance because it occupies an area close to the southern limit of colonisation by several species of plants and animals that 'belong' to Papua New Guinea rather than to Australia. The Iron Range, which lies between the Pascoe River and the coast, owes its name to the presence of haematite (iron ore) within its hills. The park encloses a segment of the range which looks down upon Weymouth Bay and some of the inner islands of the Great Barrier Reef. It contains the largest area of lowland rainforest remaining in Australia. Other types of habitat within the park include heathland, open forest and mangroves. Interesting life-forms to be seen include the insect-devouring pitcher plants, the anthouse plants, in whose bases ants make their nests, and over fifty species of orchids.

Starcke

Some 400 kilometres south-southeast of Iron Range as the crow flies, a few hours' drive from Cooktown, the smaller Starcke National Park takes in an area of sandstone plateau which rises sharply above the narrow coastal plain. This is a scenically interesting park on high ground where one of the tributaries of the Normanby River rises. It contains escarpments, narrow valleys and open eucalypt forest.

Daintree

Midway between Cairns and Cooktown is the Daintree River National Park, 'where the forest meets the reef'. This is a magnificent area, right on the coast. The rainforest stretches right down to the waterline. Daintree has been the subject of bitter battles between the Queensland Government and conservationists. The former has constructed a road through the park that threatens the stability of both rainforest and reef. An isolated park, that is suitable for day visitors or well-prepared campers. Conditions can become difficult during the wet season.

(Opposite page) Form and colour in grevillea

76

The rockpools and rainforest of Barron Gorge attract many bushwalkers (Lee Pearce)

Buttress roots of a fig tree in Barron Gorge (Lee Pearce)

Barron Gorge

The Barron Gorge National Park (formerly Barron Falls), just north of Cairns, no longer offers quite the spectacle of former times since the water falling over the 260 metre drop in the Barron River is now restrained by a dam for irrigation and hydro-electric purposes — hence the change in name to avoid disappointing visitors. Nevertheless, the views from the Cairns-Kuranda narrow-gauge railway, which snakes its way up the gorge, are dramatic.

| Bellenden-Ker | Of the several national parks close to Cairns, most notable is the Bellenden-Ker National Park, which embraces Queensland's highest and most rugged country. Here, the granite mountains of the Bellenden-Ker Range rise like a wall behind the patchwork pattern of canefields covering the coastal strip. Within the park is Queensland's highest peak, Mount Bartle Frere (1657 metres). |

Of the several national parks close to Cairns, most notable is the Bellenden-Ker National Park, which embraces Queensland's highest and most rugged country. Here, the granite mountains of the Bellenden-Ker Range rise like a wall behind the patchwork pattern of canefields covering the coastal strip. Within the park is Queensland's highest peak, Mount Bartle Frere (1657 metres).

The steepness of the Bellenden-Ker escarpment suggests that the range originated in a massive uplift, as a horst, along a fault-line. The steepness of the terrain has been its salvation, from a conservationist viewpoint, protecting it from the meddling hand of man. The tropical rainforests teem with life in many forms, from cassowaries to centipedes. The patient watcher may come across tree-kangaroos, cuscuses and many beautiful birds. A stroll through the jungle will bring you face to face with gorgeous orchids and allow you to see some of the world's largest and gaudiest butterflies.

A climb to any of the summits will take you through changing habitats, each full of interest for the nature-lover. You will discover patches of cyclone forest, where large trees have been uprooted by cyclonic winds and the spaces filled by tangled vines and stinging trees. Higher up the slopes, the forest thins out and trees become stunted, although pockets of rainforest persist where there is shelter from the easterly winds. Rainforests at altitudes above 900 metres along this section of the coast provide the only habitat of the golden bower bird. On the craggy open heights, the red-flowered rhododendron grows.

The high plateau west of the coastal range, the Atherton Tableland, owes its character to volcanic activity during the Tertiary period, over two million years ago. The basalt lava flowed for long distances before cooling and solidifying. Weathering has since broken down much of the rock into mineral-rich, fertile soil. The whole tableland was formerly covered in forest. Recent research has shown that the flora has gone through a series of phases over the past 60 000 years or so, reflecting changes in climatic conditions. In the last phase, from about 9000 years ago, tropical rainforest of the Indo-Malayan type (jungle) took over. This has gradually shrunk in area over the past 3000 years as rainfall decreased, remaining only in those localities of highest humidity.

Lake Eacham
Lake Barrine

On the tableland, 730 kilometres above sea-level and about twenty kilometres from the town of Atherton, are two volcanic craters containing lakes, both ringed by tropical rainforest. These crater lakes are Lake Eacham and Lake Barrine. Both have been reserved as national parks.

These two parks beside the Gillies Highway encapsulate all the wonders and the exotic wildlife of North Queensland jungle country in small, easily accessible reserves. At the centre of each you find the still, mysterious, almost black waters of a deep lake. The water, always sweet and cool, is perfect for swimming. The jungle, which overhangs the lake waters, contains at least eighty different tree species. More than 200 species of birds have been recorded here. Some of these are found nowhere else but in the rainforests of the Cairns region, for example, the Queen Victoria riflebird, recognisable by its iridescent plumage of black and green. The forest animals include a species of pademelon, the musky rat-kangaroo, tortoises, Boyd's forest dragon and the mountain blue ('Ulysses') butterfly. A walking track encircles each lake.

Chillagoe-
Mungana Caves

West of the tableland is a belt of limestone country, in the centre of which stands an old mining town, Chillagoe. There are nine small national parks in the vicinity, their chief attraction being their many limestone caves. Outcrops of weathered limestone rise here and there in this open countryside like battlemented towers and fairytale castles. Beneath the ground are the even stranger formations resulting from centuries of seepage and periodic flooding by rainwater.

Regular guided tours are conducted through three of the caves. Others may be visited without a guide. The Donna Cave is electrically lit. You should take a torch when exploring the others, especially if you go on your own. Your reward will be a show of grotesque and beautiful shapes and shadows: stalactites and stalagmites, curtains and columns, arches and vaults, in colours that range from white to reddish

Palmerston
Herbert River

Crystal Creek-
Mount Spec
Mount Elliot
Mount Aberdeen

Crystal Falls in the Crystal Creek-Mount Spec National Park

brown. Wildlife inhabiting the caves includes several species of bats, the children's python, which preys on the bats, and the insect-eating grey swiftlet. This bird, like the bats, uses an echo-sounding system to navigate its way safely through the caves. The swiftlets' breeding period is September to February. After that time they abandon the caves, not returning again until the following spring.

In the hills inland from Innisfail there are several small national parks containing scenically impressive waterfalls. Notable among these is the Palmerston National Park, where several falls on the Johnston River may be reached along walking tracks from the highway which cuts through the park. Further south, in the range behind Cardwell, are more small parks with waterfalls, including the spectacular Wallaman Falls, where a tributary of the Herbert River plunges 300 metres over a precipice, descending through a cloud of spray to disappear into a deep chasm.

Crystal Creek-Mount Spec National Park, south of Ingham, provides easy access to patches of rainforest. There are also stands of eucalypt forest, rock pools and short walking tracks, with picnic sites and scenic lookouts. Further south still, twenty-five kilometres out of Townsville, the Mount Elliot National Park offers similarly mixed habitats, and picnic and camping grounds. But this park encloses a wide area of wild, challenging country, attractive to the keen bushwalker and the lover of solitude. The precipitous Mount Aberdeen near Bowen also offers rough walking country, with low rainforest occurring above 900 metres, where the flora includes cabbage palms, elkhorn ferns and orchids.

CENTRAL AND SOUTHERN

In central and southern Queensland, the Eastern Highlands reach their greatest width, spreading across half the state. South from the Bellenden-Ker Range, the main divide strikes inland towards the southwest and then curves south and east in a long arc which takes it almost to the coast again beyond Brisbane. Thus the spine of the highlands forms a bow, the string of which is represented by the coastline between Coolangatta and Cairns. To the east of the divide, within the curve of the bow, many rivers run north and south through valleys divided by separate mountain ranges, outliers of the Great Dividing Range. To the west, the high country generally declines more gradually, to merge with the central lowland plain.

Within this great area of mountainous country there are approximately ninety parks administered by the Queensland NPWS. As it would be impracticable to attempt to describe all of them, just a few have been included here either for their unique importance or as being representative of their region.

Eungella

Between Proserpine and Mackay, the Clarke Range provides a wild, forested backdrop to the cultivated coastal plain. Some eighty kilometres due east of Mackay, reached by a road which passes through the sugar-growing country of the Pioneer River valley, are the township of Eungella and the main points of access to the largest national park of central Queensland, Eungella National Park.

Eungella is the name the Aborigines gave to the high southern portion of the Clarke Range. It means 'land of cloud'. The climate here is tropical, with the heaviest rains arriving between December and March. But the southeast trade winds, which blow off the sea from May to September, often bring mists and showers as they rise up the eastern ramparts of the range. This exposure to the damp coastal breezes is the secret of Eungella's special character: the tumbling slopes and deeply cut valleys are thickly covered in rainforest.

This is a park to suit all tastes. The narrow southern section, close to Eungella township, has picnic grounds and camping facilities. A number of tracks of varying lengths follow the edge of the escarpment, providing views through 'windows' in the forest, or lead you beside the Broken River, offering easy walking in delightful countryside. There are deep pools where it is not unusual to see a platypus or families of wild ducks. You may enjoy a swim in the pool close to the picnic ground or follow the self-guiding nature walk through Forest Glen with the help of a leaflet which enables you to identify many of the trees and smaller plants. Several lookouts, some easily accessible from the road, afford panoramic views of the Pioneer Valley.

For the more adventurous, the northern portion, with its extremely rugged wilderness country, offers plenty of scope for strenuous bushwalking. This part of the park contains high granite peaks, notably Mount Dalrymple (1280 metres), as well as the 300 metre deep Massey Gorge.

Prominent among the bigger trees to be seen in this park are the handsome Mackay tulip oak, straight and tall, with buttressed trunk, the red cedar, the blue quandong and the hoop pine. In the gorges you will find the white kurrajong and the Illawarra flame tree. Hibiscus, blue-flowered hovea and the pink spider flowers of hakea add their colours to the massed greenery. The foliage itself is full of variety, with palms and ferns abundant in places. Hanging gardens supported by epiphytic ferns grow high overhead, providing habitats for other epiphytic plants such as orchids.

The tree-dwelling marsupial inhabitants of the forests find daytime lodgings in these hanging gardens and in the crowns of tall palm trees. More active during daylight hours are the birds, though some are not easily seen in the twilight of the rainforest. The wompoo pigeon, for example, although clothed in plumage of bright green and yellow, blends in with the foliage. Its presence may be given away by its booming voice or by fruit raining on the ground beneath feeding flocks.

(Opposite page) Sandstone cliffs in the Carnarvon Ranges

Isla Gorge
Robinson Gorge
Carnarvon

About 400 kilometres inland in a straight line from Maryborough, where the dividing range becomes a sandstone plateau capped with a layer of basalt, there are three national parks which enclose spectacular gorges: Isla Gorge, Robinson Gorge and Carnarvon.

The geological history of this region can be traced back more than 200 million years to the Triassic period, when the sandstone, eroded from some higher, granitic hills, began to be deposited in flat beds. Much more recently, no more than thirty million years ago, a period of upheaval and volcanic eruption elevated these beds to form a basalt-capped tableland. Since that time, the elements have chiselled away at the weakest points of the rock, carving deep clefts, hollowing out caves, fretting away the cliff faces and engraving them with intricate patterns.

The porous rock of this region drains a good deal of the water which falls upon it southwestward into the aquifers of the Great Artesian Basin. In the deep, shaded ravines within the Carnarvon Range, water seeps constantly from the rock walls, forming perennial pools and creeks, providing a life-support system for a vigorous and varied flora and its associated fauna.

As you approach Carnarvon National Park by road from the south you see the precipitous white cliffs rising like a massive fortification from the plain. A narrow gash in this rampart is the mouth of Carnarvon Gorge, a cleft cut through the sandstone by the Carnarvon Creek. The gorge winds back into the tableland for a distance of thirty kilometres. Its walls stand from 50 metres to 400 metres apart and up to 200 metres high.

Dense tropical rainforest in
Eungella is home to several tree-
dwelling marsupials and a
variety of birds (Lee Pearce)

The floor of the gorge is a fertile garden, with cabbage palms and eucalypts growing straight and tall above stands of river she-oak (*Casuarina cunninghamiana*), weeping bottlebrush (*Callistemon viminalis*) and native cherry (*Acmena australis*). Where there is just enough sunlight, the broad leaves and huge yellow spikes of the rock orchid or rock lily (*Dendrobium speciosum*) sprout from rock ledges, while the daintier pink-flowered *Dendrobium kingianum* clings to cliff faces. On still higher, rockier ground grow venerable cycads (*Macrozamia moorei*) looking like squat palm trees, and grass-trees (*Xanthorrhoea* spp.).

To explore Carnarvon Gorge, you must walk. The road ends at the gorge entrance, where there is a campsite. A tourist lodge just outside the park offers cabin accommodation and sells petrol. The principal walking track leads along the floor of the gorge for a distance of ten kilometres to Cathedral Cave. This cave and the 'Art Gallery' lower down the gorge shelter important collections of Aboriginal art. In fact, some forty-four rock art sites have been identified within the park.

Tributary streams have cut several side gorges, each of which has a beauty and fascination all its own. Some of these are so narrow that you can touch both sides if you stretch out your hands. Some are dark and silent while others contain small patches of rainforest and are busy with life. Many types of ferns and mosses flourish in sheltered, moist places. One of the minor gorges, Angiopteris Ravine, is the habitat of the rare king fern (*Angiopteris evecta*).

Whiptail (or pretty-face) wallabies graze unconcernedly around the tents on the campsite. After dark, brush-tailed possums come looking for titbits. But most of the other marsupials are shy and you may have to watch patiently for them. They include grey kangaroos, brush-tailed rock wallabies, koalas, gliders and the white-spotted northern quoll (or little northern native cat). Among rocks you may see a sand goanna, a black-headed rock python or a carpet snake. The common lace monitor or tree goanna can often be seen on trunks of trees. Near water you may find the green tree-frog, the tree-snake or the freshwater snake. Look out, also, for the eastern water-dragon basking in the sun on a branch overhanging the water. You will know him by the line of saw-tooth spikes along his greyish-brown back.

The birds range from large water birds such as pelicans, herons, ibises and cormorants to small wrens and robins. Several types of honeyeaters are quite common. Flocks of squealing rainbow lorikeets swoop through the gorges. King parrots — with scarlet bodies, green wings, and blue-black tails — feed among the eucalypt branches.

The pools, too, team with life, from whirligig beetles on the surface to catfish, perch and freshwater shrimps in the depths. These creatures attract the water birds, including the azure kingfisher which you may see sitting absolutely still on a branch, staring at the water. They also provide food for the snakes.

Summer, or indeed any period of wet weather, is the wrong time to visit Carnarvon National Park. Rain makes the approach road impassable. A heavy downpour may flood the gorge and bring rocks tumbling down in landslides. You need fine weather to enable you to get here and to ensure your enjoyment of this wonderful place.

Bunya Mountains

North of Toowoomba, where the hills of the Divide rise abruptly from the high plain of the Darling Downs, midway between Dalby and Kingaroy, lies a park renowned for one particular kind of tree. The park is the Bunya Mountains National Park. The tree is the bunya pine (*Araucaria bidwillii*).

The bunya pine, an extremely handsome, symmetrical tree which grows to about fifty metres belongs to the family of pines whose members dominate most of Queensland's rainforests. This park preserves one of the last known forests of bunya pine, although specimens of this stately conifer are found in public parks and gardens as far south as Adelaide. Each of the large, pineapple-shaped cones contains a sweet white nut. In past times, the Aborigines of the Bunya Mountains used to roast the bunya nuts and eat them at special feasts, attended by large gatherings of tribes, every three years. The interval between feasts was dictated by the trees, since it was the time required for a fresh crop of cones to reach maturity.

When the white man came, he dealt with the trees more ruthlessly. From the

1870s, the bunya pine shared the fate of the red cedar, being felled in great numbers. Declaration of the Bunya Mountains National Park in 1908 saved this last forest for future generations to enjoy.

A sealed road runs along the ridge straddled by the park. Access from any direction is steep and winding. But, once on the heights, you discover splendid views over nearby valleys and gorges. Mount Mowbullan (1101 metres) stands at the southern end, Mount Kiangarow (1135 metres) at the northern end. The park has several picnic sites, campsites with piped water, and many marked walking tracks that lead through both pine and eucalypt forests to waterfalls and lookouts. A guest-house near the southern entrance provides full board and lodging, with panoramic views of the Darling Downs. Remember, when packing for your visit, that at this elevation (around 1000 metres) the weather can be chilly even in summer.

Glasshouse Mountains

In the southeast corner of Queensland, where the ranges crowd towards the coast, national parks dot the map like cherries in a cake. A number of these are within easy reach of Brisbane. For example, anyone who has driven north from Brisbane by the Bruce Highway has seen the Glasshouse Mountains. Separate national parks have been declared embracing four of these isolated volcanic plugs, including the tallest, Mount Beerwah (556 metres) and the vertical-sided Mount Coonowrin (523 metres). The craggy spires rise out of eucalypt forests with an understorey of banksias, tea-trees and casuarinas. A climb to any of the pinnacles would require the skills and equipment of experienced rock climbers, but the wild, wooded lower slopes invite your visit.

Cunninghams Gap Mount Mistake

Many of the parks of this region preserve pockets of rainforest. The Cunninghams Gap and Mount Mistake parks, for example, provide good opportunities for experiencing this type of environment. The former provides facilities for picnickers and campers, and walking tracks to mountain tops and to Gap Creek Falls The latter appeals to the serious bushwalker. These two parks are at the northern end of a chain of twenty-one national parks spaced along an arc of mountains that loops around the coastal plain upon which Brisbane and the City of the Gold Coast are situated. At the southern end, the McPherson Range extends the arc almost to the sea Holidaymakers staying at resorts along this popular coast, on either side of the state border, are well placed for visits to these parks.

Tamborine Mountain Witches Falls

The ranges close to the coastal resorts represent the residue of what was once a huge volcanic pile centred on Mount Warning, near present-day Murwillumbah. Tamborine Mountain, northwest of Southport, is a northern outlier of this system. Ten small reserves share the long ridge of this mountain with private homes and commercial market gardens producing citrus fruits, rhubarb, avocados and flowers. One of these reserves, Witches Falls, was Queensland's first national park. The reserves contain dense stands of rainforest and many scenic attractions.

Lamington

South of Tamborine, occupying that part of the McPherson Range where almost all the Gold Coast rivers rise, is the Lamington Plateau, the site of Queensland's best-known highland park, Lamington National Park. The rivers have worn deep ravines in the solidified lava on their way to the sea. Their slopes are luxuriantly overgrown with rainforest. Approach roads climb the northern spurs through eucalypt woods, entering dark green tunnels as they reach the rainforests. To the south, where the land rises to heights of more than 1000 metres, the plateau ends abruptly in a great scarp that rears high above the Tweed Valley.

To make the most of Lamington, you should spend at least a week there. Two guest-houses, Binna Burra and O'Reilly's, are situated one at either end of the plateau. The main walking track through the park connects the two and provides the backbone of the park's system of graded walking tracks. The Main Border Track, as it is called, is twenty-one kilometres long and leads you through rainforest which has stands of negrohead beech (*Nothofagus moorei*), this being the northernmost habitat of the Antarctic beeches. Lookouts at points along the track offer sweeping views of the coast, the northern hills and valleys of New South Wales, and the park's wilderness area.

There are said to be more than 500 waterfalls within this park. Walks along the forest tracks will introduce you to such attractions as Lightning Falls, Stairway Falls, Ballunjui Falls, Hidden Valley, Surprise Rock and the Talangai Caves. Around September and October you will see many lovely orchids in flower among the trees and on moss-covered rocks. More than twenty species are found in the park, ranging from the showy yellow rock lily to the delicate white orange-blossom orchid. By November the flame trees are in blossom, while the orange-red flowers of the firewheel tree add their brilliance to the green canopy through summer and into autumn.

In areas near the guest-houses some of the forest animals have become quite tame. Wallabies and possums can be fed by hand. As you explore the trails, watch out for the rare Albert's lyrebird, which is found only in this particular patch of country. This is also the domain of the satin bower bird, which paints its bower black and decorates it with blue objects. These are shy birds, however, and you are more likely to encounter the bolder, friendlier parrots, which here include crimson rosellas, king parrots and rainbow lorikeets.

The southern part of the park consists of trackless wilderness, where the bushwalker who likes to get away from it all may make his way with the help of map and compass.

Girraween
Sundown

Further west along the border are two parks of quite different character. In the region where the Queensland granite belt joins the granitic New England Tableland, Girraween and Sundown National Parks enclose environments more closely related to the mountain parks of New South Wales than those we have looked at up to this point. Girraween offers camping and walking in country which has eucalypt forests, open ridges and granite tors, and many streams, including Bald Rock Creek, whose pools offer good swimming. An information centre is open every day and rangers lead walks from time to time. The park is noted for its wildflowers (its name means 'place of flowers') and abounds in animal life. The wet gullies in this part of the ranges provide the most northerly habitat of the superb lyrebird. The remote Sundown National Park covers rugged hill country split by gorges and bearing forests of eucalypts and cypress pines. Its solitude appeals to those who take their bushwalking very seriously.

NEW SOUTH WALES

Mount Warning

Mount Warning is the remains of a volcanic plug, the solidified core of a volcano whose outpouring about twenty million years ago created a vast shield of lava which covered the surrounding countryside. Remnants of this shield are to be seen in the ring of hills formed by the McPherson, Tweed and Nightcap Ranges. Subsequent erosion has carried away much of the pile of rock and has reduced Mount Warning itself to its present height of 1157 metres. Named by Cook in 1770, when he observed it from his ship, *Endeavour*, the mountain is of striking appearance, shaped like a broad-based cone with a sharp, beak-like pinnacle.

Although only ten kilometres from Murwillumbah, Mount Warning National Park comprises extremely wild country. Wandering away from the formed tracks is not advisable. A walking track from the car-parking area leads to the summit. The return distance is nine kilometres and about four hours should be allowed. You ascend through dense subtropical rainforest which gives way to temperate rainforest. Towards the top, the track passes stands of tall Gymea lilies. The views from the summit, given clear skies, are astounding.

Bald Rock

Bald Rock National Park, further west, is in granite country over 100 metres above sea-level. Its principal feature is the great 200 metre high dome of rock known to the Aborigines as *boonoo boonoo*. A marked walking track leads to the top of the rock (two kilometres there and back), from where you can enjoy extensive views of the surrounding hills. The rest of the park is rough walking country where you

Spectacular view of Mount Warning, which appears to change colour as the sun rises and sets (Lee Pearce)

would need to take a compass. Close to Queensland's Girraween National Park, this park also has a good deal in common with the parks of the New England region. It embraces a range of habitats — wet and dry sclerophyll forests, heaths and swamps — which provide suitable country for a diverse population of native animals, from grey kangaroos and a number of species of wallabies to wombats, gliders and native cats.

South of the state boundary, the central plateau of the Great Dividing Range rises to form the New England Tableland, which extends almost 400 kilometres to the northern rim of the broad Hunter Valley. Granite is at the heart of this great highland mass and is seen in outcrops, like Bald Rock, and characteristically rounded, weathered boulders, such as the group near Glen Innes known as Stonehenge. Lava flows of the Tertiary period have left areas of basaltic soils. Much of the plateau has been occupied by pastoralists since the 1840s, so the natural vegetation has been extensively modified. The landscape consists largely of undulating grazing country with scattered clumps of eucalypts, but introduced deciduous northern-hemisphere trees, such as willows, poplars and silver birches are prominent around homesteads and towns.

On its eastern side, the tableland ends in an irregularly scalloped scarp fretted by many streams. Along these ramparts, which in places jut out across the coastal corridor, there rises a series of high peaks. The university city, Armidale, stands on the 1000 metres contour. Just forty-eight kilometres east of the city, Australia's highest waterfall plunges 470 metres into the forbidding Wollomombi Gorge. East again from here, in a knot of mountains joined to the plateau by a spur, the Doughboy Range, the New England Tableland reaches its highest elevation, 1615 metres, at Round Mountain.

There are seven national parks along this eastern scarp of the New England Highlands. All contain heavily forested hills dissected by mountain streams, several of which wind through deep gorges or tumble over rock ledges in impressive waterfalls. All possess a diverse flora and fauna. Variations in vegetation type provide a variety of habitats, ranging through subtropical and temperate rainforest, wet and dry sclerophyll forest, swamp and dry heath. The animals of the region include grey kangaroos, wallaroos (rock-kangaroos), brush-tailed rock wallabies, red-necked wallabies, swamp wallabies, and the parma or white-throated wallaby, until recently thought to be extinct. Among the strictly nocturnal animals are the sugar glider, greater glider, brush-tailed possum, ring-tailed possum and the rare marsupial mouse.

Gibraltar Range	The first of these national parks, Gibraltar Range National Park, straddles the Gwydir Highway midway between Grafton and Glen Innes. In spring and early summer it becomes a colour-splashed natural flower garden; large areas of the park are vivid with the glowing scarlet of waratahs. By December, the massed red-and-yellow trumpets of Christmas bells (*Blandfordia* spp.) are to be seen in the wetter places. The park has several picnic sites and a camping area. Formed walking tracks lead through the forests to waterfalls, swimming holes, scenically interesting rock formations and lookouts, return distances ranging from one to eight kilometres. In places, the effects on the rainforest of logging and subsequent regeneration can be observed. Vegetation features include a tree-fern forest, stands of coachwood, messmate stringybark and red cedar, and grass trees. Pademelons and parma wallabies are readily seen. The marsupial mouse, the rufous rat-kangaroo and the native tiger-cat also occur here, as do lyrebirds and bellbirds.

Gibraltar Range

The first of these national parks, Gibraltar Range National Park, straddles the Gwydir Highway midway between Grafton and Glen Innes. In spring and early summer it becomes a colour-splashed natural flower garden; large areas of the park are vivid with the glowing scarlet of waratahs. By December, the massed red-and-yellow trumpets of Christmas bells (*Blandfordia* spp.) are to be seen in the wetter places. The park has several picnic sites and a camping area. Formed walking tracks lead through the forests to waterfalls, swimming holes, scenically interesting rock formations and lookouts, return distances ranging from one to eight kilometres. In places, the effects on the rainforest of logging and subsequent regeneration can be observed. Vegetation features include a tree-fern forest, stands of coachwood, messmate stringybark and red cedar, and grass trees. Pademelons and parma wallabies are readily seen. The marsupial mouse, the rufous rat-kangaroo and the native tiger-cat also occur here, as do lyrebirds and bellbirds.

Guy Fawkes

Guy Fawkes River National Park, about fifty kilometres further south, embraces an area of true wilderness through which north-flowing rivers have etched gorges more than 400 metres deep. The picturesque Ebor Falls, which spill over a cliff of columnar basalt near the Dorrigo-Armidale Road, is on the same river system. This is a park for the adventurous and fit. The only access is on foot and all camping equipment and supplies must be carried in. Picnic and barbecue facilities are provided at Ebor Falls, outside the park, where lookouts afford views into the upper parts of the gorge.

New England Cathedral Rock

Between Ebor and Wollomombi, the road passes between Point Lookout to the east, and Round Mountain to the west. Here are two contrasting parks. The New England National Park takes in the basalt peak of Point Lookout, some cliffs of the escarpment and, far below, densely forested deep valleys drained by the upper streams of the Bellinger River. On the other side, in the Snowy Mountain Range, Cathedral Rock National Park features lichen-decorated granite outcrops and boulders set among eucalypt woods, open heath and swampland.

New England National Park offers both signposted firetrail walks and the opportunity to brave the wilderness. You can simply drive to Point Lookout and enjoy spectacular views. Or you can walk along the trails and explore the changing environments — open heath, snowgum woodland, Antarctic beech rainforest, and the luxuriant subtropical rainforests of the sheltered valleys. In spring and summer, flowering shrubs paint the bush with many colours. In winter, waterfalls freeze to form crystal curtains. You can car-camp or book cabin accommodation in advance. Campsites with fireplaces are located outside the park.

Cathedral Rock has a picnic area at Native Dog Creek. (The name is a reminder that dingoes are still found in this region.) A one kilometre walking track leads to some of the strange and fascinating rock formations. A second picnic area is located at Snowy Creek, beside the road that winds to the top of Round Mountain. The rest of the park is an open invitation to walkers and climbers.

Like its neighbour, this park presents fine opportunities for nature study. Whilst to the passing motorist the vegetation may appear to be generally much the same over the whole area, closer inspection reveals many differences. Here, on beds of granite, the commonest trees are peppermint gums and mountain gums. Swamps and heathlands support a wealth of small flowering shrubs. Several species of parrots are quite common in these parts. Look out for the yellow-tailed black cockatoo and the much rarer glossy black cockatoo. The latter, which has a distinctive red band in the tail, feeds almost entirely on seeds of casuarina trees. Other birds range from the ubiquitous wedge-tailed eagle to perky robins. In the forests you may see the tiny rose robin or the inquisitive yellow robin. On more open ground, it could be either the scarlet robin or the orange-breasted flame robin.

Dorrigo

Below Point Lookout, the basaltic Dorrigo Plateau thrusts eastward towards the sea. Now almost entirely given over to pastureland for dairying, this plateau was formerly swathed in subtropical rainforest. Today, virtually all that is left of that primordial ecosystem is contained within the Dorrigo National Park.

Two clearings in the forest provide picnic areas and give access to a number of walking tracks. A walk of about five and a half kilometres from The Glade takes you

Wollomombi Falls, on the scarp east of Armidale

91

(Opposite page) Spectacular
Apsley Gorge

through rainforest and behind Crystal Shower Falls. From the Never Never picnic area, reached by driving into the northern end of the park, thirteen kilometres of walking tracks provide opportunities to explore deep into the rainforest and to visit a number of beautiful waterfalls. Camping is not permitted.

Apsley Gorge Werrikimbe

Both Apsley Gorge National Park and Werrikimbe National Park contain rugged country typical of the New England scarp region. Both are reached from the Oxley Highway, between Wauchope and Walcha. The former encloses the gorges made by the Apsley and Tia Rivers and may be regarded as forbidding by all but the most dedicated bushwalkers. However, side roads allow you to drive to waterfalls on both rivers and look down into the rainforest-filled valleys. Picnic areas have been established just outside the park boundary at both these falls and provision is made for overnight camping. At Tia Falls there is even a river swimming pool.

Werrikimbe, the larger of these two parks, also has deep gorges and waterfalls, a wide range of habitats, and walking to suit all comers. Antarctic beech forests alternate with warm temperate rainforest dominated by buttressed carabeen and coachwood, and more open forest of tall blue gum and tallow wood. The northern part of the park has open grassland, heath, snowgum woodland and stands of ribbon gum and messmate stringybark. Animal life is correspondingly varied. Walking tracks, campsites and facilities for day visitors are provided. Bushcamping is permitted.

Barrington Tops

The southernmost bastion of the New England Tableland is formed by the high plateau of Barrington Tops. From here, streams flow towards all points of the compass: north and east to form the Manning River; south and west to join the Hunter River. This is the location of Barrington Tops National Park. Varied soils, which include some residual Tertiary basalt, sharp variations in altitude, and plentiful rain (and winter snows) give rise to a diversity of habitats. Peat bog, grassland and snow gums are found on the two linked plateaux, Barrington and Gloucester Tops. In gullies just below these heights, cool temperate rainforest occurs, with Antarctic beech dominant. Warm temperate and subtropical rainforests fill the lower valleys. Walking tracks traverse the park, conducting the walker through these changing zones and to several lookouts and waterfalls. Camping is permitted. There are picnic areas and fireplaces and an area set aside for car-camping. A guest-house is located just outside the park.

Winter in the Barrington tops region

*Mount Kaputar
Warrumbungle*

The great lava flows of the Tertiary period have left their most scenically impressive mementoes in two separate mountain ranges which reach out westward from the main Dividing Range: the Nandewars, west of Armidale, and the Warrumbungles, which hook around the southern edge of the Liverpool Plains, forming a western extension to the Liverpool Range. Mount Kaputar National Park, fifty-three kilometres by road east of Narrabri, embraces a large portion of the Nandewar Range, whilst the Warrumbungle National Park, some thirty-two kilometres west of Coonabarabran, takes in a group of the eroded volcanic peaks of the more southerly range.

The Nandewars tower above the surrounding plain, being clearly visible from as far away as Moree, some ninety kilometres to the north. More than twenty of these peaks exceed 1220 metres. The 360-degree view from the top of Mount Kaputar (1524 metres) is said to encompass one-eleventh of New South Wales. The rich volcanic soil supports an abundant and varied flora, ranging from the snow gums of the heights to wet sclerophyll forests in the gullies (eucalypts with a fern understorey). Flowering shrubs grow in profusion. The road into the park ends at Dawson's Spring, in a valley 1372 metres above sea-level. Cabin accommodation and campsites are provided.

In the Warrumbungle National Park you find yourself encircled by the most extraordinary skyline you have ever seen. Walking tracks take you through varying habitats to mountain tops and canyons. You may take a half-hour stroll or spend several days in strenuous walking and climbing excursions. The Grand High Tops of the Warrumbungles can be reached in a round-trip walk of eleven kilometres from park headquarters at Canyon Camp. From here you get a breath-taking view of all the jumbled peaks and ridges. Cabin accommodation, in converted trams, and caravan camping are available at Canyon Camp. There are also several tent-camping sites.

The Warrumbungle Range has a mixture of dry western plains and New England plant species. It provides habitats for grey kangaroos, wallaroos, red-necked and swamp wallabies and koalas. Competition from feral goats has brought the once-plentiful brush-tailed rock wallaby close to extinction. Among the particularly rich bird life, almost a third of Australia's parrot species are represented. This park is one of the last known habitats of the turquoise parrot.

SYDNEY REGION AND SOUTHERN HIGHLANDS

In the early days of colonisation, the sandstone plateau which rises to the west of Sydney presented a barrier to the expansion of the first settlement and its agriculture. The barrier was not to be breached for twenty-five years, until Blaxland, Lawson and Wentworth discovered a way across the ridges to the western slopes. Today, the Great Western Highway from Sydney crosses the Blue Mountains by the route blazed by the trio of explorers in 1813, passing through the towns of Blaxland, Lawson and Wentworth Falls on its way up the steep incline from Emu Plains.

On either side of the sinuous central ridge, the ground falls away in the precipices which continually frustrated the explorers. To the west lies the valley of Cox's River. To the north, winding through the mountains eastward towards Richmond, is the immense gorge made by the Grose River. Thanks largely to the dedicated efforts of pioneer bushwalker-conservationists in the 1930s, the countryside in these valleys below the plateau is still much as the explorers found it. Fortunately for the people of present-day Sydney (and indeed, for all who enjoy the outdoor world), huge areas of this countryside have, in recent times, been reserved within national parks. This incomparable recreational resource, a mountain environment of great scenic grandeur, is within a two-hour drive of the city.

Blue Mountains

The Blue Mountains National Park consists of three separate sections. One embraces the whole of the Grose River and its catchment area and extends northward beyond Bell and Mount Wilson to include the catchment area of the Wollangambe River. A second section, south of the Great Western Highway between Glenbrook and Wentworth Falls, reaches eastward to the Nepean River and is bounded on the south by the Erskine Creek State Forests. The remaining section extends from Katoomba to the Wombeyan Caves. The first two are accessible (to walkers only) from many points on the main roads and side roads. The third section may be entered from Katoomba. Much of it is wilderness and within the boundaries of the Warragamba Dam catchment area.

Although there are many famous lookout points on the edges of the plateau, which you can reach by car and which offer views of breath-taking magnificence, if you wish to see typical Blue Mountains countryside you must use your feet. What is more, you must climb down into the valleys and climb out again. Paths descend from many points, some representing considerable feats of engineering, often providing ways for walkers to negotiate near-vertical cliffs. All provide safe routes into the wilderness, though the climb down and the return journey are always strenuous. In many places, ladders have been provided or steps carved into the rock.

The rewards for all this effort are great. The steep, deeply dissected terrain ensures that you encounter a wide range of habitats within the compass of a day's hike. On the high ridges you find wet and dry heath and open woodland. Dwarf she-oak (*Casuarina nana*), banksias, tea-trees and various hakea species, and a varied community of smaller shrubs, including flowering heaths (*Epacris* spp.), are characteristic of the heathland. Peppermint gums, scribbly gums and many wattles occur in the open woodland, where the smaller shrubs include waratah, persoonia, grass-trees and boronias. Many high gullies contain pockets of swamp where pink heath and Christmas bells flourish. The sheer, yellow cliff-faces are ruled with horizontal green lines where shrubs sprout from the narrow layers of shales embedded between the sandstone strata. Under waterfalls, and in places where seepage keeps rock faces wet, you will find grevilleas, heath plants and ferns. Lower slopes are generally covered by the tall eucalypt forests which give these valleys their blue-misted appearance when seen from above. Deep in the narrower valleys there are temperate rainforests.

Several shrub species are endemic to the Blue Mountains. Others, such as the honey flower or mountain devil (*Lambertia formosa*), occur on sandstone plateaux throughout the Sydney region, right to the coast. Over 100 species of ground orchids have been found here, including the Blue Mountains sun orchid. The walker wending his way through these valleys is continually exhilarated by glimpses of colour: the purple and yellow of a delicate *Hardenbergia* flower dangling in a bush;

the flash of iridescent plumage as a flock of lorikeets darts overhead. And as a backdrop to every scene stand the great trees, the towering cliffs of golden sandstone, the blue-hazed gorges, the dark humps of distant peaks.

The spread of settlement has reduced the population of large ground animals in all but the more remote areas. Grey kangaroos are found in some of the southern valleys. Swamp wallabies and wallaroos are relatively common, as is the brush-tailed possum. Several other possum species are occasionally observed but probably have restricted ranges. Red-bellied black snakes are common near water, brown snakes on higher ground, but walkers seldom encounter either. Among the many types of lizards are the bearded dragon, the eastern water dragon and the common goanna. Birds include gang-gang cockatoos, yellow-tailed black cockatoos and numerous honeyeaters. The superb lyrebird occurs in open forests. Around streams you are likely to see sacred kingfishers, kookaburras and willy-wagtails.

There are many picnic and camping sites, including car-camping sites, accessible by road. Bushcamping is allowed but permits must be obtained. Hotel and motel accommodation is available in several of the Blue Mountains towns.

Mt Solitary in the Blue Mountains

Wollemi

Separated from the northern boundary of the Blue Mountains National Park only by the Windsor-Lithgow road and reaching north to the Goulburn River valley, the Wollemi National Park covers almost 5000 square kilometres of rough country centred on the catchment of the Colo River. The character of the country is generally similar to that of the Blue Mountains except that this is wholly undeveloped, forested wilderness. Four of the rivers within the park have cut deep gorges through the sandstone rock. Rainforests grow on basalt-capped peaks and in gullies. No roads or tracks exist and there are no facilities for visitors. This is a park to challenge the skills and the stamina of experienced bushwalkers, climbers and canoeists.

Kanangra-Boyd

West of the southern section of the Blue Mountains National Park, in extremely rugged country, much of it over 1200 metres above sea-level, is the Kanangra-Boyd National Park. An unsealed road reaches into the heart of this mountain stronghold to take you to Kanangra Walls, the park's most celebrated feature. Here you may stand on a high rock promontory and gaze at a scene of indescribable splendour. Waterfalls cascade into the depths of the Kanangra Gorge. An archipelago of mountains rises to the northeast: Mount High and Mighty, Mount Stormbreaker and

Kanangra Walls, overlooking the Kanangra Gorge

97

Mount Cloudmaker. To your north and west lie the great peaks of the Kanangra-Boyd Range. To the south, you look upon a sea of hills and valleys.

The park has a number of bushwalking tracks, several undeveloped limestone caves (which you need a permit to explore), and encloses a considerable section of the Kowmung River, which attracts canoeists and trout fishermen. Facilities for car-camping are provided at one site. Bushcamping is permitted. Guest-house accommodation is available at Jenolan Caves, outside the park.

South of Sydney, the sandstone plateau curves around the edge of the Cumberland Plain and reaches right to the sea. A portion of this coastal plateau is conserved within the Royal National Park (described in Chapter 1, Coasts and Islands). It is of interest to note here that the landforms and vegetation types of this and other parks adjacent to Sydney's suburbs have much in common with the highland parks of the Blue Mountains sandstone plateau.

South of Bulli, the plateau recedes inland, its steep edge rearing above the industrial city of Wollongong and the coastal plain. This is the Illawarra Escarpment. At the top, the plateau is thickly capped with sandstone. Beneath this is a layer of mixed sandstone, shale and claystone. Below this again lies the coal which provides the basis of the district's industry. This stratification underlies the national parks along this eastern edge of the Southern Tableland and can often be clearly seen in exposed cliffs.

Morton

The major park of this region, Morton National Park, occupies a scenically fascinating segment of the scarp embracing a segment of the Shoalhaven River and some of its tributaries. There are several gorges and waterfalls. Landforms, vegetation and the native fauna are generally similar to those described for the New England Tableland and the Blue Mountains. Habitats range from swamp and heath to rainforest. Igneous intrusions have left patches of more fertile soil where growth reaches its most luxuriant. Notable among the trees of the gullies is the giant turpentine (*Syncarpia procera*).

The section of the park close to Bundanoon offers picnic sites, car-camping and a variety of walks to lookouts and river beaches. Wildflowers, with species of boronias prominent, make a brave show around springtime. The spectacular Fitzroy Falls, at the northern end of the park, may be viewed and photographed from walking tracks along the east and west rims of the gorge into which the stream falls. The southern part of the park consists of wild country, ideal for those keen bushwalkers who prefer to be far away from beaten tracks.

Macquarie Pass
Budawang

The much smaller Macquarie Pass National Park, immediately to the north of Morton, occupies a portion of the scarp where the Macquarie Rivulet descends the cliffs in a series of waterfalls. The slopes are thickly forested with both subtropical rainforest and eucalypt communities. Budawang National Park extends this trio of neighbouring parks southward, embracing the rugged Budawang Range, whose peaks and slopes, formed by volcanic upheavals, support open eucalypt forests and some significant stands of rainforest.

Deua
Wadbilliga

Two further large tracts of wilderness in the southeastern ranges have been dedicated as national parks: the Deua and Wadbilliga national parks. Both preserve areas of mountainous country in which many rivers rise, cutting their courses through thickly forested slopes. The Tuross Falls and the five kilometre long Tuross Gorge are among the scenic features of Wadbilliga. Limestone caves in the Deua park attract underground explorers. Otherwise, the major attractions of both these remote parks is their potential for long, testing, bushwalking trips and bushcamping.

Mount Imlay
Nalbaugh
Nungatta

Three smaller parks in the southeast corner of New South Wales are chiefly of interest to dedicated bushwalkers and naturalists. These are the Mount Imlay, Nalbaugh and Nungatta national parks. All offer strenuous climbs to mountain summits. Apart from their recreational value, these parks serve to guard areas of natural forest from the depredations of the south-coast woodchip industry. The Mount Imlay park is the home of a rare species of eucalypt, of which only ninety-seven trees are known. It also supports an eriostemon otherwise known to occur only in Tasmania.

Weddin Mountains
Cocoparra

West of the main highlands and to the north of the Riverina there are two more national parks set in isolated ranges. Each represents an island of wilderness which has been saved from agricultural development by its ruggedness. Southwest of Grenfell, the Weddin Mountains National Park offers excellent bushwalking and bushcamping, as also does the Cocoparra National Park, near Griffith. The latter has one campsite with pit toilets and tank water. Its gullies and its forests of ironbarks and cypress pine sparkle with wildflowers in spring and summer. Both these parks provide habitats for typical western plains fauna, including grey kangaroos. Swamps in the valleys of the Weddin Range attract many water birds. Emus are also frequent visitors.

THE AUSTRALIAN ALPS

Kosciusko

In the southeast corner of the mainland, where the divide begins to curve westward in line with the coast, Australia's highlands reach their greatest heights. This is the region known as the Australian Alps. This massive plateau, created by a long, sporadic series of uplifts ending just under two million years ago and since shaped by the erosive action of ice and water, extends from the Australian Capital Territory into Victoria. On the New South Wales side of the state border lies the Snowy Mountains Range, within which is Mount Kosciusko (2230 metres), our highest peak. On Kosciusko's slopes rise the Snowy River, which loops eastward before flowing south to Bass Strait, and numerous tributaries of the great Murray River, which flows north and then west. The whole region is a labyrinth of valleys and ravines drained by swift mountain streams. Enclosing the Snowy Mountains and a number of adjacent ranges is one of Australia's largest national parks, the Kosciusko National Park.

Alpine lake fed by melting snow

Gentians in the Australian Alps

The Kosciusko area is best known as the location of the country's most extensive snowfields. Thousands of skiers come here every winter, staying at hotels and ski lodges at the well-known ski resorts, Thredbo, Smiggin Holes and Perisher Valley, all of which lie within the park. Many people, however, prefer to visit the Alps in spring and summer. After the winter snows have melted away, this high country is carpeted with flowers. Then you may walk on the roof of Australia, in the bracing mountain air, and discover the varied alpine wildlife. For the novice, there are short, guided walks and well-marked tracks. For the veteran, there is a huge area of wild, wide country: over 140 kilometres long north to south, with an average width of forty kilometres. Those prepared to carry their equipment, following the rule 'pack in, pack out', may camp almost anywhere.

Trout fishing is a major attraction. The fishing season usually opens the first weekend in October and closes the last weekend in May. Lakes Eucumbene and Jindabyne, which lie outside the park — though parts of the shores of both form park boundaries — are open for fishing all year. Licences are required. The Gaden Trout Hatchery, on the Thredbo River just above Lake Jindabyne, is of special interest to anglers.

Boating, sailing and water-skiing are also popular summer activities on the big lakes. Horseback trail riding is permitted in certain specific areas of the park.

You can motor right through the park, enjoying some of the most scenically exciting drives our country has to offer. The Snowy Mountains Highway, from Tumut, at the northeast corner, to Cooma, east of Lake Eucumbene, passes the Blowering Reservoir and the Yarrangobilly Caves. A connecting road from Kiandra takes you across to Khancoban at the western entrance to the park, from where you can follow the Alpine Way, which winds around the Murray River end of the high plateau, affording many spectacular views. A turning off the Alpine Way close to the southern shore of Lake Jindabyne leads to the park headquarters at Sawpit Creek, then to Perisher Valley and to Charlotte Pass, just below the Kosciusko summit. A branching road goes to Island Bend and Guthega in the upper Snowy River valley.

Rest areas along the roads have fireplaces and pit toilets and may be used as short-term campsites, providing bases for bushwalking expeditions. The main camping area is at Sawpit Creek, where there are showers and laundry facilities. Advance bookings are necessary for caravan sites and cabins at Sawpit Creek. Camping is not permitted in the major resort areas of Perisher Valley, Smiggin Holes, Guthega, Charlotte Pass and Thredbo, but motel or ski-lodge accommodation is available at all these places. Many of the most popular walking tracks are in this section of the park, including a twenty kilometre hike to the summit of Kosciusko.

Granitic rock predominates in the Mount Kosciusko area and much of the ground is littered with granite boulders. This is the only place on the Australian mainland to show the effects of ice action in the glacial periods of the Pleistocene epoch, between one and two million years ago, although legacies of much earlier glacial periods are found in other regions. Among the visible relics are several lakes which were formed by glaciation. They include the picturesque Blue Lake, on the southern side of Mount Twynam (2196 metres), to the north of Charlotte's Pass, Lake Albina, which drains into the deep cleft by Lady Northcote's Canyon to the north of Kosciusko, and Lake Cootapatamba ('the crystal clear waters where eagles drink'), less than 200 metres below the Kosciusko summit.

The walker encounters constant changes in his surroundings and a diverse and colourful flora. The dull greens of snow grass (*Poa labillardieri*) and alpine wallaby grass (*Danthonia nudiflora*) are brightened by patches of yellow buttercups (*Ranunculus* spp.) and billy buttons (*Craspedia* spp.), the white snow daisy (*Celmisia longifolia*), with its cushions of silvery leaves, the strong blues of gentians (*Gentiana diemensis*) and mountain bluebells (*Wahlenbergia gloriosa*), the purple and mauve of mountain violets (*Viola betonicifolia*) and alpine mint bush (*Prostanthera cuneata*) and the bright pink of trigger plants (*Stylidium graminifolium*). There are many representatives of the daisy family, including species of *Helichrysum* and *Brachycome*. Close to creeks you will find thickets of shrubs, with the woolly tea-tree (*Leptospermum lanigerum*) predominating. In wet places

stand serried ranks of creamy candle heath (*Richea continentis*). Sphagnum moss forms a brilliant light-green border to the many marshy patches. Here you may find the black-and-yellow corroboree frog, whose range is restricted to sphagnum bogs above the snowline in the Alps. Various eucalypts grow in the lower valleys, with the alpine snow gum — remarkable for its survival capacity and for its beautifully streaked, colourful bark — reaching to the limit of the tree-line at about 1850 metres.

The peak wildflower season occurs in January but you will find plants in flower here from November to March. Even at the height of the summer, you are also likely to find snow. Patches persist all year round on eastern slopes. Weather conditions are always unpredictable at these altitudes and walkers are advised to carry extra warm clothing and wet weather protection at all times.

The dry sclerophyll forests provide the habitat for grey kangaroos, red-necked wallabies and wombats. Bush rats and two species of marsupial mouse are also common, as is the echidna. Several types of possums inhabit this high country, including the rarely seen mouse-sized pygmy possums and feather-tailed gliders. Less attractive to humans are the wolf spiders (brown in colour) and black alpine funnel-web spiders, both of which burrow in the ground. Copperhead, tiger, brown and white-lipped snakes may also be encountered. All should be left alone.

Prominent among the varied bird population are many parrots, including crimson rosellas, eastern rosellas, and sulphur-crested, gang-gang and yellow-tailed black cockatoos. Many robins, honeyeaters and other birds add flashes of colour to the open woodlands. The pastel-coloured rainbow bee-eater is active near river banks. In dense gullies you may come across the superb lyrebird. One of the most interesting insects is the Kosciusko grasshopper, which changes its colour from dark blue in cold weather to light green in hotter weather. Another is the bogong moth, brown, furry and fat-bodied, which migrates from the plains in autumn to take up residence in alpine rock crevices. Massed flights of these creatures create clouds in the sky each October. They used to be followed year after year by Aboriginal tribes, for whom they were a sustaining food.

Although both the vegetation and the landscape have been extensively modified in places — by stock grazing, by the creation of dams and other works of the Snowy Mountains Authority, and by ski resort development — the Kosciusko National Park is unquestionably a national treasure. This park encloses an immense alpine region in a continent best known for its deserts and sunburnt plains, preserving an environment whose specialised flora and fauna are in many ways unique. Grazing and hydro-electric development have now ceased. By far the major proportion of the park has remained in its virgin state. And the grandeur of this high country, the sweeping vistas to be seen from its peaks and ridges, the sylvan delights of its valleys, the scenic charms of its lakes and streams, the glory of its massed wildflowers, all now enjoy the protection of belonging to our national estate.

VICTORIA

*Tingaringy
Snowy River*

The Snowy River, after passing through Lake Jindabyne and taking its eastward loop, doubles back on its tracks to cut across the southern section of the Kosciusko park. Here, bordered by sandy beaches, the river winds through a valley side by side with a road, the Barry Way, between steep slopes clothed in forests of cypress pine. On the Victorian side of the state boundary, two more national parks follow the river's course for some two-thirds of its way to the coast. The first of these, Tingaringy National Park, also takes in Mount Tingaringy (1447 metres). This is snow-gum country, as rocky and rugged as that which adjoins it across the border. The second, the Snowy River National Park, embraces a long stretch of the river as it descends between pine-clad ridges, sometimes forming placid pools fringed by broad beaches, sometimes tumbling in frothy rapids, at one point plunging through a forbidding gorge. This is a river shared by canoeists and family campers. The pine forests, and the higher forests of silver wattle and alpine ash welcome walkers.

Mount Buffalo

In Victoria, the alpine country becomes less continuous, being divided into a series of high plateaux separated by valleys. Rising abruptly from the western side of the broad Ovens Valley is the massive granite plateau of Mount Buffalo, named by explorers Hume and Hovell in 1824 because of its shape. Mount Buffalo National Park is Victoria's only alpine park. Like the Kosciusko park, it is a popular winter ski resort. From November to April, however, the climate on the plateau is mild, the flowers bloom in profusion and Mount Buffalo invites walkers, campers, rock-climbers, canoeists and anglers.

*Looking down over Ovens
Valley*

The Horn can be reached easily on foot. It allows extensive views of the surrounding countryside from the lookout.

A good sealed road climbs to the summit. The drive is delightful, taking you through a succession of different plant communities during the ascent of more than 1000 metres and giving you glimpses of waterfalls, sheer cliffs and distant mountains. Walking tracks on the plateau lead to clifftop lookouts and high points, such as Mount McLeod (1540 metres) in the north and The Horn (1720 metres) in the south. On the plateau, the mixed eucalypt forests of the lower slopes are replaced by typical alpine and sub-alpine vegetation: snow gums, alpine ash, heathlands, snow-grass plains, and bogs. The parrots, honeyeaters and other birds found at Kosciusko are all to be found here. Because this is an old-established public reserve, even the lyrebirds show little nervousness when confronted by human visitors. Wombats and smaller marsupials are easily seen. Basic camping facilities are provided in a beautiful setting beside Lake Catani. Motel and lodge accommodation are also available.

From the summit of Mount Buffalo you can see the high plains and peaks of the great mass of the Victorian Alps crowding the horizon to west and south. Although the Alps provide the state's major ski fields — on the slopes of Mount Bogong and Mount Feathertop — and some of its finest highland walking country, there is no national park here. Tourist facilities are well developed in Falls Creek, at the centre of the district, and at Mount Beauty. The area owes its development largely to the State Electricity Commission of Victoria, which has impounded the waters of the Kiewa River in the Rocky Valley Reservoir, high in the mountains, for hydro-electric power generation. Walking tracks traverse many ridges and valleys of this alpine country, much of which is a wildlife sanctuary. Permission must be obtained from the State Electricity Commission for camping or for cross-country walks lasting more than one day.

Fraser

To the southwest of Mount Buffalo, on the western shore of the man-made Lake Eildon, is the small Fraser National Park. Although formerly grazing land, the rounded hills and gentle slopes are rapidly growing a fresh cover of native trees and shrubs. Most noticeable among the animal inhabitants of the park are grey kangaroos, which can be seen feeding in large flocks on the grassy hillsides or down by the lake, often quite close to camp and caravan sites. Fire trails provide good walks and the lake attracts yachtsmen, water-skiers and anglers.

Baw Baw

South of Fraser and due east of Melbourne, rising above the brown coalfields of the Latrobe Valley to form the most southerly of those granite promontories that characterise the Great Dividing Range in Victoria, is Mount Baw Baw (1563 metres). The Baw Baw National Park takes in the plateau, popular for winter ski-touring, and parts of adjacent valleys. A walking track across the plateau forms the southern end of the Alpine Walking Track, which reaches to Tom Groggin on the New South Wales border.

The Alpine Walking Track, Baw Baw National Park

Mustering Flat. Ski-touring is popular in Baw Baw

105

Grampians

One of Victoria's newest, and also its largest national park is the Grampians, covering some 167 000 hectares. The absence of a national park in the Grampians was for long a sore point with conservationists in Victoria. The declaration of the park brought important variety of native flora and fauna, plus Aboriginal rock art sites, under permanent protection. The scenery of the Grampians is perhaps its greatest visitor attribute: the rugged peaks are equalled only by those in the alpine regions of the north-east. Facilities in the park are very good, and cater effectively for both day visitors and camping groups. Be sure to make a visit to one of the states most beautiful waterfalls, MacKenzie Falls.

TASMANIA

Two-thirds or more of Tasmania consists of uninhabitable highland country. Consequently, the island state has retained a larger proportion of its total area in a wild, relatively unspoilt condition than has any other Australian state. Some 10 per cent of the land area is protected in national parks. With minor exceptions, these parks all embrace mountainous terrain.

Joined to the mainland by an isthmus across Bass Strait during several past glacial periods and separated again each time thawing ice raised the sea-level, Tasmania has been an island continuously for about the last 9000 years. This isolation, together with climatic factors, has resulted in the evolution of a distinctive flora and fauna, with a considerable number of endemic species.

Our most southerly state has a different climate from that of the rest of Australia. This outlying fragment of the world's driest continent experiences rain all year round, with snow cover persisting on high ground for many months. This is the part of Australia furthest from the tropics, closest to the Antarctic. With the South Island of New Zealand and the southern portion of South America, it is one of only three significant land masses in the track of the 'roaring forties'. These winds bring almost constant rain to Tasmania's west coast.

The gnarled and furrowed landscape of Tasmania as we see it today owes its form to the events of a long and complex geological history. Its mountains were probably built by the same processes that built the Transantarctic Mountains, at a time when Australia and Antarctica were still joined. Over hundreds of millions of years limestones, sandstones and shales were deposited, and great intrusions of molten rock appeared, solidifying as granite or the darker dolerite. Successive ice ages reshaped the hills, the sliding ice carving out hollows, moving masses of rock debris, forming lakes and valleys. Streams and rivers fed by the wet winds have flowed continuously since the last glacial period ended about 9000 years ago, etching their way through the rocks.

The result of all these influences is a region markedly different from the rest of Australia — a region of great scenic interest and drama, carrying an exuberant vegetation and a varied animal life.

Much of the Tasmanian countryside is forested. You cannot drive far in this state without passing through lush green forests or meeting timber jinkers carting logs to the sawmills. As in other states, eucalypts dominate the scene over large areas. Of the twenty-nine species found, fifteen are endemic to the state. About half of all the forested area consists of temperate rainforest, in which Antarctic beech (*Nothofagus cunninghamii*) dominates. This relative of the European beech tree, known in Tasmania as the myrtle or myrtle-beech, is a spreading, evergreen tree with a dense, deep-green foliage of heart-shaped leaves and a broad, smooth, grey-green trunk. The rainforest understorey is often thickly grown with shrubs, which may include native laurel (*Anopterus glandulosus*), musk daisy-bush (*Olearia argophylla*) or soft tree-fern (*Dicksonia antarctica*). The floor of these wet forests is usually covered with moss, which also spreads over the trunks of the trees.

Other trees of the Tasmanian rainforests are the southern sassafras (*Atherosperma moschatum*), celery-top pine (*Phyllocladus aspleniifolius*) and leatherwood (*Eucryphia lucida*). The latter's big white blossoms are the source of Tasmania's most distinctive honey. Forests of pencil pines (*Athrotaxis cupressoides*) and King William pines (*A. selaginoides*) surround highland lakes. The endemic huon pine, once widespread but thoughtlessly massacred for its rotproof timber, now occurs only in remote valleys of the west. The world's tallest flowering plant, the noble mountain ash (*Eucalyptus regnans*), reaches its most vigorous growth — sometimes topping ninety-five metres — in the valleys of the central south, where it is cut to provide the raw material for newsprint manufacture. Tasmania's only deciduous tree, *Nothofagus gunnii*, known locally as the tanglefoot, grows beside tarns and streams in the mountains of the southwest, where its foliage adds glowing colour to the autumn scene.

Buttongrass (*Mesomelaena sphaerocephala*) covers broad stretches of treeless sedgeland in the west, where many flowering shrubs — chiefly *Boronia, Baeckia, Epacris* and *Leptospermum* species, line the stream banks. In wet gullies of the southwest, densely tangled horizontal (*Anodopetalum biglandulosum*) and wiry bauera scrub makes penetration by walkers virtually impossible. In many large moorland areas above 1000 metres, particularly in the central highlands, only alpine plants survive, commonly including dark-green cushion plants (*Dracophyllum* spp.), several endemic *Richea* species and dwarfed conifers. One of the most remarkable of Tasmania's mountain plants, the pandani (*Richea pandanifolia*), sometimes takes a dwarf form but may reach a height of ten metres or more, when it looks much like a palm tree. The striking, deep-red flowers of the Tasmanian waratah (*Telopea truncata*) are also seen in the mountains.

With its vast areas of untamed country, Tasmania naturally has a wealth of native animals. The largest marsupial is the forester kangaroo, closely related to the great grey kangaroo of the mainland. Groups may be seen grazing on open slopes close to eucalypt forests. The Bennett's wallaby, grey with a chestnut patch on the back of the neck, inhabits open forests, while the smaller rufous wallaby, greyish brown with orange underneath, prefers dense forest and scrub-grown gullies. Brush-tailed possums are very common and, indeed, are snared by the thousand during the open season each year (in areas outside national parks). Three other possum species, and the related sugar glider, are fully protected.

The island state has no dingoes. The Tasmanian devil, however, roams the remoter parts of the west and north in substantial numbers. A stocky, short-legged marsupial, black-furred with white patches, its screaming cry often disturbs the night silence. Wombats, bandicoots and echidnas are widespread. Marsupial mice inhabit the plains and forest edges. The attractive white-spotted native cat and the larger tiger cat are much more common than on the mainland and sometimes wander into camping areas at night, where they readily accept meat scraps.

Most colourful among the birds of the forests is Tasmania's own green rosella, which is lemon-yellow underneath, blackish-green above, red-browed, with flashes of light blue. On buttongrass sedgelands, the green-and-black speckled ground parrot may often be found, usually running away from the observer along a track. The rare orange-bellied parrot, much smaller, may also be seen, particularly in the west coast region.

The Tasmanian devil, a carnivorous nocturnal marsupial which grows to about a metre in length and feeds on birds, lizards and other small animals
(Lee Pearce)

Four species of honeyeaters are endemic to Tasmania, including Australia's largest honeyeater, the yellow wattlebird, which favours eucalypt forests. Colourful smaller birds include robins, pardalotes, the fire-tailed finch (or beautiful firetail) and the perky little silvereye. Larger birds include black currawongs (endemic to Tasmania), yellow-tailed black cockatoos, sulphur-crested cockatoos and that majestic high-flyer known right across Australia, the wedge-tailed eagle.

The central and western highlands, which contain most of the state's highest mountains, sprawl across more than half the main island, reaching right to the southern and western coasts. Scores of streams rise among these hills, running off to north, east, south and west, feeding most of the major rivers. Hundreds of lakes and tarns spangle the landscape. This is the region in which Tasmania's two largest national parks are located; one lies in the very heart of the highlands, reaching south from Lake Dove and Cradle Mountain to Lake St Clair, and the other encompasses a huge slice of southwest wilderness between Lake Pedder and the sea.

Cradle Mountain-Lake St Clair

Cradle Mountain-Lake St Clair National Park is essentially for walkers. The celebrated Overland Track traverses the whole length of the park, a distance of eighty-five kilometres. Five days is the recommended time for the walk. Huts are placed at intervals along the track to provide overnight shelter. However, these are primitive and too small to accommodate all visitors in the summer months. Walkers must therefore carry tents and sleeping bags, as well as food for at least five days' meals, plus extra clothing and wet weather gear. Nevertheless, if you are reasonably fit and accustomed to bushwalking, this walk should be within your capacity.

This is one of the great experiences of Australian bushwalking. The well-defined track takes you across moors and mountain ridges, through eucalypt, pine and beech forests, beside lakes and waterfalls. Side tracks lead to neighbouring valleys and to the summits of several mountains, including Tasmania's highest, Mount Ossa (1617 metres). If you can carry sufficient food, you may happily spend extra days exploring and climbing.

Inexpensive accommodation is available at both the northern and southern ends of the park — at Cradle Valley and Cynthia Bay (Lake St Clair) — though advance bookings are necessary. As an alternative to walking the Overland Track, you may stay at Cradle Valley and take one- or two-day walks from there.

Waterproof boots, woollen trousers, a waterproof parka with a hood, gloves and a balaclava are considered essential equipment for the walker in this high country, though not all of these items will be needed all the time. The weather is fickle and can change rapidly. Blizzards occur even in summer. Muddy ground is often encountered. When you venture into these highlands on foot, it is wise to be prepared for all these eventualities.

Lichen and moss form miniature gardens on rocks at Cradle Mountain (Lee Pearce)

Franklin — Lower Gordon Wild Rivers

Joining Cradle Mountain — Lake St Clair and Southwest National Parks is the famous Wild Rivers National Park. The centre of the stormy High Court battle between state and federal governments, Wild Rivers is now listed as part of the World Heritage area, as are its two neighbours.

As its name suggests, this is an area of wild, untamed rivers, the Franklin and Gordon. Dr Bob Brown described the Franklin as a 'wild and wondrous thing', a statement that holds true for the whole park. Aboriginal sites so far discovered in the park date back at least 20 000 years, and are claimed to be more comprehensive than any others in Australia.

Southwest

Tasmania's largest national park, the Southwest National Park, is also for walkers. It embraces country which has been described as 'one of the world's last remaining true wilderness areas'. Until the 1950s this region had not even been fully mapped. Then in the 1960s the interest taken in it by the Tasmanian Hydro-Electric Commission and the HEC's ultimate victory against the conservationists, gave this wild corner of Australia worldwide notoriety. The flooding of the valley of the Serpentine River, which enlarged the ten square kilometre Lake Pedder into a vast waterway of 233 square kilometres, was one of the most controversial and bitterly resented actions ever taken by a government-owned authority in Australia.

Today, Lake Pedder is a recreational resource much appreciated by boat-owners and fishermen. A road constructed by the HEC places the lake and the northern boundary of the national park within two to three hours' drive from Hobart. The journey takes you through forests of towering mountain ash, across buttongrass plains, and in and out of Antarctic beech rainforests.

The national park stretches to the ocean, taking in the extensive shoreline around Port Davey and Bathurst Harbour. This is extremely rugged country, packed with mountain ranges, cut by many rivers and gorges, with many valleys overgrown with impenetrable bauera and horizontal scrub. There is also buttongrass and wet heathland, wet sclerophyll forest, rainforest and montane vegetation communities. All camping gear and supplies must of course be back-packed in. Intending expeditioners are advised to consult local walking clubs before tackling this challenging country. (More information about Southwest National Park and its walking tracks is included in Chapter 1, Coasts and Islands.)

Frenchmans Cap

West of the central plateau, where the Lyell Highway runs along the floor of a valley between two rows of mountains, the startlingly white quartzite peak of Frenchmans Cap (1443 metres) dominates the scene to the south of the road. The mountain gives its name to a national park of which it forms the central feature. Accessible only on foot, this is a park strictly for dedicated walkers and climbers. A typical range of habitats is encountered on the way up from the base to the glacier-eroded peak. A 300 metre-high sheer rock face on the eastern side of the cap presents an irresistible lure to competitively minded rock-climbers.

Ben Lomond

Ben Lomond National Park takes in the high plateau in the northeast of the state which is separated from the central and western highlands by the pastoral midlands. Dense forests flank the lower parts of the park. The plateau itself is covered by alpine moorland. Within easy reach of Launceston, this is Tasmania's principal winter skiing area.

Several of the southern state's coastal national parks embrace mountainous country and therefore merit a mention in this chapter also. On the east coast, Freycinet National Park, incorporating the whole Freycinet Peninsula and Schouten Island, offers the pink granite magnificence of The Hazards. In spring and summer, the heathlands come alive with wildflowers. Mount William National Park, in the northeast corner of Tasmania, has a cover of heath and dry sclerophyll vegetation, providing habitats for a diverse animal community. The smaller Asbestos Range National Park, on the central north coast, comprises hilly country whose abundant wildlife includes the forester kangaroo. Maria Island National Park off the east coast, and Strzelecki National Park on Flinders Island, also enclose hilly country, the latter being of an extremely rugged character, the former providing somewhat gentler slopes but a very varied range of habitats.

Russell Falls, picturesque in the sunlight, in Mount Field National Park (Lee Pearce)

SOUTH AUSTRALIA

The city of Adelaide stands on a narrow coastal plain beside Gulf St Vincent, hemmed in on the east by the green hills of the Mount Lofty Ranges. This line of low hills is in fact a plateau with stepped scarps along its eastern and western sides. Technically it is described as a horst: a zone of ancient rock which was long ago thrust up in a block beside a fault line. The land to the west of the fault sank, allowing the sea to penetrate at Spencers Gulf and Gulf St Vincent and resulting in low-lying salt lake basins further inland. The spine of mountains which starts at the tip of the Fleurieu Peninsula, opposite Kangaroo Island, continues northward between Lake Torrens and Lake Frome, finally sinking into the desert plains of the country's 'dead heart'. In these mountains are South Australia's highland national parks, quite different in character from those of the Eastern Highlands and Tasmania.

The hills close to Adelaide are now sprinkled with towns which stand in a chequered pattern of orchards and farms. The pre-settlement character of the country has been preserved, however, in a number of parks and reserves. Just thirteen kilometres southeast of Adelaide, surrounded by suburban development, lies the state's oldest public reserve, formerly known as The National Park but now called Belair Recreation Park. Here, despite tennis courts, barbecue areas and a museum, the visitor may enjoy the unspoilt beauty of the bush. Creeks are bordered by stands of South Australian blue gum (*Eucalyptus leucoxylon*) and river red gum (*E. camaldulensis*), while higher slopes carry open woodland of peppermint box (*E. odorata*) and messmate stringybark (*E. obliqua*) with many smaller shrubs.

Cleland Conservation Park, only nine kilometres southeast of the city, contains a fauna reserve in which visitors may observe native animals at close quarters in segments of the park which correspond to the animals' natural habitats. This park also offers strolls through eucalypt forest and to the summit of Mount Lofty (727 metres), highest point in the Adelaide district. Morialta Conservation Park, to the east of the city, provides a patch of rough bushwalking country.

Mount Remarkable

Further north, where the hills come close to the eastern shore of the narrowing Spencer Gulf, the northern Mount Lofty Ranges merge into the southern Flinders Ranges. About half-way between Port Pirie and Port Augusta, Mount Remarkable towers 963 metres above sea-level. Most of this mountain, and adjacent areas which take in gorges cut in the sandstone rock by the Mambray and Alligator Creeks, is enclosed within the Mount Remarkable National Park. This is good walking country, its scenic values enhanced by woodlands of South Australian blue gum and sugar gum (*Eucalyptus cladocalyx*), several mallee species and a wide variety of smaller flowering shrubs — wattles, fringe myrtle (*Calytrix tetragona*) and bottlebrushes (*Callistemon* spp.). Walkers may share it with red kangaroos, euros or hill kangaroos and, in rocky terrain close to the gorges, the rare yellow-footed rock wallaby. Gnarled river red gums line the creeks, while cypress pines (*Callitris columellaris*) and the smaller drooping she-oak (*Casuarina stricta*) grow on rocky hillsides.

You may come across the mallee fowl, a solemn and solitary bird which (if a male) spends much of its life working on its nesting mound, a heap of leaves, twigs and sand covering an area about four metres in diameter. Or you may hear the four-note call of the male western whipbird, followed by the answering three-note call of the female.

Mount Remarkable National Park is closed between November and March because of the high bushfire risk.

Colour and stark grandeur in the Flinders Ranges

Brachina Gorge, Flinders Ranges

Flinders Ranges

Further inland, beyond the town of Hawker, you come to the great Flinders Ranges National Park, right in the heart of the South Australian highlands. Here the jumbled peaks and ranges thrust up starkly from flat plains, the summits mostly bare quartzite crags, the valleys a labyrinth of rocky gorges. Annual rainfall, even in the hills, averages less than 400 millimetres. The streams are intermittent, most of them dry or a mere trickle for most of the time, becoming wild torrents for brief periods after rain.

The folding of strata that produced these rugged hills was a complex process and it has resulted in a strange and fascinating landscape. Many great domes were formed, with hollow basins where the strata dipped. Some 500 million years of erosion have worn down the softer rock, leaving a pattern of ridges and hollows, and a number of crater-like formations known locally as 'pounds'. Best known of these, and one of the most spectacular features in any Australian mountain range, is Wilpena Pound, lying within the Flinders Ranges National Park.

This oval basin rimmed with jagged mountain walls is sixteen kilometres long and eight kilometres wide. Unlike much of the surrounding countryside, it is well covered with vegetation, including groves of cypress pines and eucalypts. On the outside, the walls rise steeply from the plain, in places to a kilometre or more high. These walls are breached in only one place, where the Wilpena Creek has scoured a gorge through the eastern rim.

At the entrance to the pound stands the Wilpena Pound Motel and, nearby, a campsite beautifully situated among river red gums. From here, five well-marked walking tracks begin, leading into the pound to various points of interest, such as the old Wilpena Pound station homestead, Edeowie Gorge, and several peaks. One walk takes you to the summit of St Mary Peak (1165 metres), highest point in the Flinders Ranges. This is a strenuous twenty kilometre return trip but one which rewards you with memorable views of the pound, the vast red sea of hills and the surrounding country, including the gleaming white saltpan of Lake Torrens to the west.

The larger, northern section of the park, known as the Oraparinna section, contains the park headquarters, reached by gravel road from Wilpena. (Both sections were formerly sheep stations.) Within the Oraparinna section are the Heysen and Trezona Ranges and the Bunyeroo, Brachina and Wilkawillana Gorges. Several gravel roads cross the park, providing access to many creekside sites suitable for camping. These make good bases from which to launch exploratory bushwalks. The roads are linked at many points by walking tracks.

Wildflowers in the Flinders Ranges

The dry-country vegetation is noticeably different from that further south. White cypress pine is still present, with some eucalyptus species, notably peppermint box, and casuarinas, including the belah (*Casuarina cristata*). But the smaller shrubs such as wattles and bottlebrushes are replaced by saltbush (*Atriplex* spp.) and bluebush (*Maireana sedifolia*), with stands of yellow-flowered cassias. In spring, whole hillsides glow bright red with massed flowers of an introduced weed, the Flinders Ranges hop.

Red kangaroos and emus are conspicuous animal inhabitants of open plains, with euros and western grey kangaroos in more rugged terrain. Yellow-footed rock wallabies may be sighted on steep slopes around the gorges. Many parrots brighten the scene in these brown hills. Coloured clouds of budgerigars or galahs or corellas may rise up as you approach. You may be lucky enough to see the lovely scarlet-chested parrot, occasionally present in large flocks but unobtrusive in habit. The majestic and relatively rare pink (or Major Mitchell's) cockatoo may also visit these parts.

Gammon Ranges

Similar flora and fauna are found in the smaller Gammon Ranges National Park further north, between Copley and Arkaroola. This covers extremely rough country, taking in an extensive plateau with numerous gorges attractive to hardened bushwalkers. Permission is needed for entry.

Winter and spring are the best times for walking in the Flinders Ranges. Summer can be distressingly hot and occasional thunderstorms can cause problems. Also, a total ban is placed on lighting fires in the open at that time. You should always carry your own fresh water.

WESTERN AUSTRALIA

Western Australia is both the largest and the flattest state of Australia. Underlying its whole area is the Great Western Shield, many of whose exposed rocks have been dated at 600 million years old. Sand covers much of this ancient landscape, forming dunes up to thirty metres high in the inland deserts. There are also many salt lakes, their beds usually dry. In general, the inland area is a plateau sloping gently eastwards, dipping low in the central north to form the Canning Basin, which is covered by the Great Sandy Desert. Here and there, isolated patches of highland country rise above the generally flat plateau; these outcrops are mostly composed of granite which has resisted the thousands of centuries of weathering that wore down the rest of the land surface.

Along the southern coast there are several ranges of low hills separated from the plateau by a narrow coastal plain of sedimentary rock. Where the plateau curves inland, the sea covered the edge of the continent for periods during the Eocene and Miocene epochs. These inundations resulted in the deposits of limestone which now cover the Nullarbor Plain and which are also found in many places along the south coast. The headlands and coastal mountains of this region, however, are of granite and gneiss (the metamorphosed form of granite), as are the offshore islands.

Cape Arid

Biggest and most easterly of the national parks of this coast is the Cape Arid National Park, which extends inland to embrace much of the Russell Range, including its highest peak, Mount Ragged (585 metres). This steep-sided mountain does not easily submit to climbers, its sides being scree-covered, but the view from its summit repays the effort. Like the Cape Le Grand and Fitzgerald River National Parks further west, Cape Arid National Park contains a diversity of habitats, including sandhills, sandy heath, swamp, woodland and open mountain sides. These reserves are rich in wildlife, one unusual animal being the tiny honey possum or noolbenger. This agile, mouse-size marsupial has a long snout which it thrusts into blossoms, using its bristle-tipped tongue to gather nectar. (More information about these coastal parks is included in Chapter 1, Coasts and Islands.)

Mount Ragged, the highest peak of the Russell Range

The southwest corner of the continent, a high rainfall area, is justly famous for its great forests of karri (*Eucalyptus diversicolor*) and jarrah (*E. marginata*). The karri shares with the mountain ash of Tasmania and Victoria the distinction of being the world's tallest hardwood tree, growing to ninety metres or more. It owes its specific name of *diversicolor* to its appearance in late summer when, as the bark is shed, the tall, straight trunk wears a patchwork of yellow, orange, white and grey. The smaller, but equally straight-growing jarrah occurs over a wider range than the karri, being found from Albany to Gin Gin, north of Perth. Both these trees produce white flowers, those of the karri secreting the nectar which yields Western Australia's most prized honey.

Stirling Range

This corner of the state is also renowned for its wealth of wildflowers. Nowhere is this better displayed than in the Stirling Range National Park, seventy kilometres north of Albany. Of more than 500 plant species identified, at least one hundred are endemic to this southwest region. Several are unique to the Stirling Range and some specific to a particular peak within the range. The park encloses the whole range which rises abruptly from the plains in a series of sharp and grotesquely shaped quartzite peaks, extending sixty-five kilometres from east to west but with a maximum width of only fifteen kilometres. This is the highest part of the southwest, five of the peaks reaching over a kilometre above sea-level, the highest being Bluff Knoll (1073 metres), towards the eastern end of the range.

The Albany-Borden road intersects the park, crossing the range at the Chester Pass. Several side roads lead into the park, including the Stirling Range Drive, which winds around shoulders of mountains and through timbered valleys to link with Red Gum Pass Road. You may drive almost to the summits of Bluff Knoll and Toolbrunup Peak (1052 metres) to enjoy splendid views which reach to the cool blue waters of the Southern Ocean. There are several formed walking tracks, some offering short walks (of about two hours' duration) from picnic sites to nearby peaks, others covering much longer distances. Walking need not be restricted to the tracks. A lot of open country and numerous untrammelled mountains invite the less inhibited bushwalker. Be warned, however, that climbs are generally steep and the going rough. Many cliff faces present challenges to experienced rock-climbers. In summer, water should be carried. In winter and spring, when light snow or hail may be encountered on the peaks, extra clothing should be carried. Overnight camping is allowed at only one site, near the ranger's house beside Chester Pass Road. A caravan park with some on-site vans is located close to the northern park entrance.

This area has a prolific bird life, including several colourful parrot species — western rosellas, purple-crowned lorikeets, red-capped parrots — and more than a dozen types of honeyeaters. The glory of the Stirlings, however, is their covering of shrubs and trees. The lower valleys are clothed in forests of jarrah, the pink-flowered marri (*Eucalyptus calophylla*), and wandoo (*E. redunca*). A dense shrub cover extends from the swamps and sandplains right up to the higher slopes. Around September and October in particular, the park is awash with colour. Dainty spider orchids and greenhoods grow on the forest floor. On the mountainsides you will find mountain bells (*Darwinia* spp.), with flowers of yellow, pink, orange, red or red-and-white — the various colours occurring on different peaks — and such characteristic western shrubs as red-and-green kangaroo paws (*Anigozanthos manglesii*). Other tall shrubs, some of which occur in species restricted to this area, include banksias, grevilleas, dryandras, acacias and peaflowers. On rocky slopes you see groups of 'black gin' (*Kingia australis*), a small tree of the grass-tree family. It grows to about three metres, its knobbly trunk topped by a grass skirt of rush-like leaves and crowned with a ring of creamy-white flower heads held up on stalks, like drumsticks.

Porongurup

Closer to Albany, the lower and more compact Porongurup Range — about twelve kilometres long and reaching a maximum height of 670 metres — also extends in an east-west line. The Porongurup National Park, which encloses the range, contains some rough walking country offering strenuous hikes over the rounded granite peaks. Walks of two or three hours' duration may be made from several picnic sites, which can all be reached by car. The major feature of this park is a luxuriant karri

Starkly beautiful kangaroo paw

Birdflower

forest which covers almost the whole range. Rainfall is higher here than in the Stirlings and a lush understorey of flowering shrubs is present In spring, the forest glades are brilliantly decorated with the purple flowers of *Hovea elliptica* and *Hardenbergia comptonia*, the yellow of *Bossiaea aquifolium* and the cream blossoms of the hazel tree, *Trymalium spathulatum*. In gullies, where the forest trees are the lower-growing jarrah and marri, the diversity of wildflowers becomes even greater. Here you may also see western grey kangaroos and bush wallabies.

The narrow coastal plain upon which the city of Perth stands is bounded on its eastern side by a long scarp, running more or less parallel to the coastline. This is the western edge of the shield plateau. The people of Perth see it as their flat eastern horizon. It is also the hill country; here are located the city's water storages, a timber belt carrying extensive forests of valuable jarrah, and places to go for Sunday afternoon picnics. This is the Darling Range. It extends southward almost to Collie and rises to 582 metres at Mount Cooke, southeast of Perth.

John Forrest

A number of small pockets of this scarp country have been reserved and declared national parks, though some of these consist of no more than a patch of ground from which you may enjoy a good view of the coastal plain. Others protect important stands of wildflowers. Still others contain scenic waterfalls. One of the most valuable is the John Forrest National Park, the original forty-three hectares of which were the state's first national park, declared in 1895. Covering 1577 hectares, it contains open woodland of jarrah and marri. A scenic drive, entered from the Great Eastern Highway, meanders through much of the park. Natural swimming pools in the Jane Brook provide one of the park's major attractions for Perth suburbanites. Another is the massed display of wildflowers from late winter to spring. Among these are some species whose natural range is confined to this particular locality, notably the spindly grevillea (*G. endlicherana*), and conesticks (*Petrophile biloba*), both of which have become popular garden plants throughout Australia.

Western Australia's highest land lies in the northwest, in a region best known to the world for its great iron mines. Yet it also possesses great beauty. The region's major physical feature is the Hamersley Range, a massif some 450 kilometres long, separated from the Pilbara region by the low grasslands of the Fortescue River valley. The hump-backed peaks of the Hamersleys rise from a generally flat or undulating landscape to heights of 1200 metres or more. Along its northern edge the range plunges precipitously to the floodplain of the Fortescue. Like all the rivers of this semi-arid region, the Fortescue remains dry for much of the time.

Rock dominates the scene more completely here than in any other region of Australia. The vegetation cover is generally sparse, consisting mainly of clumps of porcupine grass (*Triodia* spp.) and occasional straggly acacias, although cases of greenery are found in the deep canyons, where pools of water lie in cool shade. This is one of the oldest land surfaces on Earth. Yet over most of it relatively little soil is visible. Instead you find rock, largely reddish-brown in hue and also all shades of red, brown, purple and black; rock that has weathered into steps, sharp-edged boulders, splinters and sheets of slate. Sandstone is the predominant material but a rich variety of ancient sediments and igneous intrusions has accumulated over many aeons. You can see the variegated strata clearly in the rock cliffs and stepped walls of the gorges. And the great trainloads of iron ore currently being dug out of parts of this range, and the blue asbestos which was mined here until the late 1960s, attest to the presence of haematite and crocidolite.

Hamersley Range

This is a land of gorges — deep clefts that were cut through the rock by streams at a time when the climate was very much wetter. Many of these spectacular gorges and much of the gnarled grandeur of the Hamersleys are enclosed within the Hamersley Range National Park, one of Australia's greatest national parks and the second largest in Western Australia (the largest is Rudall River, near the edge of the Great Sandy Desert).

Wittenoom, once the township for an asbestos-mining enterprise, makes an ideal base for excursions into the park. Camping is allowed in designated areas. Roads provide access to some of the places of scenic interest, which include the Wittenoom, Yampire, Hancock and Dales gorges and the Joffre and Fortescue falls.

The Hamersley Range. Enthusiastic walkers will gain great pleasure from exploring gorges and waterways in this area.

This still leaves a wealth of wild, wide-open country to be explored on foot and a number of other uniquely formed gorges to be discovered by the enthusiastic walker.

Conditions in this hot, dry province are not easy for living things, including humans. You must carry water with you. If you are lucky enough to see the countryside after spring rain you may enjoy the surprising sight of flowers blooming among the spiky yellow grasses. These could include the mauve parakeelya (*Calandrinia polyandra*), members of the *Eremophila* family, the crimson Sturt's desert pea and a three metre tall shrub native to the northern part of the state, the bird flower (*Crotalaria laburnifolia*), whose large, yellow-green peaflowers resemble birds. Deep in the shaded ravines you will be soothed by the lush greenery of ferns. Crooked, white-trunked ghost gums (*Eucalyptus papuana*) grow from high crevices on the walls of brilliantly coloured rock. Near streams and pools you may find white-trunked river red gums and slender, straight, often close-packed cajuputs (*Melaleuca leucadendra*).

Ground animals generally keep out of sight while the sun is out but you may come across red kangaroos, wallaroos, dingoes or some of the smaller creatures, including many reptiles. You will notice no lack of birds, though some, such as the red-browned pardalote which is able to tunnel into the hard-baked earth, do not often reveal themselves.

Collier Range	In the hills of the inland northwest there are two other major national parks. Southeast of the Hamersley Range park, reached from the Great Northern Highway some 250 kilometres north of Meekatharra, the Collier Range National Park covers high country between the upper streams of the Ashburton and Gascoyne Rivers. Accommodation is available at the nearby Kumarina Motel.
Chichester Range	To the north of the Hamersley Range, on the other side of the broad rift valley of the Fortescue River, lies the Chichester Range. The road from Wittenoom to the coast passes through the Chichester Range National Park. The mountains here are lower than those to the south but this is harsh, rocky country nonetheless. By contrast, two verdant, shaded picnic sites beside the road invite the traveller to pause for refreshment. First, at Millstream, a national park in its own right, you come upon a series of permanent pools on the Fortescue River lined with river red gums, graceful cajuputs and fan-palms of a type which grows nowhere else, *Livistona alfredii*. To add to the charm of the place, there are also lily ponds. Further along, within the Chichester Range park, you will find the Python Pool, another cool, green oasis, at the foot of a granite cliff. Aboriginal rock carvings at both sites testify to their long history as welcoming watering places.

Journeys in the northwest must be carefully planned to allow for long distances between settlements where supplies of food, water and petrol may be replenished. Even when travelling on main roads, motorists should carry sufficient water and food to sustain each member of the party for at least forty-eight hours. Keep in mind that in this area you are close to the heat centre of the continent. The best time to take a holiday trip in these parts is between May and October, when days are warm and nights cool.

Drysdale River	The triangular bulge pointing into the Timor Sea, which forms the far north of Western Australia, contains one of our country's most rugged and desolate regions, the Kimberleys. This whole province consists of a plateau of very ancient rock, predominantly sandstones, with some basalts and vitrified lavas, which has been deeply scored by many rivers. High scarps of bare red rock are common landforms. Tree cover includes woodlands of Darwin stringybark (*Eucalyptus tetrodonta*) and spinifex gum (*E. dichromophloia*), and scattered Kimberley pines (*Callitris intertropica*), with an occasional bulbous-trunked baobab or bottle tree (*Adansonia gregorii*) in wetter spots. In the northern part of this region lies the vast Drysdale River National Park, which embraces the Ashton Range and the forty-eight kilometre long Carson Escarpment. This is remote country which can be reached only in the dry season and then only by four-wheel-drive vehicle. The state authorities have no plans to develop this park in any way at present.

At the southwestern corner of the Kimberleys, the Great Northern Highway skirts the Oscar Range. This low range, quite different in formation from the Kimberley plateau, is a relic of the time, some 350 million years ago, when the sea invaded the land and marine creatures built a limestone reef here. The Fitzroy River, in its long, curving course from the heart of the Kimberleys to King Sound, has carved through this limestone barrier to create one of Western Australia's most celebrated scenic features, Geikie Gorge.

Geikie Gorge	Geikie Gorge National Park, although only eight kilometres long by just over three kilometres wide, is a very special and valuable national park. It is easily accessible by car — at least, in the dry season, between April and December — being just twenty kilometres from Fitzroy Crossing on the Great Northern Highway. Popular as it is, you should not omit this park from your itinerary on any tour of the northwest.

Unlike the gorges of the Hamersleys, Geikie Gorge is wide and open to the sun. The mood here is not so much one of drama as of peace. The river, whose flow ceases during the Dry, at this point forms a series of pools which reflect the clear blue of the sky, the white and cinnamon of the cliffs, the many greens of the riverside vegetation. Cajuputs and river red gums contrast in size, shape and coloration with native figs and screw palms, reeds and freshwater mangroves. Living in the water are freshwater sharks, stingrays and Johnston's (freshwater) crocodiles. Flying above the water, you will see parrots, cormorants, darters, red-backed kingfishers, blue-winged

Tunnel Creek
Windjana Gorge

kookaburras and a multiplicity of other birds. Many of the trees are draped with colonies of 'flying foxes' (fruit bats). You may also see rock wallabies, agile (or sandy) wallabies recognisable by their light tan colour and white-striped flanks, and the more robust, darker brown euros. Much of the park is a wildlife sanctuary from which human visitors are barred.

Do not attempt to visit Geikie Gorge in the months of the Wet. At this time, the river becomes a savage torrent which swirls through the gorge, rising a dozen metres up the limestone walls, flooding the campsite, carrying trees on its frothing surface. Come here during the Dry, when the river is tranquil, and take a two-hour boat trip through this superbly beautiful gorge. And bring your camera.

A detour via Leopold Downs on your way from Fitzroy Crossing to Derby will enable you to see two other impressive features of the limestone belt: Tunnel Creek and Windjana Gorge. Both are contained within national parks. At the first a creek has bored a tunnel 750 metres long through the rock. During the Dry, you may walk through it. (Take a torch with you.) Stalactites hang from the roof. In the middle, a shaft has opened in the roof, leading to the summit of the range. Windjana Gorge, gouged out by the Lennard River, has a broadly similar character to that of Geikie Gorge, although it is about one quarter the length and its cliffs somewhat more imposing, rising almost vertically to heights of about eight metres. Its name is a reminder of the gorge's former importance to the Aboriginal people — though, sadly, in the latter years of last century, this place was the scene of conflict between natives and settlers, and saw blood shed. Caves in the towering limestone cliffs contain galleries of ancient rock paintings in black, white, yellow and red pigments, depicting stylised animals and mythical heroes. The caves have also revealed other evidence of the long occupation of the area by the earliest Australians.

NORTHERN TERRITORY

The Territory's major highland region (purists would say its *only* highland region) is situated in the Centre, which is the subject of Chapter 4, The Centre. There are two important national parks in the north of the Territory, however, which cannot be ignored in any consideration of highland parks. Both owe their character to the presence of an upland area which, although its average elevation is less than 350 metres, is the Top End's nearest equivalent to a highland region. This is the Arnhem Land Plateau, which explorer Ludwig Leichhardt described as '. . . tremendously rocky country. A high land composed of horizontal strata of sandstone [which] seemed to be literally hashed, leaving the remaining blocks in fantastic figures of every shape; and a green vegetation, crowding deceitfully within their fissures and gullies . . .'

Standing on the ancient basement rocks of the Great Western Shield, the plateau consists of sandstones deposited in the Precambrian era, some 1600 million years ago, which were uplifted as a block, with little folding. The 'hashed' effect to which Leichhardt referred is the result of thousands upon thousands of years of weathering which has penetrated joint lines, creating a rectangular pattern of valleys.

Many rivers rise in this plateau region, following north, east and west to the sea. From December to March, fed by the torrential monsoon rains of the Wet, the streams become roaring torrents, plunging down from the plateau to spread in sea-like floods across the flat coastal plain. At its western edge, the plateau ends in a craggy escarpment. This combination of factors results in some of Australia's most impressive and dramatic scenery.

Katherine Gorge

Katherine Gorge National Park, thirty kilometres from the town of Katherine, embraces a large section of this sandstone plateau and escarpment country, including thirteen kilometres of gorges cut by the Katherine River. High cliffs with weatherbeaten, pinkish-brown faces bracket the broad green river along a series of straight reaches which end in right-angled bends. Here and there the cliffs descend cleanly into the depths of the river pools. At other points, heaped boulders form rapids and cascades, or the river's edges are fringed with screw palms (*Pandanus basedowii*), paperbarks (*Melaleuca* spp.) and other tropical rainforest shrubs.

Sheer sandstone cliffs rise from the Katherine River to form Katherine Gorge

The Katherine River can be explored by boat and offers opportunities for swimming and fishing

Regular daily excursions in flat-bottomed tourist boats take visitors through a considerable length of the gorges during the months of the Dry (April to November). At the end of the lower gorge, passengers disembark and walk past a series of low waterfalls to board another boat in the second gorge, which turns out to be even grander than the first. Near the change-over point there are galleries of magnificent Aboriginal rock paintings.

The Katherine is a perennial stream, although its flow is very much reduced in the dry season. In the five months of the Wet, when almost all of the annual total of about 900 millimetres of rain falls, the Katherine and its tributaries become swollen and turbulent. The muddy water rises up the sandstone walls, waves up to two metres high pounding the rock. However, unless major floods cut the roads, the national park remains accessible to motor vehicles. Launch tours still operate but are restricted to the lower gorge. The tours include a visit to one of the larger waterfalls, where you can enjoy a swim and an inspection of rock art sites. Many of the fascinating Aboriginal paintings, here seen on open rock faces above flood levels rather than in the shelter of caves, show human figures and animals life-size or larger.

One of the bonuses of taking a boat trip on the Katherine is the opportunity it gives you to observe freshwater crocodiles (*Crocodylus johnstoni*) at close quarters. The Johnston's crocodile is a fish-eater, harmless to man, which grows to a maximum length of about two and half metres. This species is also known as the Australian crocodile, for it is found nowhere else in the world. In this national park they are seen in large numbers, especially on sunny days, basking on rocks, banks and fallen logs close to the water. Formerly almost shot to extinction, this species has been protected by law since 1964. The Katherine Gorge population has apparently been lucky enough to find ideal conditions for survival.

The park has more than 100 kilometres of clearly marked walking tracks, most of which lead to points on the escarpment providing views into the gorges. One of these is the Wilderness Walk of seventy-two kilometres to Edith Falls and back. Overnight camping is permitted on some of the walks, with the ranger's approval. Those with a taste for water-borne adventure may try taking an air-mattress to a point upriver and floating back.

In size, and in its role as a reserve protecting a range of tropical habitats and a related spectrum of flora and fauna, the Katherine Gorge National Park is one of this country's most important national parks.

Kakadu

Further north, where the escarpment curves eastward and the Territory's coastal plain is broadest, a remarkable national park — Australia's biggest by far — has been established as the result of an agreement reached in 1979 between the Australian National Parks and Wildlife Service and the Northern Land Council. This, the Kakadu National Park, embraces a portion of the plateau and its scarp, together with a large slice of the coastal plain. However, since most of the park occupies lowland country, it would not be appropriate to discuss it at length in this chapter. A detailed description of Kakadu is to be found in Chapter 3, The Outback

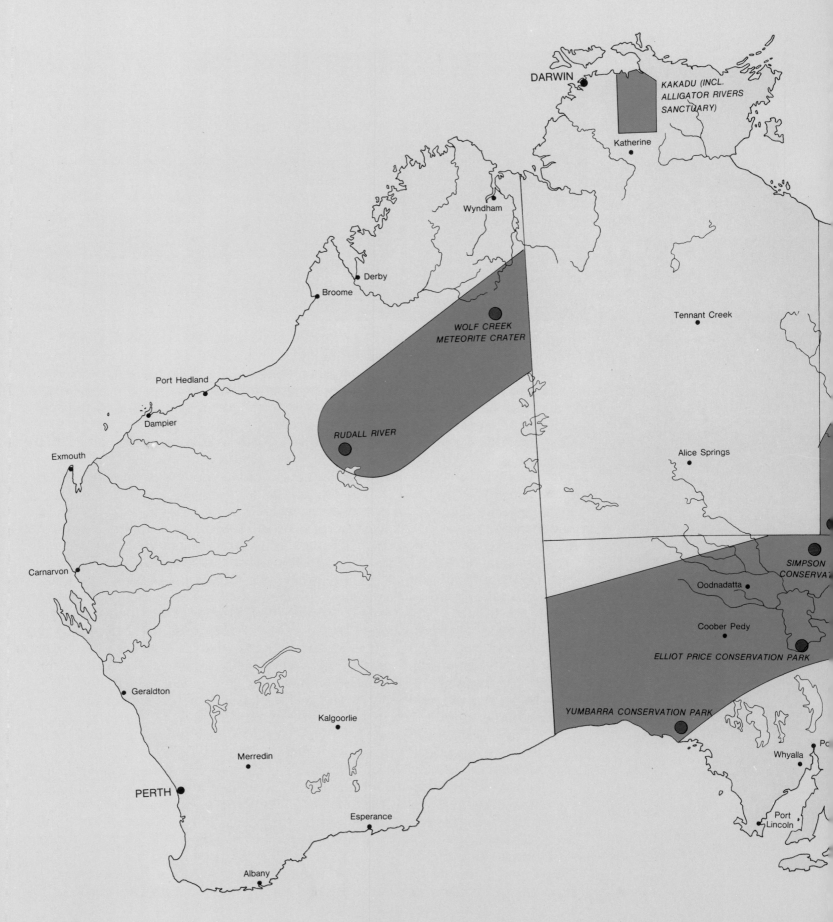

DARWIN

KAKADU (INCL.
ALLIGATOR RIVERS
SANCTUARY)

Katherine

Wyndham

Derby

Broome

WOLF CREEK
METEORITE CRATER

Tennant Creek

Port Hedland

Dampier

RUDALL RIVER

Exmouth

Alice Springs

SIMPSON
CONSERVA

Carnarvon

Oodnadatta

Coober Pedy

ELLIOT PRICE CONSERVATION PARK

Geraldton

Kalgoorlie

YUMBARRA CONSERVATION PARK

Whyalla

Merredin

PERTH

Po

Esperance

Port
Lincoln

Albany

Mou

128

3 THE OUTBACK

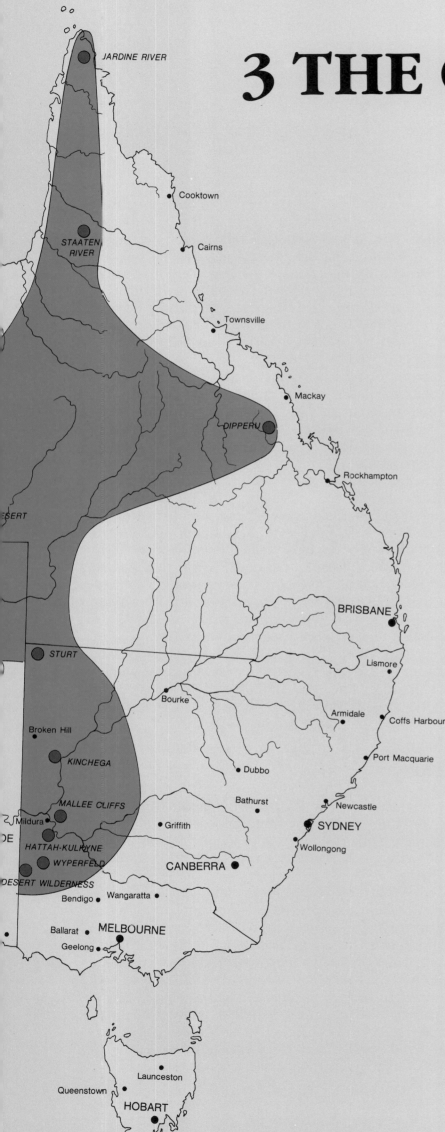

JARDINE RIVER

Cooktown

STAATEN
RIVER

Cairns

Townsville

Mackay

DIPPERU

Rockhampton

DESERT

BRISBANE

STURT

Lismore

Bourke

Armidale

Coffs Harbour

Broken Hill

Port Macquarie

KINCHEGA

Dubbo

MALLEE CLIFFS

Bathurst

Mildura

Newcastle

Griffith

SYDNEY

HATTAH-KULKYNE

Wollongong

WYPERFELD

CANBERRA

DESERT WILDERNESS

DE

Bendigo   Wangaratta

Ballarat   MELBOURNE

Geelong

Launceston

Queenstown

HOBART

Australia is both the flattest and the driest of the world's continents. Some seven-tenths of the land area fall within the arid zone, where annual rainfall averages less than 380 millimetres (15 inches). Throughout this zone, which extends in a broad band from the shoulder of Western Australia across to the western slopes of the Great Dividing Range and the shore of the Bight, level plains and low plateaux predominate. If there is a characteristic Australian landscape, then it is this flat, dry inland. It is 'outback'. Yet the great majority of Australia's national parks reserve segments of coast or areas of hill country, and a high proportion of these enclose or abut lakes or permanent rivers.

This imbalance reveals something about Australians as a people. It is related, of course, to the fact that most of us live near the coast and close to hills — which, in turn, reflects the fact that the arid and infertile interior could not support a high density of population. But it seems also to indicate a low level of interest in the type of environment to be found in our outback regions. We have been eager, from the beginning of our national parks movement, to reserve areas which are accessible to us and which appeal to us as being suitable for our preferred recreational activities — places where we can bushwalk, climb, camp, swim, boat, ride horses, ski, or simply goggle at the scenery. Outback landscapes, in general, are not as appealing.

In recent years, national parks authorities in all states have turned their attention increasingly to outback areas. If national parks are to fulfil the purpose of preserving representative samples of all Australia's different types of landscape and ecosystem, it is important that portions of outback regions remote from population centres should be included in the system. In this chapter, we focus attention upon some of these more remote parks.

The scenic variety to be found in these parks is much wider than the generalisations of our opening paragraph might suggest. Some parks in desert areas are included, but a number of our outback reserves are in fact in regions with a reliable regular rainfall. And, with only a few exceptions, to describe any of them simply as 'flat', without considerable qualification, would be both misleading and unjust.

QUEENSLAND

Jardine River

It will come as a surprise to many Australians to learn that the Jardine River, the most northerly river system in the continent, which flows into Endeavour Strait some fifty-five kilometres from the tip of Cape York, is the largest perennial river in Queensland. Most of the catchment area of this great river is contained within the large Jardine River National Park.

This is a region which has proved unattractive to Europeans ever since James Cook described it in 1770 as a 'low and barren land'. In fact, it is far from barren, supporting a prodigious plant life. Tropical rainforest with its wealth of different plant species, notably many palms and tall hoop pines (*Araucaria cunninghamii*) also found in Papua New Guinea, covers large areas of the low hills close to the east coast. Extensive heathlands occur around the headwaters of the Jardine and its tributaries, their flowering grevilleas and banksias attracting many birds, including several species of honeyeaters, also natives of New Guinea. Pandanus palms growing in sandstone areas near the sea provide food for the handsome black palm cockatoo and nesting sites for bar-shouldered doves (also known as pandanus pigeons). Both these birds are common in New Guinea. The pitcher plant, whose leaves form

cylindrical 'pitchers' in which unwary insects are trapped and digested, grows in swampy ground, as does another insect-devouring plant, the sundew. Open forests of Darwin stringybark (*Eucalyptus tetrodonta*) north of the river attract many different birds from time to time, including the pale-headed rosella, with its distinctive yellow head, blue and black wings and flash of red in its undertail coverts.

In open woodlands throughout Cape York Peninsula, termite mounds stand among the grasses like gravestones in some neglected graveyard. Red kangaroos, agile wallabies, emus and bustards are all inhabitants of this country. The handsome bustard, or plains turkey, is usually seen on the ground rather than on the wing, though it is a strong flyer. An adult male stands over a metre tall and has a wing-span in excess of two metres. Formerly common right across Australia, the bustard is now found only in grassland districts where there has been little or no human intrusion and consequent competitive pressure from grazing sheep and cattle or introduced rabbits. Cape York Peninsula is one of the few places where it may still be found in substantial numbers.

Archer Bend

Queensland's five biggest national parks all come within the scope of this chapter. Four of these — including the Jardine River park — are located in Cape York Peninsula. Archer Bend National Park, fifth largest, is situated on the western side of the peninsula, south of the bauxite mining town of Weipa. The park takes in the alluvial plains around the middle reaches of the Archer and Coen Rivers. Here, as happens around all the rivers flowing across these lowlands to the Gulf of Carpentaria, much of the country is flooded every year throughout the months of the Wet.

The Archer River and its swamp and lagoons usually retain some water during the Dry, attracting many water fowl and sustaining families of freshwater crocodiles. These reptiles nest during the dry season, excavating a hole in the sand. Quite harmless to man, the freshwater (or Johnston's) crocodile is not easily distinguished from the more dangerous estuarine or saltwater type. The clues to the difference are the 'freshie's' narrower snout and a row of four scales across the back of its head. Fully grown specimens are about three metres long — big enough to be frightening but still smaller than a mature 'saltie' which could be as much as twice that size. Vine forests line the river, providing a habitat for many birds, including the palm cockatoo, which here reaches the southern limit of its range. Away from the rivers, vegetation is mainly tea-tree scrub or eucalypt woodland, the home of agile wallabies and antelopine kangaroos.

Mitchell and Alice Rivers
Staaten River

Mitchell and Alice Rivers National Park, further south, and Staaten River National Park, further south again, similarly embrace the middle reaches of rivers on the floodplain. Habitats range through those already mentioned, with strips of riverine rainforest.

132

Lakefield

On the eastern side of the peninsula, Lakefield National Park reaches in a huge 'L' shape from the township of Laura to the shore of Princess Charlotte Bay. Covering more than half a million hectares of land, this is Queensland's largest national park. It encompasses much of the broad plain of the Normanby River, an area formerly used for cattle-grazing. With its southernmost point close to Laura and a road passing along its whole length, this is the Cape York Peninsula's most accessible national park.

Lakefield contains examples of all the varied habitats, with their associated flora and fauna, that characterise the tropical far north. You can find rainforest, paperbark woodland, swamp, mangroves and mudflats, open grassy plains and forests of stringybarks. In the wet season, all the rivers overflow and join to form massive lakes. In the dry season, there is still enough water to support a wealth of wildlife. Both estuarine and freshwater crocodiles are numerous. Lily-covered lagoons support large populations of magpie geese, pygmy geese, burdekin ducks, ibises, spoonbills, egrets and colonies of the stately black-and-white jabiru. The brolga is an inhabitant of this region, and the rather similar but slightly larger sarus crane, once thought to live only in Malaysia, may also be found here.

Parrots abound, adding life to the open woodlands with their brilliant colours, their busy movements, their excited cries. Among those most often seen are galahs, red-tailed black cockatoos and red-winged parrots. The latter, with its bright green plumage and gorgeous scarlet wing-coverts, moved naturalist John Gould to write, 'It is beyond my power to describe the extreme beauty of the appearance of the red-winged lory . . .' The equally splendid golden-shouldered parrot makes its nest in termite mounds. Ground animals include grey kangaroos, agile wallabies, northern nail-tailed wallabies and dingoes. Offshore lies the warm, shallow lagoon of the Great Barrier Reef, teeming with colourful marine life.

Magnetic ant hills in Lakefield National Park

Dipperu

The relatively small Dipperu National Park, southwest of Mackay, reserves a typical sample of the region's belah and brigalow scrub and flooded lagoon country. The birdlife of this wetland region is prolific, making this a park with particular interest for the naturalist.

Simpson Desert

In the far west of the state, close to the South Australian border, is one of Australia's most renowned outback settlements: Birdsville. Some 500 kilometres westward from

there, the slender tentacle of railway line from Port Augusta to Alice Springs snakes across one of the loneliest and driest regions of all. Between lies the Simpson Desert. Half a million hectares of this desert are reserved in the Simpson Desert National Park.

If true wilderness is still to be found on our continent — and some will argue that, according to their definition, it is not — this is surely one of the most important examples of it. Named by C. T. Madigan, who in 1939 led the first expedition to cross it, the Simpson is a land of massive red sand dunes that reach to the horizon in endless, parallel ridges. The dunes, as Madigan observed, can be up to thirty metres high and as wide, or wider, at the base. They run on continuously, sometimes converging, aligned southeast to northwest. Aerial photography has revealed that this orderly alignment is part of a distinct pattern found throughout Australia's deserts and apparently linked with prevailing wind directions. The dunes of the great ring of deserts which encircle the Centre form a huge whorl, like the petals of a rose.

Although surface sand is still moved by the winds, the dune system originated in ancient times, probably during periods of aridity between episodes of raised sea-levels in past ice ages. The red colouring comes from the thin coating of iron oxide on the quartz grains, developed over long periods of hot, dry conditions. Close to creek beds, where aridity has been less constant, the sand becomes lighter in colour, shading to white.

The Simpson Desert is far from being lifeless. Desert cane grass (*Zygochloa paradoxa*) grows on the unstable dune crests, sometimes accompanied by mulla mulla (*Ptilotus* spp.), also known as lambs' tails because of its fluffy flower heads. Lower down the dune flanks, porcupine grass (*Triodia* spp.) forms hummocks, whilst thickets of stunted gidgee (*Acacia cambagei*) — called 'stinking wattle' for its offensive perfume — spread over flat areas between the dunes, where clay soils retain moisture. When summer storms bring rain, a riot of growth follows, large areas of red sand disappearing beneath a flood of flowering plants such as parakeelya, everlasting daisies, white paper daisies and yellow-top (*Senecio gregori*). A botanist on a visit here in 1966 recorded eighty-five plant species.

This burgeoning of vegetation after rain triggers a remarkable expansion in the bird and insect populations. Many beautiful, colourful birds live in the desert, moving nomadically throughout the region. One of the smallest, the brilliantly hued crimson chat, travels in small flocks, living mainly on insects but also collecting nectar from flowers. Its relative, the orange chat, has similar habits but is more likely to be seen on saltbush flats close to salt lakes. Surprisingly, there are also many honeyeaters, all of which include insects in their diets. The handsome red-backed kingfisher is thoroughly at home here. Zebra finches, budgerigars, galahs and little corellas may be seen from time to time in large flocks.

The park's fauna has not yet been fully investigated, but it is likely to include small marsupials such as the various desert mouse and rat species (*Antechinus, Sminthopis* and *Notomys* spp.) and such common desert-dwelling reptiles as the desert death-adder, the bearded dragon and the two largest Australian lizards, the sand goanna and the perentie. The region's most commonly encountered ground animals are red kangaroos.

No roads lead into the Simpson Desert. In fact, unless you are specially equipped for desert travel and can bring enough water with you to meet your needs, you will not be able to visit this park. Its importance is not so much recreational as educational. It preserves intact an environment which has remained unaffected by man and whose value lies not in what we can produce from it but what we can learn from it. Its very inaccessibility and inhospitableness provide the best guarantee that this value will be maintained.

The Simpson Desert National Park occupies the corner of Queensland which borders South Australia and the Northern Territory. The desert itself extends into all three states. On the South Australian side, an even larger slice of the desert has been placed under the control of that state's National Parks and Wildlife Service and has been designated a Conservation Park. These puzzling differences in nomenclature from state to state are indicative of the lack of agreement among the various administrations about precisely what a national park is.

NEW SOUTH WALES

In the far northwest corner of New South Wales, where the borders of the state come closest to the deserts of the Centre, the barren, gibber plains of Sturt's Stony Desert merge into the dry grass plains of the North Darling lowlands. This is the legendary 'back o' Bourke' country. Here, occupying over 300 000 hectares reaching from Cameron's Corner, at the junction of the state borders, to thirty kilometres east of the small town of Tibooburra, is Sturt National Park.

The name commemorates explorer Charles Sturt, who first described this part of the country to the outside world after his expedition of 1845, when he penetrated as far as the southeast corner of the Simpson Desert. Sturt established a base camp at Fort Grey, now within the national park.

Pastoralists began to move into this Corner region in the 1880s. Heavy grazing from the 1890s on, coupled with the depredation caused by introduced rabbits, stripped the country of its saltbush and bluebush, leaving the so-called galvanised (or copper) burrs (*Bassia* spp.) dominant. The natural wildlife was also affected, though some species, especially the red kangaroo, gained from the improved availability of water once the graziers had sunk bores to water their stock. Since the withdrawal of stock and the declaration of the national park in 1972, the natural vegetation has showed signs of regenerating. Saltbush, bluebush and Mitchell grass are spreading again. Regeneration of tree growth will be a slower process. Mulga (*Acacia aneura*), gidgee (*A. cambagei*) and dead finish (*A. carnei*) all grow naturally in this environment, but during a century of pastoralism thousands of trees were cut down for fence posts, whilst the mulga provided stock-feed in drought years.

The eastern half of the park consists mainly of undulating red-soil gibber plains broken by low, flat-topped hills, known locally as 'jump-ups'. (More strictly termed 'mesas', they are capped with a silicrete duricrust.) The western half is largely covered by sand dunes, within which lies Pinaroo Lake. Beds of ephemeral creeks are lined with river red gums and coolabahs (*Eucalyptus microtheca*).

Several roads pass through the park, including the unsealed Silver City Highway. Roads in this region become impassable after rain and some are suitable only for four-wheel-drive vehicles. Choose your time carefully (April to October is recommended), and a visit to Sturt could prove most rewarding. A drive through the park can include an inspection of the old homestead, which gives an insight into the life of the outback pioneers.

Drive slowly, for this is kangaroo country. Keep a sharp lookout for the 'big reds' and the female 'blue flyers' around dusk and early in the morning. It is also lizard country. Watch for the stumpy-tail or shingle-back, which has a bad habit of sunbaking in the middle of the road. In rocky gorges flanking dry creek beds you may see euros. Emus wander these plains, sometimes in large flocks, more usually in smaller family groups. Birds of prey, including eagles and kestrels, are almost always hovering somewhere in the sky. (The swoop of an eagle close to you sounds for all the world like a car racing by at high speed.)

As you walk around the area you will come across many birds on the ground: blue wrens, pipits, bronzewing pigeons. Two birds which choose the open gibber plains for their nesting sites are the pratincole (also known as the swallow-plover or the ground-runner) and the inland dotterel. The pratincole, a graceful bird with an upright stance, is a migrant which arrives here about September and leaves in December or January, travelling in large, high-flying flocks. The dotterel breeds in winter, covering its eggs with twigs or sand when leaving them unattended. Dotterels stand around dozing in the sun during the day, becoming active at night.

You may camp inside the park, but you must be completely self-sufficient. Water is scarce in this region and all travellers should carry their own supply. Talk to the ranger in Tibooburra first to check road conditions. Accommodation is available in the town.

Stumpy-tailed lizard

Red kangaroos in Kinchega National Park

Kinchega

(Opposite page) In Mungo National Park

The lakes in Kinchega National Park are breeding grounds for vast numbers of waterbirds, including cormorants, ducks, herons, ibis, spoonbills, egrets and pelicans (Lee Pearce)

Western New South Wales has four more national parks occupying former grazing land. Kinchega National Park, on the west bank of the Darling River close to Menindee, reserves part of what was once Kinchega station. At this point, the Darling forms a system of overflow lakes. The park encloses the two largest, Lakes Menindee and Cawndilla, while its eastern boundary follows the tortuous line of a long stretch of river.

Kinchega is perhaps the best place of all in which to experience the western plains environment. Here you can camp beside the Darling among spreading river red gums and take breakfast in the company of ducks, waterhens, cormorants, egrets and pelicans. The lakes support a very large breeding population of water birds. Varying habitats within the park are inhabited by red kangaroos, grey kangaroos, emus, possums and birds of many types.

At times of flood, the river spills over its banks, inundating the campsite. At any time, a sudden storm can close all the roads. For most of the year, however, this area is dry and the roads are sound. If you can arrange your visit for late winter or early spring, before the weather becomes unbearably hot — and, ideally, when recent rains have brought life to the landscape — you will see Kinchega at its best. Dirt roads lead you from the blacksoil floodplain to the red sandplains around the lakes, where picnic sites have been provided. A woolshed built in the 1880s stands as a reminder of the park's sheep-raising past.

About 130 kilometres northeast of Broken Hill is a site which enjoys the protection of the New South Wales National Parks and Wildlife Service though it is not classified as a national park: Mootwingee Historic Site. This reserve encloses the upper valley of the Nootumbulla Creek, in the isolated and rugged Bynguano Range, a rocky oasis in a flat, arid land of gibber plains and sandplains. The Wilyakali tribe, which formerly lived in the area, has left behind a wealth of ancient tribal art. Rock caves contain scores of paintings and stencils. One sandstone rockface, now sadly cracking and splitting apart into fragments, carries thousands of engraved designs depicting human figures, animals and other subjects. Walking tracks lead to the various rock galleries.

Mootwingee has a ranger station, a visitor centre with a theatrette, and campsites shaded by river red gums. Cold showers, toilets and fireplaces are also provided.

Willandra

Willandra National Park, sixty-four kilometres northwest of the little town of Hillston, lies on the northern edge of the Riverina Plain. The park covers a portion of what was formerly one of the biggest stud merino stations in Australia. Within the park, the buildings of the homestead complex include the historic rams' shed where, at shearing time, you may watch sheep from neighbouring properties being shorn. Grazing stock is now excluded from the park. A motor trail enables you to drive around the eastern section of the park, crossing the plain and following the meandering course of the Willandra Billabong, whose banks are fringed with coolabahs and black box (*Eucalyptus largiflorens*). All the animals of the inland plains are to be seen here, including many species of waterfowl and parrots. The billabong is well stocked with fish, including yellowbelly and perch.

Renovated former staff quarters provide lodge-style accommodation. Camping is permitted. No food is available and you must bring all your supplies with you.

Mallee Cliffs

Mallee Cliffs National Park, near the Victorian border at Mildura exists not so much for the benefit of people as for the benefit of a strange race of mound-building birds. The mallee fowl, which is found no further east than western New South Wales, is naturally adapted to living in the type of country characterised by the growth of stunted eucalypts in the form called — from an Aboriginal word — 'mallee'. The word does not refer to a single species of eucalypt but describes a style of growth in which many stems spring from one woody underground root, called a lignotuber. Mallee grows in sandy soils in areas where annual rainfall is less than 431 millimetres.

The mallee fowl, like the scrub fowl and scrub turkey of the northeastern rainforests and monsoon forests, constructs a nesting mound on the ground. Its range, however, is confined to the southern half of the arid zone of mainland Australia. The bird has lost much of its habitat to the clearing of land for wheat-growing, introduced foxes have reduced its numbers by eating the eggs, and rabbits and sheep have competed for its food supply. If this rare creature is to survive it must be allowed some protected living areas. This is the principal purpose of the Mallee Cliffs National Park. Human visitors are not provided for.

Mungo

Evidence of the earliest known human occupation of Australia has been found within Mungo National Park, northeast of Mildura. This remote park has in recent years become a centre for archaeological and earth sciences studies which are attracting worldwide scientific interest. Investigators have found traces of man's presence dating back more than 35 000 years. Fascinating discoveries have been made about burial rites and tools used by Aborigines in past ages.

The region possesses a chain of ancient lakebeds which have been continuously dry for the last 15 000 years, but which formerly held fresh water to depths of as much as ten metres. When last filled, the lakes covered more than a thousand square kilometres. The Aboriginal inhabitants lived on the shores, taking fish and mussels from the lakes, hunting land animals and collecting emu eggs.

As at Lake Menindee, in Kinchega National Park, the eastern shores are marked by crescent-shaped sand dunes known as lunettes. The park's most prominent feature is a section of a thirty kilometre lunette formation which has been given the name of the Walls of China.

No facilities are provided for overnight camping. Visitors usually inspect the buildings of the old Mungo sheep station, including the shearing shed, built in 1869, and drive ten kilometres through the park to the Walls of China. Regular bus tours to Mungo National Park operate from Mildura.

VICTORIA

Hattah-Kulkyne
Murray-Kulkyne

Mallee country extends through large parts of Victoria and South Australia and covers an even larger area in the southern half of Western Australia. Part of this mallee region occupies the northwest corner of Victoria, where it is known as the Sunset Country, presumably because it is so flat that nothing obscures the setting sun. On the eastern edge of the Sunset Country, about fifty kilometres south of Mildura, two adjoining national parks extend from the Calder Highway to the banks of the Murray River. These are the Hattah-Kulkyne and the Murray-Kulkyne National Parks. The terrain includes former grazing land, now regenerating, an extensive lake system surrounded by river red gum forest with a mixture of other eucalypts, notably black box, and a long segment of the tortuous south bank of the Murray River.

You may camp at the lakeside (though you should bring your own drinking water) and enjoy a holiday of bushwalking, boating, fishing and observing the wealth of wildlife to be found in the varied habitats. There are walking tracks and a nature drive. Both grey and red kangaroos are to be seen in this area, as are emus and mallee fowls. Birdlife is prolific, especially the many types of waterfowl which nest around the waterways: ibises, spoonbills, egrets, herons, ducks and many more. The Murray Valley is remarkably rich in bird species and especially noted for its many honeyeaters and parrots.

Pink Lakes in spring

Pink Lakes

A group of colourful saltpans, surrounded by saltbush flats, sand dunes and dry grass plains, forms the central feature of Pink Lakes National Park, to the west of Ouyen, in the Sunset Country. Salt is harvested from two of the lakes. Grazing also continues within the park but is to be phased out. Bushcamping is permitted in certain areas.

South of the Sunset Country, in the region known as the Big Desert, Victoria has three more outback national parks: Wyperfeld, Big Desert Wilderness and Lake Albacutya. Further south, close to Dimboola, Little Desert National Park reserves an area of similar country — largely mallee scrub and sandy heathland.

Wyperfield and Big Desert Wilderness are two of Victoria's largest parks, exceeded in size only by the Grampians National Park. Each park exceeds 100 000 hectares. It is noteworthy that Wyperfeld was originally reserved specifically to protect the habitat of the mallee fowl. As agricultural development has steadily spread into this corner of the state since the establishment in the 1950s of the Wimmera-Mallee Stock and Domestic Water Supply, these parks may yet become islands in which the unique ecosystem of the region may be preserved beyond the twentieth century. When development laps around them, their size may be just enough to give some of the flora and fauna species a fighting chance of survival. Fortunately, the conservation value of Big Desert Wilderness National Park is enhanced by the existence of adjacent conservation parks with a total area of more than a quarter of a million hectares, on the South Australian side of the state border.

Lake Albacutya is part of the Wimmera River system. This river, which rises in the Grampians and flows northward, disappears into the ground at Wyperfeld. Lake Hindmarsh, to the south, feeds Lake Albacutya through Outlet Creek. The usually dry creek-bed continues through the park, opening out in a series of shallow depressions flatteringly called lakes. Some of these lakes have contained no water since the 1920s, though some were filled as recently as 1975. Nevertheless Lake Albacutya is a popular place for boating, swimming, fishing and water-skiing.

You drive into Wyperfeld alongside the bed of Outlet Creek, passing through groves of black box and native pine to reach the park headquarters and the camping area, set in a circle of tall river red gums. Roads radiate from here to take you to lookout points and walking tracks. From a lookout tower you can gaze across the astonishing mallee landscape which inevitably invites comparison with the sea. This is a sea of sand dunes. The colour is grey-green, for the crests are heath-covered while the intervening hollows are wooded with the stunted mallee, with tea-trees, wattles and pines. Below the trees, when you walk into this landscape, you will discover a diverse vegetation which comprises many flowering species, and which is bustling with life. Over 200 bird species have been noted in Wyperfeld.

The other parks of this region possess generally similar landscape, for they also cover parts of the mallee country. Whilst the Little Desert park has campsites, picnic areas, a nature trail and an information centre, Big Desert Wilderness, as its name implies, has no developed facilities to provide for the comfort of the human visitor. If you enter it you must do so on foot, prepared to be entirely self-sufficient. Note that daytime temperatures between December and March in this region are usually far too high for safe bushwalking.

Your reward for venturing into one of these parks will be the memorable experience of coming into intimate contact with an environment that is like no other and in which the native wildlife is as free as you are. You will discover that an area which men call 'desert' can be home to a multitude of living things and a place rich in colour and beauty. Watch out for the lovely mallee ringneck parrot. Also, this is one of the few regions of Australia where you may still see large flocks of the superb pink (or Major Mitchell's) cockatoo.

TASMANIA

As Tasmania has no areas which can strictly be described as outback, its out-of-the-way national parks have been discussed in Chapter 1, Coasts and Islands, and Chapter 2, Highlands and Forests.

Mallee ring-necked parrot

Major Mitchell cockatoos

145

SOUTH AUSTRALIA

South Australia has a higher proportion of its area within the arid zone than any other Australian state. Some eighty-seven per cent of the state receives less than 250 millimetres of rain each year. Much of outback South Australia is consequently desert country, vast areas covered with mallee or silver-grey mulga scrub. Mulga (*Acacia aneura*) survives through long droughts, even when no rain falls for several years. It rarely grows taller than five metres, except in the better watered parts of its range.

Although South Australia has only ten national parks (most of which have been described in Chapter 1, Coasts and Islands, and Chapter 2, Highlands and Forests), the state's National Parks and Wildlife Service is also responsible for managing no less than 168 conservation parks with an aggregate area of almost four million hectares. Although these parks are defined as 'areas where visitor development is kept to a minimum', in many cases their character and use seem to be appropriate to what would be called a national park in other states. In fairness to South Australia, some of these have been included in our review.

The Naracoorte Caves Conservation Park, in the southeast, is a good example. This park has a camping ground, with shower and toilet facilities and powered caravan sites, a kiosk, a picnic area, a wildlife enclosure, a museum and an information centre where visitors can watch scientists working on fossils. Three of the famous limestone caves are open for inspection. Although the caves provide the park's main attraction, the above-ground area conserves a eucalypt forest habitat in which a diverse community of native animals can be observed. Two marsupials survive here which were once believed extinct in South Australia: the koala and the brush-tailed phascagole (marsupial rat).

Not all of South Australia's conservation parks are freely open to the public. If Naracoorte Caves Conservation Park, with its facilities for visitors, is seen as representing one end of a scale of accessibility, then some of those which are most characteristic of the South Australian outback are at the opposite end of the scale. This category includes the state's two largest reserves: Simpson Desert Conservation Park and an unnamed conservation park along part of the western border which reaches into the Great Victoria Desert. These two parks together cover 2 825 000 hectares. Entry to them is by permit only and should not be attempted except by properly equipped expeditions.

The primary importance of these desert and semi-desert reserves lies in their rôle as flora and fauna sanctuaries. A secondary value is their usefulness to man as open-air laboratories for the study of that flora and fauna and its environment, to help us to enlarge our understanding of our world, before we modify it out of existence. Opening up such areas to mass incursions by the sight-seeing public would, of course, quickly destroy these complex and fragile ecological systems.

There are, nevertheless, parks accessible by car and open to the public, where you may come face to face with environments of equal barrenness. The Eyre Highway, which reaches along the southern perimeter of the continent from Port Augusta into Western Australia, will lead you to three of these. About 140 kilometres from Port Augusta, on the northern side of the highway, lies the long, shallow depression called Lake Gilles, more often than not a dry saltpan gleaming in the sun. The Lake Gilles Conservation Park spans the highway and extends north along half the length of the lake. This is sand-dune country, sparsely covered by low-growing myall (*Acacia sowdenii*) and black oak (*Casuarina cristata*) woodland, with some areas of mallee.

Further west, reached via an unsealed track which turns inland off the highway beyond Ceduna, is Yumbarra Conservation Park. The landscape here is filled to the horizon with long sand ridges with some outcropping crags of granite. Vegetation is confined to open hollows between dunes, which support mallee and other low shrubs. Nomadic animals of the outback roam freely here; most noticeable are emus, red kangaroos and western grey kangaroos (whose fur is slightly more reddish than that of their eastern cousins).

Still further west, beyond the Yalata Aboriginal Reserve, is Nullarbor National Park. Gazetted in 1979, this park occupies 230 000 hectares of land formerly leased for grazing. The highway runs clean through the middle of the park, which extends to the high cliffs of the coast all along its southern boundary.

The Nullarbor Plain has often been described as Australia's most monotonous landscape. Nowhere else is the land so flat and featureless over such great distances. The Trans-Australian Railway, which crosses the plain some 100 kilometres north of the highway, includes the world's longest straight stretch of line. This flatness is characteristic of ancient limestone formations; the Nullarbor is the uplifted portion of the world's biggest single slab of limestone bedrock. This compacted mass of coral skeletons accumulated on a sea-bed through two separate epochs of the Tertiary period, beginning some forty to fifty million years ago. At a much later time, the plain was raised by earth movements, the strata remaining remarkably horizontal. The ocean cliffs reveal the stratification clearly, showing a marked contrast between the yellow-white, chalky rock at lower levels, which was laid down in the Eocene epoch, and the younger Miocene rock above, which is grey.

The uniform hardness of the rock has prevented the formation of valleys. No water courses cut across the surface. Rain, when it falls, soaks rapidly into the porous limestone. Over the centuries it has hollowed out underground caves where the water collects in lakes, eventually seeping out through the cliffs to the south. Caves are found only along the coastal margin, where rainfall is highest. Even so, in this dry region, moisture penetration has been insufficient to form the extensive decorations found in limestone caves elsewhere.

The Nullarbor caves have other claims to fame. Zoologists have been able to learn much about the wildlife and the climate of past ages through study of fossilised and, in some instances, well-preserved remains of animals which fell into the caves through holes formed when cave roofs collapsed. Today, many animals of the treeless, waterless plain use caves as homes. Blowholes are a strange feature of this region — cave openings which sometimes suck in air, sometimes expel air, in response to changes in atmospheric pressure.

The name Nullarbor, formed from the Latin words *nulla* and *arbor* and meaning 'not trees', expresses the desolation of this desert plain. Large expanses of country are absolutely treeless, the red soil being thinly covered with clumps of saltbush and bluebush. Near the coast, some growth of mallee scrub occurs. Rain does fall from time to time. The coastal strip has an annual average rainfall of about 250 millimetres which occurs mostly, but unreliably, in winter. The occasional heavy storm produces a lush growth of grasses and a brief burst of colour from flowering desert plants.

The absence of trees and surface water makes the Nullarbor as inhospitable to most animals as it is to man. Ground animals are mainly nocturnal. This is the domain of the hairy-nose wombat, which has long since disappeared from other parts of Australia. Slightly smaller than other types of wombat, the hairy-nose has the ability to survive without water for many months. On cool, fine days, hairy-nosed wombats may be seen (by the quiet observer) lying in the sun outside their burrows.

WESTERN AUSTRALIA

Apart from the forested southwest and the tropical eucalypt woodland of the Kimberleys, Western Australia has no extensively timbered areas. Inland from the wet southwest corner, the vegetation changes from eucalypt woodland to mallee scrub and heath. North of Kalgoorlie, mulga scrub takes over, giving way in turn to saltbush or porcupine grass with sparse tree growth and shrubs such as hakea. Then comes the desert country.

Deserts form a broad ribbon of barrenness across the state, from Eighty Mile Beach in the northwest to the southern cliffs of the Nullarbor Plain. The arc of human settlement curves around this vast expanse of desert, leaving more than half the state unoccupied and without roads. Naturally enough, almost all the state's national parks are found in the south and west. Notable exceptions (already dealt with in Chapter 2, Highlands and Forests) are those in the ranges of the northwest — the Hamersley, Chichester and Collier Range National Parks — and Drysdale River National Park, in the north Kimberleys.

Coastal heathland, Badgingarra National Park

Badgingarra

Before turning our attention to the western state's more remote parks, mention must be made of the dozen or more national parks and other reserves whose essential purpose is to preserve areas of exceptional floral interest or samples of particular vegetation zones. For example, Badgingarra National Park, northeast of Cervantes, has been reserved to protect the black kangaroo paws (*Macropidia fuliginosa*) which grow there. The flowers of this Western Australian plant are not in fact black, as the name suggests, but green, the flowers and stems being densely covered with black hairs.

Wolf Creek Meteorite Crater, second largest of its kind in the world (G Deichmann / Auscape)

Rudall River

For those adventure seekers who wish to get right away from civilisation, Western Australia's National Parks Authority has provided an answer: Rudall River National Park. This huge park — the state's biggest, with an area of more than one and a half million hectares — is situated on the edge of the Great Sandy Desert over 200 kilometres east of Nullagine. The ephemeral Rudall River rises in the Broadhurst Range and disappears in the direction of Lake Dora, normally a dry saltpan. Without special training and equipment, few of us brought up in a twentieth-century urban environment could survive for long in such a place.

Wolf Creek Crater

Before leaving Western Australia, we must take a look at a small national park which contains a unique feature: the world's second largest meteorite crater. (The largest is in Arizona.) Wolf Creek Crater National Park sits at the northeastern corner of the Great Sandy Desert, 134 kilometres south of Halls Creek, close to the Alice Springs Road. The circular crater, left by the impact of a meteorite which hit the Earth some 50 000 years ago, measures 854 metres across by about 50 metres deep. Approaching the crater, you see a low hill, an oddity in this flat, featureless landscape. Climb the slope and gaze into the deep, symmetrical hole in the red ground; you will find it an eerie experience. A nearby homestead offers camping facilities and supplies.

NORTHERN TERRITORY

Kakadu

The national parks of the Centre are described in Chapter 4. The other principal reserves controlled by the Northern Territory Conservation Commission have been included in previous chapters. To conclude this present chapter, we put the spotlight on the nation's biggest national park — one which, although located in the Northern Territory, about 200 kilometres east of Darwin, is under the management of the Australian National Parks and Wildlife Service and was declared a national park under an Act of the Commonwealth Parliament. This is Kakadu National Park.

Proclaimed on 5 April 1979, Kakadu National Park covers an area of 1 307 393 hectares. In other words, it is more than five times the size of the Australian Capital Territory. The boundaries of the park may be extended even further in the future. The present park abuts the Arnhem Land Aboriginal Reserve, embracing the middle reaches of the South Alligator River and the greater part of the courses of its major tributaries, the Nourlangie, Deaf Adder, Jim Jim and Barramundie Creeks. It takes in a portion of the Arnhem Land Plateau and a long segment of the plateau's dramatically scarped edge, together with areas of lowland and floodplains and, in a separate northern section, tidal mangrove flats at the mouth of the East Alligator River. Its boundaries have been drawn around the uranium deposits at Jabiluka, Jabiru (Ranger) and Koongarra.

An important fact to keep in mind about Kakadu is that this is Aboriginal property. The Kakadu Aboriginal Land Trust, representing the traditional owners, has leased most of the land comprising the park to the Commonwealth Director of National Parks and Wildlife for 100 years from November 1978, to be managed as a national park. The owners also gave their consent for mining of uranium. One of the managing authority's more difficult tasks will be to protect the park from the effects of that mining.

The many-hued cliffs of the Kakadu escarpment are the eroded edges of the vast Arnhem Land Plateau (Lee Pearce)

Aboriginal painting at Obiri Rock, Arnhem Land

Nourlangie Rock, Kakadu National Park

Kakadu is scenically magnificent. It also has outstanding value as a part of Australia's natural heritage in terms of its wildlife, its vegetation and its importance to research in climatology, geomorphology and archaeology.

The park contains what must be regarded as the finest known collection of Aboriginal rock art in the whole country, a cultural treasure of immense importance. Hundreds of cave walls and rock faces are richly decorated with fascinating paintings, in a wide range of styles, including X-ray figures, stick figures and elongated, sumptuously adorned figures. The scenes depict many aspects of life as experienced by the people of the area in past times, from hunting to encounters with Macassan fishermen and with Europeans. Some of the pigments have been dated at 18 000 years old, making the galleries of Kakadu comparable in importance with those in such renowned sites as the Lascaux Cave in southwest France.

There are also rock engravings and rock arrangements with special significance for the Aborigines. The people living in the locality today still regard many of these sites as sacred and access to some by park visitors is therefore restricted.

Excavations of archaeological sites and examination of the cave paintings are revealing much about the earliest known human inhabitants of our continent and much about the wildlife and the climate of past ages. Some traces of human occupation are thought to date back 25 000 years and evidence has been found of the earliest known technology of edge-ground axes.

Fine examples of cave paintings can be seen and photographed by visitors at two sites which are relatively easy to reach: Obiri Rock and Nourlangie Rock. Both are outliers of the great sandstone escarpment which is the dominant landform of the area. The paintings should not be touched. The park authorities are working hard to preserve this fragile inheritance, carrying out such tasks as removing wasps' nests and installing silica drip lines to divert water flow as these paintings are at least as precious and irreplaceable as anything hanging in the Louvre.

The area has an incredible abundance and variety of plants and animals. Many of the flora and fauna species reveal affinities with those of Southeast Asia and New Guinea. Some species are endemic to the region, their range being confined to particular habitats within it. For example, the banded fruit-dove and the white-lined honeyeater are found only in the pockets of monsoon rainforest and its adjacent shrubbery on the plateau. The stony escarpment country is the home of a recently discovered python, the Oenpelli python, whilst the black wallaroo, the rock wallaby, the rock possum and several other marsupials are confined to the escarpment and its rock outliers. The hooded parrot and the Gouldian finch, both rare and declining species, have been observed in the eucalypt woodlands on the undulating plains below the escarpment. The yellow chat, also declining in numbers, is found only in the floodplains around this corner of the Top End.

Much of the character of the park and its wildlife is dictated by the monsoonal climate. Average annual rainfall at the coast is about 1300 millimetres, most of this falling between November and March. Average summer maximum temperature is 34° C and this drops only a few degrees in the dry months of 'winter'. During the Wet, vast areas of the floodplains are inundated as the rivers and creeks overflow. This excess of water attracts myriad water birds. By February, the wetlands are alive with large populations of magpie geese, burdekin ducks, wandering whistling ducks, green pygmy-geese, jabirus, brolgas, pied herons, white-faced herons, large egrets, black ducks and pelicans.

The best time to visit Kakadu is between April and July. In the first few weeks following the end of the Wet there is still plenty of water around and plenty of life. The waterfalls that plunge over the escarpment are at their spectacular best. But you may have to restrict your routes to all-weather roads. By May, the ground is drying out, the waters are shrinking back into the permanent pools and the skies are often thick with smoke from bushfires. By August, the seasonal streams have become dry beds of sand and the desiccating heat is hard on animals and men alike.

You can drive into Kakadu on the Arnhem Highway from Darwin or the unsealed road from Pine Creek. The latter is often closed in the wet season, as are some of the roads inside the park. Light planes can land at airstrips within the park. There are several campsites, and accommodation, petrol and general supplies are available

Yellow Water, on the Alligator River, is the largest of the billabongs and lagoons strung throughout Kakadu National Park (Lee Pearce)

at several points inside or close to the park. The park headquarters is at Jabiru, where a new town is being developed to cater both for tourists and for the uranium mining industry. A four-wheel-drive vehicle would be of considerable advantage when visiting this area but you should be able to travel widely within the park even in an ordinary car.

At any time of year, extended bushwalking excursions in this region can be extremely hard on anyone not fully acclimatised to the tropics. Before setting out on any walk you should discuss your plans with a ranger. This is wild, implacable country and it would be foolish to put yourself (and others) at risk by underestimating the severity of the conditions. Also, the rangers can give you invaluable advice to help you get the most out of your visit and to ensure that you do not unwittingly trespass upon areas of special significance.

The glories of Kakadu are its wildness, its diversity, its fecundity, its spaciousness and its scenic and artistic uniqueness. There are dangers, too, which should not be ignored. Buffaloes should be given a wide berth. Saltwater crocodiles — which roam well beyond the saltwater estuaries, often being found in freshwater lagoons and swamps — do not make good swimming companions. They are, however, entitled to be left in peace in their own habitat. Come here to watch the sun rise over the crags of the escarpment, to see the great communities of water birds busy on the lagoons, to explore the fascinating and lively world of the mangroves by boat, to observe the rare and beautiful small things, such as the orange and blue Leichhardt's grasshopper (the explorer passed through here in 1845) or to enjoy the colours — of water lilies, paperbark and gum blossoms, parrots and rainbow birds — and you will have the time of your life.

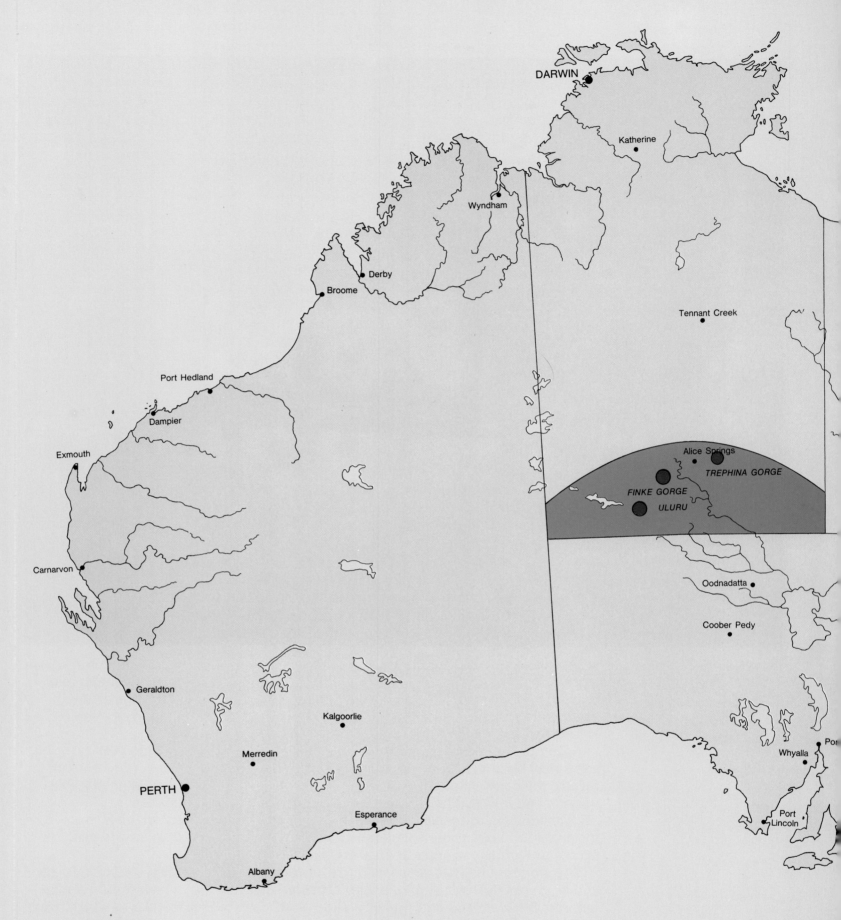

4 THE CENTRE

The subject of this chapter — the southern part of the Northern Territory — lies in the middle of Australia's arid zone, surrounded by deserts. This is country unlike any other, in which ancient mountains rise from sandy plains, their valleys and chasms containing oases of green life in the otherwise harsh red landscape. There are natural features scattered around the Centre so unique and spectacular in character they attract armies of tourists from all over the world each year.

Explorer John McDouall Stuart, in 1860 the first European to penetrate this region — at his fourth attempt — had the rare good fortune to find the Centre's major river in flood. He named it the Finke River, to honour one of the two patrons of his expedition. Apparently he had not learnt of the melodious name by which the Aborigines already knew it: Larapinta.

Stuart paid tribute to his other patron in the name he gave to a remarkable slender column of sandstone thirty metres tall which stands among the sandhills of the Finke. He called it Chambers Pillar. It now enjoys the protection of the Conservation Commission of the Northern Territory in the Chambers Pillar Historical Reserve.

By 1872 the Overland Telegraph had been built, linking the northern and southern shores of the continent, and white men were living in the Centre, operating a telegraph station beside the Alice Spring. Settlers soon followed, bringing livestock with them. By the turn of the century the area had become established beef-producing country. Camels were brought in to transport goods. Before the railway from Port Augusta reached Alice Springs in 1929, most property owners kept herds of goats as a source of milk and meat. These animals did considerable damage, consuming everything that grew. All these influences modified the region's natural balance and its appearance, stripping it of trees and grasses. Many of the Centre's national parks are on land formerly used for grazing where the natural vegetation is now slowly regenerating.

Alice Springs, the region's main town, provides a convenient base from which to visit the parks and reserves of the Centre. 'The Alice' has a relaxed, friendly atmosphere and offers all kinds of accommodation. You may stay in a hotel, a motel or a caravan park, or pitch your tent at a campsite. You may even book yourself into a tourist centre eighty kilometres east of town which is a restored pioneer homestead with air-conditioned log cabins.

The real Alice Springs, the semi-permanent waterhole in the Todd River beside which the telegraph station was built in 1871–72, is four kilometres north of the town. It is now the centrepiece of a public reserve. You may wander through the collection of colonial-era stone buildings, which have been carefully restored, and learn something of the lives of those earliest settlers in the Centre. There are picnic and barbecue facilities, marked walking tracks and, from May to September, guided tours of the historical section.

The town itself is situated in a hollow in the eastern hills of the MacDonnell Ranges, beside the Todd River. Like all the rivers of this region, the Todd flows only occasionally and then usually for no more than a few days. The rest of the time it is nothing more than a broad ribbon of sand. On maps it is marked as a wavy line meandering southeast from the MacDonnells into the Simpson Desert, where it vanishes.

The MacDonnells, one of Australia's major mountain chains, extend for more than 300 kilometres in a great east-west arc along the Tropic of Capricorn. These ancient, gnarled hills have been shaped by millions of centuries of weathering. They reach their highest point (115 metres) at Mount Zeil, in the west.

Much of the region's special character derives from past wetter periods in earth's history. The most obvious examples are to be seen in the numerous scenic gorges and gaps in the ranges, all cut long ago by streams much larger and more continuous in their flow than the intermittent streams of today. These canyons provide most of the major tourist attractions of the MacDonnells. Many of them have been incorporated into public reserves.

Reds predominate in the colours of the Centre's landscapes. On every side you are confronted by red sand dunes, red claypans, red rock. The redness results from the formation over long periods of time of an iron-oxide coating on the grains of material of which both rocks and desert sands are composed. This process — in which two of the commonest elements, iron from the earth and oxygen from the air, are combined — occurs only in hot, dry conditions. In wetter climates, leaching prevents it.

The ruddiness is not, however, all-pervasive. The Centre is a kaleidoscope of many colours. Distant hills appear blue, shaded with purple, becoming chocolate-brown, cinnamon or ochre as you approach them. Clumps of yellow-grey porcupine grass (*Triodia irritans*) — popularly, but erroneously, called spinifex — and saltbush (*Atriplex* spp.) bristle above the red sandplains in company with the silvery mulga trees (*Acacia aneura*). Everywhere you will see trees and shrubs, often bright with blossoms. These, in turn, attract a pageant of birds.

Most majestic of the region's trees is the river red gum (*Eucalyptus camaldulensis*), often found in company with ghost gums (*E. papuana*). High on rock slopes, the tallest tree is generally the white cypress pine (*Callitris culumellaris*), easily recognised by its dark-green foliage and its conical shape. Twisted white ghost gums are also found on many slopes, growing from crevices in rock faces. On sandy plains and claypan flats, you find the bloodwood (*Eucalyptus terminalis*), the beefwood (*Grevillea striata*), the whitewood (*Atalaya hemiglauca*) and the ironwood (*Acacia estrophiolata*). One of the most attractive trees is the erect, black-trunked desert oak (*Casuarina decaisneana*), to be seen growing on the dunes near Mount Olga and Ayers Rock. Or you may prefer the corkwood (*Hakea suberea*), which bears clusters of sweetly scented creamy yellow flowers.

The domes of Mount Olga, called 'the mountain of many heads' by the Aboriginals (Lee Pearce)

Some would give first prize for beauty to one of the several species of *Eremophila* or *Cassia* found in these parts. The eremophilas (the name means 'desert-loving') bear tubular flowers in various colours; cassias have buttercup-like yellow flowers. Or perhaps your choice would be the desert grevillea (*Grevillea juncifolia*) for its masses of vivid orange flowers held high on tall stems among its long, slender leaves. Others might choose the native fig (*Ficus platypoda*) or a smaller herbaceous plant which similarly favours rocky hillsides, the *Nicotinia ingulba*, a relative of the tobacco plant. Its tubular white flowers perfume the night air. Aborigines use its lush leaves as chewing plugs.

Rain, when it comes in this region, comes in a deluge. And it transforms the country. The hard, smooth claypans become gleaming yellow lakes of shallow water. Torrents pour through previously dry creek-beds. Waterholes expand. When the skies clear and the sun comes out again, all the rocks glisten, their many facets displaying new, bolder tints. Waterfalls tumble down cliff faces. The beauty of many a scene is doubled by reflections in still pools. And, in one of Nature's cleverest conjuring tricks, grasses and flowering plants erupt from the russet ground and rapidly spread across the open spaces.

Among the wide variety of ephemeral plants which spread, from time to time, in living carpets across the sands of the Centre, the suburban gardener will find many familiar faces. Very widespread is the pink or mauve-flowered parakeelya (*Calandrinia balonensis*). You will recognise several members of the daisy family: pink, white and yellow 'everlasting' daisies of the genus *Helichrysum*, white paper daisies (*Helipterum* spp.), and the poached egg daisy (*Myriocephalus stuartii*). Unmistakable is the Sturt's desert pea (*Clianthus formosus*), a trailing plant whose scarlet-and-black flowers stand erect on short stalks, giving them the appearance of miniature, red-coated soldiers.

The Centre's pools and creeks teem with life in many forms, from water insects to tadpoles and frogs. Some of the frogs and even fish manage to survive long dry spells by burrowing into the mud of creek beds and lying there inert, until the water flows again. A small crustacean, the shield shrimp, has evolved an adaptation technique much like that of the ephemeral plants. Its eggs remain dormant, buried in mud or dried clay, until heavy rain fills the claypans with enough water for the creature to fulfil its whirlwind life-cycle. Once hatched, the shield shrimp must grow to maturity, mate and produce eggs before the merciless sun dries up the water in which it lives. As the ponds shrink, the shrimps die in thousands around the muddy edges. At these times, flocks of herons and egrets arrive to indulge in a banquet.

Waterholes and creeks are the essential natural reservoirs upon which virtually all life depends. All the animals need water from time to time, though some are able to survive for long periods without it. Even the creatures that roam widely, such as kangaroos and the flightless, nomadic emus, must have access to a water supply, or die.

The water patches of the Centre are almost always busy with birds: insect-eaters such as willy-wagtails, cuckoo-shrikes, swallows and martins, or flocks of budgerigars, galahs or other parrots. One of those most often seen is the Port Lincoln parrot, a talkative and inquisitive bird. It is recognisable by its distinctive black head with vivid cyan cheek patches and yellow neckband. The rest of the body is bright green, shading to yellow underneath with some blue in wings and tail.

There are quieter, less obtrusive parrots to be observed also. You may come across, for example, the mulga parrot, bright green with flashes of blue and small patches of orange on the shoulders, or Bourke's parrot, brown above with blue leading edges to wings and rose-pink belly. Or you may be lucky enough to observe a pair of rare princess parrots. These are birds of exceptional beauty, with back feathers of light olive green shading to bright yellow on the wings, sky-blue crown, coral-pink bill and throat, tail shading from green to royal blue and pale blue belly tinged with yellow.

Watch out also for colourful finches: the zebra finch, often seen in flocks of thousands, and the painted firetail. There are honeyeaters, robins, notably the red-capped robin, wrens, including a sub-species of the splendid wren, and several doves

(Opposite page) Frilled lizard

Monitor lizard of Central
Australia (Lee Pearce)

and pigeons. And you will often see a red-backed kingfisher sitting patiently on a
branch watching for prey, which may be insects, a frog or a small reptile.

This is reptile country. Lizards come in all sizes, from small geckoes to the
splendidly patterned, yellow-and-brown perentie. This, the largest Australian lizard,
can grow to a length of two and a half metres. A neatly marked smaller lizard often
seen darting about among clumps of porcupine grass during the day is the military
dragon, coloured to tone with the red desert sands, with black and cream spots and
two white or pale cream lateral stripes on either side of its body. The highly
venomous desert death adder, reddish-brown in colour, is not easy to see in its
natural habitat among clumps of porcupine grass. It is nocturnal in habit, as is the
rock (or children's) python which may be encountered in rocky country. Average
length is about one and half metres. Colouring is dull olive green with darker spots.

Mobs of red kangaroos will be seen grazing on mulga flats and grasslands. The
smaller, darker, stockily built euro is found singly or in small groups in rocky
country. In the hills of the MacDonnell Ranges, the kangaroo family is represented
by the black-flanked rock wallaby. When disturbed, the rock wallaby is a fast and
agile mover, making long leaps from rock to rock.

The dingo, introduced some 10 000 years ago by Aborigines, is more often heard
than seen. Other animals introduced in the last 200 years and widespread throughout
the area include rabbits, feral cats, foxes and camels.

Rain may fall at any time of year, though usually much of the annual average
rainfall (less than 250 millimetres) comes in summer thunderstorms. Average January
maximum temperature at Alice Springs is 36.6° C, minimum 22.2° C. Corresponding
figures for July are 19.3° and 4.5°. Summer daytime temperatures occasionally reach
the mid-forties. Winter night-time temperatures sometimes fall below zero. Alice
Springs, which is 550 metres above sea-level — much the same altitude as Canberra
— has several frosty nights each winter.

The best time for touring the Centre is between July and September. No-one
drives long distances for pleasure in this part of the country in summer. Anyway,
sudden storms at that time of year may make roads impassable. Winter is the ideal
time for camping — but remember to bring a snug sleeping bag to keep out the cold.

(Opposite page) Desert death
adder, Acanthopis pyrrhus

Some of the gorges and gaps in the Macdonnell Ranges have been designated as reserves or nature parks. Nearest of the gap reserves to Alice Springs is the Emily and Jessie Gap Nature Park, thirteen kilometres east of town, in a beautiful section of range and enclosing two attractive gaps. Here you may camp, picnic or barbecue.

Similar facilities are available at Trephina Gorge Nature Park further west, eighty-five kilometres out of town. This park encloses the red-walled gorge from which it takes its name and the John Hayes Rockhole. Wild donkeys, cattle and rabbits still run free here and many years of careful management may be needed to restore the area to its natural condition. Nevertheless, this a place of quiet beauty. The nutmeg faces of towering rock cliffs are framed between blue sky and white beaches, and splashed with green where native figs sprout from their crevices. White-trunked ghost gums add graceful highlights. Parrots bustle among the leaves. Fairy martins build mud nests on the rock walls and can be seen darting acrobatically through the air, catching flying insects. Cracks in the walls shelter bats and lizards.

Simpsons Gap

The most spectacular gorges are to be found west of Alice Springs. One of the best known, Simpsons Gap, is just eighteen kilometres from town and at the centre of the region's third-largest public reserve, Simpsons Gap National Park. This park is open only from 8 am to 8 pm. But it is so close to Alice Springs that you can quite conveniently spend a full day here and return to your hotel or campsite in town. Walking tracks lead to a number of gaps in the Runutjirba Ridge and to various other beauty spots and places of interest. The only road leads to a parking area at Simpsons Gap.

A day's ramble here provides a good introduction to the countryside of the MacDonnells. Most of the trees and shrubs of the area are represented. You may see red kangaroos, euros, black-flanked rock wallabies and many types of lizards. Bird life ranges from the great wedge-tailed eagle to many colourful small birds such as the scarlet-breasted mistletoe bird and the pretty red-browed pardalote.

Recommended walks include such alternatives as following the course of Rocky Creek to Spring Gap, about twenty kilometres from the park entrance, and a wander through gentle hills to Wallaby Gap, eleven and a half kilometres in another direction. At Spring Gap you are at the foot of Mount Lloyd, which offers good climbing for those seeking more strenuous activity. North of the Runutjirba Ridge is wilderness, best reached by making your way through one of the several gaps. The gaps, with their pools of still, sometimes icy cold water, provide peaceful and picturesque locations where you may relax, take photographs, study the flora and fauna, or simply picnic in the shade of an old river red gum. You may even enjoy a cooling swim.

To make the most of a holiday in this fascinating part of Australia, you should allow yourself several days' stay in the West MacDonnells. As you head west from Alice Springs, you encounter a series of nature reserves and parks, each established around one of the gorges. Every one has its own character and should not be missed. Standley Chasm, forty-six kilometres from Alice Springs, although not set in a public reserve, is deservedly popular with tourists and well worth a visit. Sheer rock walls rise about eighty metres high and form a natural corridor a mere four metres wide. The sun shines directly into the chasm for only a few minutes each day as it passes directly overhead. At this time, the walls glow a brilliant red.

Continuing westward, you reach in turn Ellery Creek Big Hole Nature Park, a good spot for a swim, a picnic or an overnight camp, Serpentine Gorge Nature Park, where barbecue facilities are provided, Ormiston Gorge and Pound National Park (see below), Glen Helen Gorge Nature   Park — one of the most scenically satisfying of the gorges — and Redbank Nature Park, where you may camp.

Ormiston Gorge and Pound

Although it covers less than 5000 hectares, the Ormiston Gorge and Pound National Park nevertheless contains some of the wildest country and some of the most striking natural features of the West MacDonnells. The gorge itself is a deep cleft carved through quartzite hills by the Ormiston Creek, a tributary of the Finke River. The rock walls of the gorge hold considerable interest for students of geology. Ormiston Pound, beyond the gorge, is a hollow in the hills some ten kilometres across, a natural amphitheatre ringed by high ridges. A walk through the gorge (six to eight

Ormiston Gorge has been carved by the action of Ormiston Creek, revealing rock formations of great geological interest

(Over page) Walking through Ormiston Gorge provides excellent opportunities for observing diverse wildlife and varied terrain

Simpsons Gap; rock wallabies live on the rugged cliffs and birds flock to the waterholes

kilometres and back) brings you the reward of many splendid views and allows you to observe a variety of wildlife in a variety of habitats. Birds especially will be seen in abundance.

There is plenty of scope for an extended bushwalk. You may, for example, take a walk of some eighteen kilometres to Bowmans Gap and back, or follow a winding creek bed across the Pound and climb Mount Giles (1283 metres), which involves a trek of about forty-two kilometres.

There are facilities for day visitors, including gas barbecues and toilets. For those wishing to stay longer there is a small campsite with showers and laundry water. Drinking water should be brought with you. Note that the campsite is unsuitable for caravans. Also, the access road may be closed in wet weather.

To the south of the West MacDonnells, the Finke River has cut a meandering course through the rock of the James and Krichauff Ranges, creating a long chain of twisting gorges. A large area of this rugged country (almost 46 000 hectares) has been set aside as a national park: the Finke Gorge National Park. Most of the park area is inaccessible to all but the most intrepid latter-day explorer — who may follow the course of the river, when it is dry, either on foot, or on horseback (as explorer Ernest Giles did in 1872), or in a four-wheel-drive vehicle. The more popular portion of the park is the Palm Valley section, at the northern end. Here you can see living evidence of the fact that Central Australia was once partly covered by sea. And you can walk among some of the most impressive and colourful scenery the Centre has to offer.

The park entrance is 138 kilometres from Alice Springs, some sixteen kilometres south of the Hermannsburg Mission. Although tourist buses visit the park regularly, the road from the mission is unsealed and is suitable for four-wheel-drives only. In fact, it follows the bed of the river. Access is therefore not possible when the river is flowing. For most of the time, however, the track is dry but sandy. Advice about road conditions should be obtained before attempting to drive to the park.

If you are able to reach it, this park is well worth a stay of more than one day. You must, however, bring your accommodation with you. There is a campsite with toilet, shower and gas barbecue facilities.

Off-road vehicles may be driven a considerable way into Palm Valley in dry conditions. But the best way to see this unique place is with your feet on the ground. A short walk from the parking area takes you to Initiation Rock, from where you look into the huge natural hollow known as the Amphitheatre. A longer walk (six kilometres in each direction) takes you right through the valley. Cliffs of bright red sandstone rise sheer above you. At the foot of the cliffs, beside pools in the sandy creek-bed, grow the noble palms for which the valley is famous. The brilliance of the sunlit greenery seen against the contrasting red walls, the reflections in still water of blue sky and the graceful trees, tall-stemmed with crowns of fan-like leaves, all combine to create a scene of memorable loveliness.

The palms, which are endemic to this valley only, are *Livistona mariae*, also known as the red-leaved palm because of the reddish colouring seen in younger fronds. They bear creamy flowers, followed by dark-brown fruit. Related to (but not the same species as) the familiar cabbage-tree palm of the east coast, they grow here in great profusion, relics of an age when the climate of this place was very much wetter than it is now — when such trees as these looked out upon an inland sea.

Pale-green cycads (*Macrozamia* spp.), ferns and mosses also grow here. In addition to the palms, you will find many other trees, notably the white-trunked river red gums and ghost gums. The varied animal population includes wallabies, dingoes, brumbies (wild horses) and many kinds of birds, with parrots especially conspicuous. Over 400 plant species have been recorded within the park.

Bushwalkers who camp here will find many of the side valleys equally beautiful and worthy of exploration. The many waterholes provide opportunities for swimming. Drinking water should be brought in, as should firewood.

Uluru
(Ayers Rock —
Mount Olga)

(Opposite page) Ayers Rock

Some 470 kilometres by road southwest of Alice Springs, set in a rolling, red sand plain, is Australia's most famous natural feature, Ayers Rock. The Rock has always struck awe into the hearts of men: it sits alone upon the surface of the plain like some immense crouching animal, consisting almost entirely of bare rock coloured an even, startling, deep crimson. To the Aborigines it was *Uluru*, its many caves and waterholes rich in totemic symbolism. To the geologist it is the upper part of a buried sandstone mountain, one of the peaks of a buried range now visible only in the three great tors of the Centre, the others being Mount Olga and Mount Conner. The three lie, like all the other mountain chains of Central Australia, in an east-west line. Of sedimentary origin, they are believed to have been formed by glaciation, their material having been scraped off the older Musgrave Ranges to the south.

The Centre's largest national park encloses two of the three great tors, Ayers Rock and Mount Olga, within 126 000 hectares of sand-plain country. This is the Uluru (Ayers Rock-Mount Olga) National Park. Visitors come here in large numbers, year after year, to see the world's largest monolith. And it is indeed impressive. No matter how many pictures you may have seen of the Rock, only when you stand below its cliffs will you fully appreciate the immensity and the wonder of it.

You need to stay here at least two nights, but preferably longer, to see the rock and Olgas. A week's stay in this park would not exhaust all its possibilities. Many new facilities have been constructed here over the last few years, the most impressive being the Yulara Village. Hotel accommodation is now equal to anything found in the capital cities. The level of development at the rock has come in for a degree of criticism, some of it justified, but it is a conscientious attempt to cater for a high level of tourism, while still maintaining the character of the place.

One of the most important facets of the new developments is that they are located at a respectable distance from the rock itself. In the past, development was allowed too close, destroying much of the rock's scenic beauty (there were even proposals for buildings *on top of the rock*!).

The Olgas; these beautiful domes can be explored on foot or viewed from the air by plane

Facilities at Yulara include three separate motels, visitor centre, police station, camping area and service station. Roads to the complex from Alice Springs are very good, but the road from the rock to the Olgas is, at present, unsealed.

Management of Uluru is vested in the ANPWS, who have leased the land from the traditional owners, an issue which has been the subject of bitter debate.

A visit to Ayers Rock has two essential components: a guided tour around the base of the Rock, which takes up most of a day, and a climb to the top, for which you should allow at least two hours. The Rock is more than eight kilometres in circumference and its summit is 353 metres above the plain. It is encircled by a road, so you may drive right around it, seeing the great monolith from all sides. This, however, is no substitute for a guided walking tour in which a park ranger points out the many caves and other features, and explains their significance for the Uluritdja, the Aborigines who formerly dwelt in this locality.

Many features of the mountain had mythological associations for the Uluritdja. In a ravine above the permanent waterhole (now called Maggie Springs) in a cleft on the southern side of the Rock, is the sacred rock-hole of Uluru. Many caves on the northern side are known as 'chest caves' because they are said to symbolise the chests of the Mala (kangaroo-rat) people as they waited the start of a ritual dance. Much of one version of the mythology tells of a battle between the Kuni (carpet snake) people and the Leru (poisonous snake) people. However, to begin to appreciate the relationship between the Rock and its people, as explained in the ancient myths, you must hear the stories told as you stand in the presence of the Rock itself.

If you choose to explore the base of the Rock on your own, take the northern side during the morning, before the heat of the day. Save the shaded southern side for the afternoon.

Unlike its two neighbouring peaks, Ayers Rock has vertical stratification, clearly visible even at a distance. This indicates that the mountain was tilted through almost ninety degrees by some upheaval process, in past geological time, from the horizontal position in which the layers of sediment were originally laid down. At close quarters, the conglomerate nature of the rock is obvious. You can see grains of sparkling quartz and white feldspar cemented together — like fruit in a Christmas pudding — by brown and red oxides of iron.

Although steep in parts, especially at the bottom, the climb to the top of the Rock is well worth the effort for those who are sound in wind and limb. A chain handrail has been provided on the steepest pitches. Beyond that, a painted white line shows you the way. The top is undulating, with deeply weathered furrows between the strata, resulting in a dune-like formation whose ridges run northwest to southeast. Wandering away from the marked path can be dangerous. Special care is necessary in windy weather.

From the summit, the surrounding country has the appearance of a dun-coloured sea blotched with dark green (though new colours appear after a shower of rain). Mountain ranges are seen as blue smudges on the horizon, like far-off shores, while the flat-topped hump of Mount Conner to the east, and the domes of Mount Olga (known as the Olgas) to the west, are neighbouring islands. As you stand here, high above the sand dunes, you may find yourself looking down upon soaring eagles or hawks, or a flock of finches.

The Olgas — called Katatjuta ('many heads') by the Aborigines — lie twenty-seven kilometres away towards the setting sun. For many, this bizarre group of rounded rocks holds an even greater fascination than Ayers Rock. Explorer Giles described them as: 'Most grotesque, like five or six enormous pink haystacks, all leaning against each other, or the backs of several elephants kneeling.' Viewed from a distance, their colours change constantly, so that at one moment you are sure they are blue or violet; at another, they become bright red.

The major peak, Mount Olga, reaches a height of 546 metres — almost 200 metres taller than Ayers Rock. The group is seven kilometres long by about five kilometres wide, with a total circumference of twenty-five kilometres. Wandering around in this unique cluster of ancient rocks is a spellbinding experience. The towering domes

The abundant vegetation and animal life found amongst the Olgas contrast with the stark desert surrounding them (Lee Pearce)

rise sheer above you like great tombstones, their gnarled surfaces stark against the sky. Some are divided by narrow ravines, some by green valleys grown over with grasses, shrubs and trees, their colours vibrant and fresh against the rust-brown rock. Moisture is held in the ground here long after the surrounding plain has dried to a desert, so in many places the vegetation is quite dense. After a shower, when the waterholes are full and the creeks running, this is a distinctly separate world from the plains that await you beyond its shadows — a world astir with life.

You will have heard of Sunset Strip, where tourists gather in their hundreds every evening throughout the Dry to photograph Ayers Rock as it glows red in the light of the setting sun. If you can ignore the presence of the other people and simply drink in the glory of the view — of either the Rock or the Olgas, either at sunset or sunrise — you will be taking in the Centre's most awe-inspiring sight. And you will begin to feel something of the reverence which the people of this land in ancient times felt for these mountains.

DIRECTORY

This section lists in detail the national parks of Australia. Because of the difficulties of defining what a national park is, some important recreation areas, conservation parks and reserves have also been included.

For easy reference, all the parks described in the first part of the book are marked with an asterisk in the directory.

Where no contact address for individual parks is given in the directory, further information can be obtained from state national parks authorities, whose addresses appear at the beginning of each state section.

The state maps show the location of the parks. However, due to the problems of scale, some of the smaller parks listed in the directory are not included on the maps.

The tranquil waters of the Gordon River belie the stormy battle waged in the High Court to protect this World Heritage Area (J–P Ferrero/Auscape)

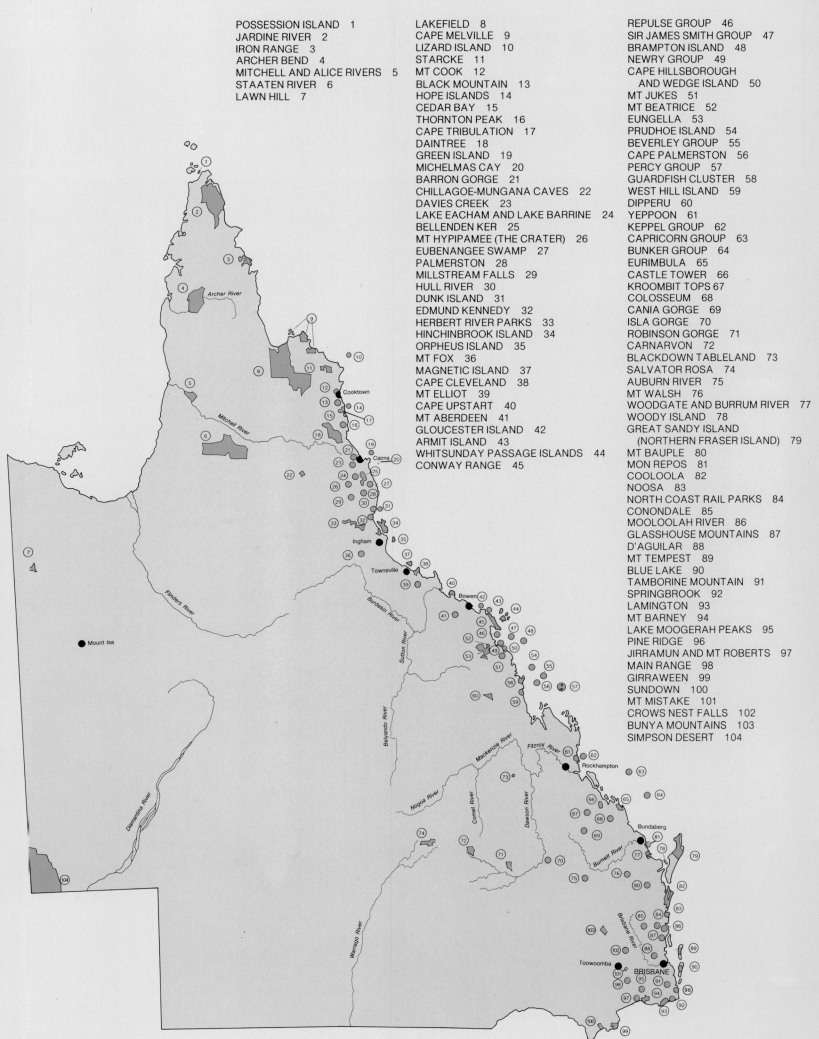

POSSESSION ISLAND 1
JARDINE RIVER 2
IRON RANGE 3
ARCHER BEND 4
MITCHELL AND ALICE RIVERS 5
STAATEN RIVER 6
LAWN HILL 7

LAKEFIELD 8
CAPE MELVILLE 9
LIZARD ISLAND 10
STARCKE 11
MT COOK 12
BLACK MOUNTAIN 13
HOPE ISLANDS 14
CEDAR BAY 15
THORNTON PEAK 16
CAPE TRIBULATION 17
DAINTREE 18
GREEN ISLAND 19
MICHELMAS CAY 20
BARRON GORGE 21
CHILLAGOE-MUNGANA CAVES 22
DAVIES CREEK 23
LAKE EACHAM AND LAKE BARRINE 24
BELLENDEN KER 25
MT HYPIPAMEE (THE CRATER) 26
EUBENANGEE SWAMP 27
PALMERSTON 28
MILLSTREAM FALLS 29
HULL RIVER 30
DUNK ISLAND 31
EDMUND KENNEDY 32
HERBERT RIVER PARKS 33
HINCHINBROOK ISLAND 34
ORPHEUS ISLAND 35
MT FOX 36
MAGNETIC ISLAND 37
CAPE CLEVELAND 38
MT ELLIOT 39
CAPE UPSTART 40
MT ABERDEEN 41
GLOUCESTER ISLAND 42
ARMIT ISLAND 43
WHITSUNDAY PASSAGE ISLANDS 44
CONWAY RANGE 45

REPULSE GROUP 46
SIR JAMES SMITH GROUP 47
BRAMPTON ISLAND 48
NEWRY GROUP 49
CAPE HILLSBOROUGH
  AND WEDGE ISLAND 50
MT JUKES 51
MT BEATRICE 52
EUNGELLA 53
PRUDHOE ISLAND 54
BEVERLEY GROUP 55
CAPE PALMERSTON 56
PERCY GROUP 57
GUARDFISH CLUSTER 58
WEST HILL ISLAND 59
DIPPERU 60
YEPPOON 61
KEPPEL GROUP 62
CAPRICORN GROUP 63
BUNKER GROUP 64
EURIMBULA 65
CASTLE TOWER 66
KROOMBIT TOPS 67
COLOSSEUM 68
CANIA GORGE 69
ISLA GORGE 70
ROBINSON GORGE 71
CARNARVON 72
BLACKDOWN TABLELAND 73
SALVATOR ROSA 74
AUBURN RIVER 75
MT WALSH 76
WOODGATE AND BURRUM RIVER 77
WOODY ISLAND 78
GREAT SANDY ISLAND
  (NORTHERN FRASER ISLAND) 79
MT BAUPLE 80
MON REPOS 81
COOLOOLA 82
NOOSA 83
NORTH COAST RAIL PARKS 84
CONONDALE 85
MOOLOOLAH RIVER 86
GLASSHOUSE MOUNTAINS 87
D'AGUILAR 88
MT TEMPEST 89
BLUE LAKE 90
TAMBORINE MOUNTAIN 91
SPRINGBROOK 92
LAMINGTON 93
MT BARNEY 94
LAKE MOOGERAH PEAKS 95
PINE RIDGE 96
JIRRAMUN AND MT ROBERTS 97
MAIN RANGE 98
GIRRAWEEN 99
SUNDOWN 100
MT MISTAKE 101
CROWS NEST FALLS 102
BUNYA MOUNTAINS 103
SIMPSON DESERT 104

QUEENSLAND

Administered by the National Parks and Wildlife Service of Queensland (NPWS) these parks total over 1 200 000 hectares. They include large areas of unexplored forest, small plots of historical or cultural significance, environmental parks, nature reserves, refuges and wildlife sanctuaries. Each contributes to the State's natural and cultural heritage. Information about these parks is obtainable from Regional Offices of the NPWS, from The Director, National Parks and Wildlife Service, 138 Albert Street, Brisbane, Qld 4000, or from the ranger at the relevant local park administration centre.

Archer Bend
Cape York Peninsula region.
166 000 ha. Features swamps, lagoons, abundant birdlife and freshwater crocodiles along the Archer River plus tall vine forests, eucalypt woodland and flat alluvial plains.
Contact: Cairns Regional Office, NPWS.

Armit Island
Off Bowen near Hayman Island.
129 ha. Includes rocky Armit Island plus nearby Saddleback (45 ha), Gumbrell (105 ha) and Double Cone (40 ha) islands.
Stunted rainforest, tussock grass and windswept rock.
Contact: District Ranger, NPWS, Mackay.

Auburn River
389 ha of open woodland with large granite boulders cut by a scenic river. Access via main Hawkwood road to turnoff 32 km southwest of Mundubbera.
Contact: District Ranger, Maryborough.

*Barron Gorge
Kuranda–Cairns railway, which winds up the gorge through rainforest, is best access.
2784 ha.
Contact: Ranger, Lake Eacham National Park.

*Bellenden-Ker
Undeveloped park, featuring Queensland's highest mountain, Mount Bartle Frere (1657 m), on eastern slopes of Bellenden Ker Range.
31 000 ha of dense rainforest. Numerous waterfalls and streams.
Contact: NPWS, Cairns.

Blackall Range
3 small parks, Kondalilla (75 ha), Obi Obi Gorge (80 ha) and Mapleton Falls (26 ha), on the Blackall Range west of Nambour. Remnants of rainforest and wet eucalypt forest.
Contact: District Ranger, Maryborough.

Blackdown Tableland
A sandstone plateau at the junction of 3 ranges, near Dingo, covering some 23 000 ha. Waterfalls of interest and good walking trails. Access is suitable for conventional vehicles, but not for caravans. Ranger is present and water is available, but food should be taken in.
Contact: District Ranger, Blackdown Tableland.

Blue Lake
The lake from which this park takes its name is a water table window, situated in sand dunes some 10 km east of Dunwich on Stradbroke Island. Facilities are scarce in this 501 ha park, but graded walking tracks are provided and access is easy. Popular for day visits.
Contact: Brisbane Regional Superintendent, Moggill.

Bunya Mountains
Over 11 000 ha of rainforest and grassland, situated between Kingaroy and Dalby. Well-developed facilities for campers and day visitors, but unsuitable for caravans. Winter nights can be quite cold.
Contact: District Ranger, Bunya Mountains via Dalby.

Burleigh Heads
A small park covering 24 ha, but still showing great floral diversity. Full day facilities are provided.
Contact: District Ranger, Burleigh Heads.

Cania Gorge
Twenty-six kilometres from Monto, near Maryborough. Noted for its sandstone gorge and lush vegetation. Only some 1000 ha, no camping facilities, but day visitors catered for.
Contact: District Ranger, Maryborough.

Cape Hillsborough
Hoop pine rainforest, eucalypt forest and mangroves over 800 ha near Mackay. Good access, but no camping facilities.
Contact: District Ranger, Mackay.

Cape Tribulation
Coastal rainforest covering 16 965 ha. Access is by ferry over the Daintree River. Best visiting time is outside the Wet season.
Contact: District Ranger, Cape Tribulation or phone NPWS Cairns.

Carnarvon
Four major parks, totalling 217 000 ha, in the vicinity of Carnarvon, 400 km west of Maryborough. Includes Carnarvon Gorge, Mt Moffat, Salvator Rosa and Ka Ka Mundi. Access is good for all centres, with facilities well-developed at Carnarvon Gorge.
Contact: District Ranger, Carnarvon Gorge; District Ranger, Mt Moffat; District Ranger, Springsure (Salvator Rosa and Ka Ka Mundi).

*Cedar Bay
Between the Endeavour River and Rattlesnake Point.
5650 ha of densely vegetated and undeveloped coastal area.
Contact: NPWS, Cairns.

*Chillagoe-Mungana Caves
240 km west of Cairns.
1900 ha. Includes remarkable limestone cave system.
Contact: NPWS, Cairns.

Clump Point
North of Tully off State Highway One.
301 ha traversed by a walking track to Bicton Hill. Views of coast, rainforest, mountains and offshore islands.
Contact: NPWS, Cairns.

Colosseum
Off the Bruce Highway near Miriam Vale and accessible from Colosseum Railway siding by gravel road 5 km to the south. 840 ha. Encompasses Mt Colosseum and a stand of hoop pine forest.
Contact: Regional Superintendent, Rockhampton.

Conondale
Southwest of Conondale on the Conondale Range.
2126 ha of west eucalypt forest and rainforest preserving typical flora and fauna.
Contact: District Ranger, NPWS, Maryborough.

Grass trees in Bunya Mountains National Park (Barry Slade)

176

*Conway Range
On western and mainland edge of the Whitsunday Passage. Facilities located near the road to Shute Harbour, foot access to the northern end.
23 800 ha of tall lowland rainforest and eucalypt forest, coastal scenery and island views.
Contact: District Ranger, NPWS, Mackay.

*Cooloola
Noosa area, access by sand road 5 km south of Rainbow Beach through State Forest to Freshwater Lake, or by boat up the Noosa River from Noosa, Tewantin or Boreen Point.
39 400 ha of sand dunes, heathland, rainforest, ocean beaches and freshwater lake supporting varied animal life.
Contact: District Ranger, NPWS, Maryborough.

Crows Nest Falls
6 km east of Crows Nest.
949 ha with boulder-strewn creek dropping into a steep granite gorge. Spring wildflowers and eucalypts growing along the ridges.
Contact: District Ranger, NPWS, Maryborough.

Crystal Creek–Mount Spec
Off the Bruce Highway between Ingham and Townsville. Picnic areas 4 km along the Paluma Road off the Highway and at The Loop, a further 12 km.
7224 ha of extremely rocky park with eucalypt forests and rainforest patches.
Contact: Townsville NPWS, Pallarenda.

D'Aguilar
A group of parks west of Brisbane on the D'Aguilar Range. Eventually to be absorbed into a forest recreation park extending from Mt Coot-tha to Mt Glorious.
Includes Maiala (1140 ha) Manorina (139 ha) Jolly's Lookout (12 ha) and Boombana (38 ha).
Contact: Brisbane Regional Superintendent, Moggill.

Daintree and Mossman Gorge
On the Great Dividing Range's eastern slopes, 56 450 ha of truly unique wilderness. Extensive areas of rainforest, dissected by the Daintree River. Rainforest grows down to hightide mark in some places, virtually joining with spectacular coral reefs. Few facilities, therefore suitable for well-prepared walkers only, leaving from Daintree or Mossman; dry season only.
Contact: District Ranger, Cairns.

Davies Creek
West of Cairns.
468 ha of eucalypt forest growing on a granite outcrop, and a 100 m waterfall on Davies Creek which bisects the park.
Contact: Lake Eacham Park Ranger, Yungaburra.

*Dipperu
Near the main Mackay-Clermont Road some 130 km from Mackay.
11 100 ha of brigalow and belah scrubs, and vast areas of 'flooded country' around Bee Creek.
Contact: District Ranger, Mackay.

Edmund Kennedy
Beside the Bruce Highway, north of Cardwell.
6200 ha of mangroves, dense rainforest, tea-tree, sedge, fan palm and sword grass swamps.
Contact: NPWS, Cairns.

Etty Bay
On the Moresby Range, traversed by a road between Coquette Point and Etty Bay.
244 ha of rainforest and fan palm stands.
Contact: NPWS, Cairns.

Eubenangee Swamp
Located north of Innisfail.
1520 ha of swampland, herbland fringed by lowland rainforest and open eucalypt with abundant birdlife, particularly waterfowl.
Contact: NPWS, Cairns.

Eungella
6 km from Eungella 83 km west of Mackay via the Pioneer Valley.
49 610 ha of tropical rainforest, grassy eucalypt woodland with exceptional fern growth, prominent peaks and rocky gorges.
Contact: District Officer, NPWS, Mackay.

* Eurimbula
110 km southeast of Gladstone and
27 km east of Miriam Vale on the 1770
road.
7270 ha of hoop pine forest on sandy
soils a few feet above sea-level.
Contact: Ranger, NPWS, Miriam Vale.

* Girraween
On the Granite Belt, 246 km southwest of
Brisbane, 10 km north of Wallangarra on
the New England Highway.
11 400 ha. Includes massive granite tors
and boulders, dense cover of flowers,
shrubs and eucalypt trees.
Contact: Brisbane Regional
Superintendent, Moggill.

* Glasshouse Mountains
70 km north of Brisbane, accessible by
unsealed roads from Bruce Highway.
700 ha. Features 4 eroded volcanic
plugs, topped by heath and popular with
climbers.
Contact: District Ranger, Maryborough.

Gloucester Island
A continental island accessible by boat,
20 km east of Bowen.
2460 ha of undeveloped open eucalypt
woodland and rocky mountainous terrain.
Contact: District Ranger, Mackay.

* Great Sandy Island (Northern Fraser
Island)
Boat access from Urangan and Inskip
Point or by air from Orchid Beach.
52 400 ha on the northern part of the
world's largest sand island.
Contact: District Ranger, Maryborough.

* Green Island and Reef
Access by boat from Cairns.
3000 ha of coral cay and surrounding
reef, rainforest, fringing casuarinas,
pandanus and tournefortias.
Contact: NPWS, Cairns.

* Herbert River Parks
Located 50 km west of Ingham via the
Lannercost Range Road.
14 814 ha. Feature river gorge scenery
and falls: Herbert River Falls (2428 ha),
Yamanie Falls (9712 ha); the Falls of
Herkes Creek, Sword Creek, Garrawalt
and Broadwater Creek (each 518 ha); and
Wallaman Falls (602 ha) which has
Australia's largest single falls (278 m).
Contact: Townsville NPWS, Pallarenda.

* Hinchinbrook Island
Queensland's largest island national park,
accessible by boat from Cardwell and
Lucinda Point.
39 350 ha of rugged rock mountain,
rainforest, beach and eucalypt forest.
Contact: NPWS, Cairns.

Hope Islands
On inner part of Great Barrier Reef
northeast of Cedar Bay and 35 km
southeast of Cooktown.
174 ha of coral cays
Contact: Director, NPWS, North Quay, or
Cairns Regional Office.

Hull River
Off the Mission Beach Road.
1060 ha of typical lowland vegetation on
granite soil.
Contact: NPWS, Cairns.

* Iron Range
Cape York region via the Janet and Tozer
Ranges.
34 600 ha of largest true wilderness in
Australia. Includes lowland rainforest,
mangrove, heath and open forest.
Contact: NPWS, North Quay, or Regional
Office, Cairns.

* Isla Gorge
South of Dawson Range. Access 60 km
along Leichhardt Highway, northeast of
Taroom.
7800 ha. Includes scenic gorge.

ISLAND GROUPS

Beverley
85 km southeast of Mackay.
550 ha. Features 10 rocky masses mainly
covered with stunted eucalypts and
rainforest patches.
Contact: District Ranger, NPWS, Mackay.

* Bunker
Three islands just south of Capricorn
Group.
Undeveloped coral cays. Important
gannet nesting sites. Permit needed (not
issued between September and
February).
Contact: Regional Superintendent,
NPWS, Rockhampton.

*Capricorn
180 km from Rockhampton and 80 km from Gladstone. A group of coral cays. Heron Island is the only national park in the group.
Contact: Regional Superintendent, NPWS, Rockhampton.

*Dunk Island
Access by boat from Clump Point or by air from Townsville and Cairns.
730 ha partly national park.
Surrounded by island national parks of Purtaboi, Mung-um-nackum and Kumboola.
Contact: NPWS, Cairns.

*Guardfish Cluster
80 km southeast of Mackay.
708 ha. Includes 6 rocky continental islands with fine beaches, and grassy open forests of bloodwoods, Moreton Bay ash and tea-tree on Curlew, the largest island.
Contact: District Ranger, NPWS, Mackay.

*Keppel
25 km from Yeppoon. Access by boat or tourist launch service from Rosslyn Bay.
11 continental islands comprising 900 ha.
Contact: Regional Superintendent, NPWS, Rockhampton.

*Newry
7 km northwest of Seaforth.
485 ha. 5 small, largely undeveloped continental islands with open eucalypt vegetation and sandy beaches.
Contact: District Ranger, NPWS, Mackay.

Percy
112 km southeast of Mackay.
South Island (1619 ha) and North East Island (308 ha). Rocky and precipitous.
Contact: District Ranger, NPWS, Rockhampton.

*Repulse
In Repulse Bay, 72 km northwest of Mackay.
187 ha. Includes 3 islands with rainforest, eucalypt forest and mangrove areas.
Contact: District Ranger, NPWS, Mackay.

Sir James Smith
North of Mackay in the Cumberland Channel.
1830 ha. Features 14 small, rocky, precipitous islands with low eucalypt forests. Undeveloped.
Contact: District Ranger, NPWS, Mackay.

*Whitsunday Passage
Access by launch from Shute Harbour and nearby coastal towns. Aircraft from Proserpine and Mackay to some of the highly developed tourist islands such as Lindeman and South Molle.
An extremely large cluster of 39 islands.
Contact: Ranger, NPWS, Mackay.

*Jardine River
Near Cape York Peninsula in the Jardine River catchmen area.
253 000 ha of wilderness containing small watercourses and swamps, varied vegetation, including tall healthland, open forests with high termite mounds and evergreen rainforest areas, and abundant bird and animal life.
Contact: NPWS, North Quay, or Cairns Regional Office.

Jirramun
At the end of Teviot Brook with access via the Killarney-Boonah Road 26 km east of Killarney.
385 ha. Features Wilsons Peak and its rugged rainforest surrounds.
Contact: Brisbane Regional Superintendent, NPWS, Moggill.

Kroombit Tops
West of Miriam Vale.
455 ha covered by rugged rainforest and young hoop pines and cliffs over 100 m high to the west.
Contact: Regional Superintendent, NPWS, Rockhampton.

Kurramine
Located north of the Kurramine Road, north of Murdering Point.
910 ha of coastal sand plain containing tall melaleucas, grassy eucalypt forest, sedge savannah and swamp.
Contact: NPWS, Cairns.

*Sunset over Mount Warning
(Brett Gregory)*

* Lake Eacham
On the Gillies Highway.
A lake in an extinct volcanic cone,
surrounded by tropical rainforest. 490 ha.
Lake Barrine (491 ha) another crater lake
also surrounded by tropical rainforest is
6 km beyond Eacham. East Barron, a
5 ha rainforest park, and Topaz Road, a
37 ha park, are also in this area.
Contact: National Park Ranger,
Yungaburra.

* Lakefield
In Cape York Peninsula. Take the first
road to the right after passing through
Laura.
537 000 ha. Contains stringybark forest,
mudflats, open grass plains, and vast
areas of open water in the wet season.
Contact: NPWS, North Quay, or Cairns
Regional Office.

Lake Moogerah Peaks
Located 16 km southwest of Boonah.
A group of small undeveloped parks
comprising Mt French (63 ha), Mt Greville
(129 ha), Mt Moon (119 ha) and Mt
Edwards (364 ha).
Contact: Brisbane Regional
Superintendent, NPWS, Moggill.

* Lamington
Accessible through O'Reilly's entrance,
40 km south of Canungra (115 km from
Brisbane) or Binna Burra entrance 9 km
south of Beechmont (96 km from
Brisbane via Nerang).
20 100 ha of rainforest, eucalypt, and
heathland, waterfalls, walking tracks and
spectacular views.
Contact: District Ranger Lamington,
Beechmont, via Nerang.

Lawn Hill
Situated between Camooweal and
Burketown in the north-west. Covers
12 200 ha, and includes sandstone
gorges and rainforest pockets.
Contact: District Ranger Lawn Hill.

* Lizard Island
24 km from the mainland, 240 km
northeast of Cairns, 1012 ha.
A continental island almost surrounded
by fringing reefs, it features a tourist
resort and research station.
Contact: Director, NPWS, North Quay, or
Cairns Regional Office

*Magnetic Island
Off Townsville.
The National Park section of the 2709 ha island contains rugged boulder-strewn hillsides covered with hoop pine and eucalypts.
Contact: Townsville NPWS, Pallarenda.

Main Range
A 10 500 ha park, approximately 110 km west of Brisbane on the Cunningham Highway. Two noted attractions are Cunningham's Gap and the Queen Mary Falls. Most of the area's facilities are centred on Cunningham's Gap.
Contact: District Ranger, Main Range, Warwick.

Michelmas Cay
Although only 3 ha or so, Michelmas Cay, along with nearby Upolo Cay, forms a vital nesting area for seabirds. Access is restricted to everywhere but the beach areas, which can only be reached by boat.
Contact: District Ranger, Cairns.

Millstream Falls
1 km off the Ravenshoe-Mt Garnet Road, 6 km from Ravenshoe.
372 ha of open eucalypt area traversed by a bottlebrush-bordered stream and the 65 m wide falls.
Contact: Lake Eacham National Park Ranger, Yungaburra.

*Mitchell and Alice Rivers
Southeast of the Edward River Mission at the junction of the Mitchell and Alice rivers.
37 100 ha. Contains stands of tall 'gallery forest', extensive alluvial flood plains with open grassland and woodland.
Contact: Director, NPWS, North Quay, or Cairns Regional Office.

Mon Repos
One of the smallest and most important of Queensland's parks, Mon Repos is only 23.5 ha, located on the coast 14 km east of Bundaberg. Vital breeding area for loggerhead turtles; nesting from November to January; hatching January to March. No camping except for researchers, but accommodation nearby.
Contact: District Ranger, Maryborough.

Mooloolah River
5 km south of Mooloolaba. Access by rough road from the Bruce Highway near the Buderim turnoff or via Bundilla Lakes.
676 ha of Mooloolah River landscape and associated vegetation.
Contact: District Ranger, NPWS, Maryborough.

Mossman Gorge
On the Great Dividing Range's eastern slopes. 8 km west of Mossman.
56 450 ha of wilderness area with peaks over 1300 m.
Contact: NPWS, Cairns.

*Mount Aberdeen
Southwest of Bowen.
1667 ha of open eucalypt forests surrounding a 990 m mountain with low rainforest on the upper portion. West of Mt Aberdeen is another area of national park, 1242 ha in size.
Contact: Townsville NPWS, Pallarenda.

Mount Barney
Near the NSW-Queensland border.
Access via the Mt Lindesay Highway to Rathdowney 100 km southwest of Brisbane and then 32 km further. The park is 11 400 ha. The same route takes you to Mt Maroon–Mt May (1800 ha) and Mt Lindesay (243 ha) located south of Rathdowney.
Contact: Brisbane Regional Superintendent, Moggill.

Mount Bauple
Near the Bruce Highway, 4 km south of Bauple.
505 ha mountain park of eucalypts and rainforest.
Contact: District Ranger, NPWS, Maryborough.

Mount Beatrice
65 km northwest of Mackay near Yalboroo.
1117 ha of rugged ranges, open eucalypt forest and rainforest.
Contact: District Ranger, NPWS, Mackay.

Mount Cook
2 km south of Cooktown.
494 ha. Includes Mt Cook (430 m) covered with rainforest on the upper slopes.
Endeavour River, a 1840 ha park north of Cooktown with a unique tall scrub plant community, is nearby. Both areas are of scientific and historical importance.
Contact: NPWS, Cairns.

*Mount Elliot/Bowling Green Bay
Access 7 km along a partly sealed road off the Bruce Highway 25 km south of Townsville.
55 300 ha of true tropical rainforest.
Contact: Townsville NPWS, Pallarenda.

Mount Fox
68 km west of Ingham and accessible via the Mt Fox Range road.
214 ha with a conical shaped volcanic crater (365 m).
Contact: Townsville NPWS, Pallarenda.

Mount French
Popular with rock climbers, Mt French is easily accessible from Boonah by a sealed road. Impressive lookouts and graded walking tracks in this 63 ha park.
Contact: District Ranger, Boonah.

Mount Hypipamee (also called The Crater)
South of Atherton along the Kennedy Highway, 364 ha.
A crater-like depression of geological interest.
Contact: Lake Eacham Ranger, Yungaburra.

Mount Jukes
35 km northwest of Mackay via Kuttabul.
229 ha of undeveloped area.
Mt Mandurana–The Leap (103 ha), visible from the Bruce Highway 11 km northwest of Mackay; and Mt Blackwood, 31 km northwest of Mackay near Kuttabul, are in the vicinity.
Contact: District Ranger, Mackay.

*Mount Mistake
North of Cunninghams Gap. Access from Allora through the state forest at the head of Dalrymple Creek (dry weather only).
4260 ha of rainforest and tall eucalypt forest.
Contact: Brisbane Regional Superintendent, Moggill.

Mount Roberts
Access via the Killarney–Boonah Road 26 km east of Killarney.
1790 ha of grassy eucalypt and rainforest patches on the eastern slope of the Great Dividing Range.
Contact: Brisbane Regional Superintendent, NPWS, Moggill.

*Mount Tempest
On Moreton Island, access by ferry from several suburbs and North Quay, Brisbane, or by air from Eagle Farm airport.
9360 ha of coastal sand dune reaching 285 m.
Contact: Brisbane Regional Superintendent, Moggill.

Mount Walsh
8 km south of Biggenden with limited access.
2987 ha with botanically interesting vegetation and prominent (645 m) scenic mountain.
Contact: District Ranger, NPWS, Mackay.

*Noosa
160 km north of Brisbane and 67 km south of Gympie with road access through Noosa township.
432 ha of coastal scenery and varied vegetation including rainforest growing on sand.
Contact: District Ranger, NPWS, Mackay.

North Coastal Rail Parks
Four small undeveloped parks: Dularcha (138 ha) north of Landsborough; Eudlo Creek (43 ha) north of Eudlo; Tuckers Creek (53 ha) on the northern outskirts of Nambour; and Ferr Tree Creek (20 ha) north of Tuckers Creek
Contact: District Ranger, NPWS, Mackay.

Orpheus Island
In the Palm Island group east of Ingham. Access by launch from Lucinda Point.
1368 ha of continental island with scenic beaches backed by low rainforest and open eucalypt forest.
Contact: Townsville NPWS, Pallarenda.

*Palmerston
Southwest of Innisfail on the Johnstone River. Also McNarree Creek and Palmerston Rocks near the Fishers Creek Bridge on Palmerston Highway about 15 km west of Innisfail.
2556 ha with various picnic spots amid luxurious jungle.
Contact: Lake Eacham Park Ranger, Yungaburra.

Pine Ridge

An environmental park of 109 ha, Pine Ridge contains the last remnants of coastal lowland on the Gold Coast. A boardwalk enables wheelchair access, and full day facilities are provided.
Contact: District Ranger, Burleigh Heads.

*Possession Island

Cape York, where James Cook hoisted the English flag in 1770.
510 ha with historical significance.
Contact: NPWS, North Quay, or Cairns Regional Office.

Prudhoe Island

A rocky continental island 50 km southeast of Mackay.
518 ha of tussock grassland.
Contact: District Ranger, NPWS, Mackay.

Ravensbourne

Although only 100 ha, Ravensbourne contains an important slice of remaining rainforest in the Crows Nest area. Situated on the Hampton-Esk Road. Walking tracks and water available.
Contact: District Ranger, Crows Nest.

*Robinson Gorge

On a tributary of the Dawson River.
8903 ha containing mostly sandstone ridge country.
Contact: Brisbane NPWS, North Quay.

Rokeby

An unsealed road, best left to 4-wheel drive vehicles, and then only in the Dry, leads to the 291 000 ha Rokeby National Park. Situated between the McIlwraith Range and Archer River, close to Archer Bend National Park. Ranger staff and campsites, but no facilities.
Contact: District Ranger, Cairns.

St Helena Island

Access to this historic area in the mouth of the Brisbane River is restricted to water craft, and then only with permission. The island was used as a high security prison from 1867 to 1932. Provisions and fuel are available on the island.
Contact: Brisbane Regional Superintendent, Moggill.

Salvator Rosa

On the eastern slopes of the Great Dividing Range, forming part of the Buckland Tableland.
26 270 ha. Contains weathered sandstone formations and sweeping views from the higher ridges.
Contact: Brisbane NPWS, North Quay.

*Simpson Desert

Far west of the state.
555 000 ha of arid central Australian land with long unbroken sand ridges and claypans in the valleys.

Springbrook

A group of parks located 100 km south of Brisbane in the mountainous hinterland of the Gold Coast.
Comprising: Warrie (599 ha), Gwongorella (534 ha), Wunburra (140 ha), Mt Cougal (674 ha) and Natural Bridge (212 ha).
Contact: District Ranger, Lamington National Park, Beechmont, via Nerang.

*Staaten River

Cape York Peninsula, about 400 km west of Cairns. Access very difficult — through private property, so permission needed for entry.
About 530 000 ha of unspoilt bushland. Bushcamping (permit needed).
Contact: Ranger, NPWS, Cairns.

*Starcke

North of Cooktown.
7960 ha rising sharply above the coastal plain with sandstone plateaux, escarpments, gentler slopes and narrow valley floors.
Contact: Director, NPWS, North Quay, or Cairns Regional Office.

*Sundown

Enclosing part of the Severn River and only accessible by foot.
6680 ha containing densely forested slopes, rugged gorges and bare rock outcrops.
Contact: Brisbane Regional Superintendent, Moggill.

* Tamborine Mountain
Ten parks 70 km south of Brisbane and 45 km west of the Gold Coast, totalling 594 ha.
Features remnants of the original vegetation.
Contact: District Ranger, Lamington National Park, Beechmont, via Nerang.

Thornton Peak
In the highland area north of the Daintree River.
2331 ha with 1375 m Peak.
Contact: NPWS, Cairns.

* West Hill Island
A continental island 130 km south of Mackay close to the coast at the mouth of West Hill Creek. Access by boat.
398 ha of eucalypt, tea-tree and rainforest vegetation. The creek mouth contains another 345 ha park with a fine beach; access by foot from Carmila or by boat.
Contact: District Ranger, NPWS, Mackay.

* Woodgate
40 km east of Childers via Goodwood and Burrum River Park, across the river, reached via the Burrum Heads Road, 16 km north of Burrum.
5490 ha with beach scenery backed by sand dunes and heath.
Contact: District Ranger, NPWS, Mackay.

Woody Island
Accessible by boat from Urangan. Park contains Little Woody Island to the south.
660 ha rocky island with open eucalypt forest and some fringing mangroves.
Contact: District Ranger, NPWS, Mackay.

Yeppoon
Comprised of two parks: Double Head and Bluff Point, 8 km south of Yeppoon on the Yeppoon–Emu Park Coast Road, and Mulambin south of Double Head.
115 ha of coastal scenery.
Contact: Regional Superintendent, NPWS, Rockhampton.

Sand dunes, Simpson Desert (M Jensen/Auscape)

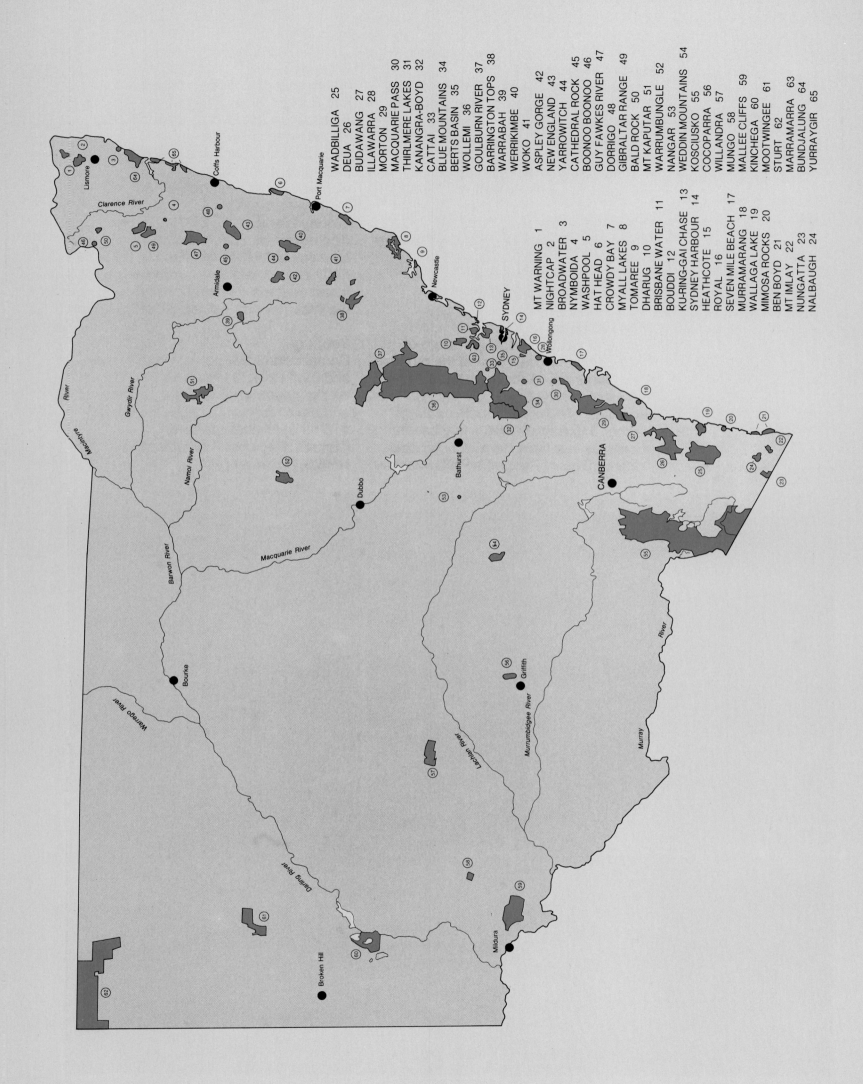

MT WARNING 1
NIGHTCAP 2
BROADWATER 3
NYMBOIDA 4
WASHPOOL 5
HAT HEAD 6
CROWDY BAY 7
MYALL LAKES 8
TOMAREE 9
DHARUG 10
BRISBANE WATER 11
BOUDDI 12
KU-RING-GAI CHASE 13
SYDNEY HARBOUR 14
HEATHCOTE 15
ROYAL 16
SEVEN MILE BEACH 17
MURRAMARANG 18
WALLAGA LAKE 19
MIMOSA ROCKS 20
BEN BOYD 21
MT IMLAY 22
NUNGATTA 23
NALBAUGH 24

WADBILLIGA 25
DEUA 26
BUDAWANG 27
ILLAWARRA 28
MORTON 29
MACQUARIE PASS 30
THIRLMERE LAKES 31
KANANGRA-BOYD 32
CATTAI 33
BLUE MOUNTAINS 34
BERTS BASIN 35
WOLLEMI 36
GOULBURN RIVER 37
BARRINGTON TOPS 38
WARRABAH 39
WERRIKIMBE 40
WOKO 41

ASPLEY GORGE 42
NEW ENGLAND 43
YARROWITCH 44
CATHEDRAL ROCK 45
BOONOO BOONOO 46
GUY FAWKES RIVER 47
DORRIGO 48
GIBRALTAR RANGE 49
BALD ROCK 50
MT KAPUTAR 51
WARRUMBUNGLE 52
NANGAR 53

WEDDIN MOUNTAINS 54
KOSCIUSKO 55
COCOPARRA 56
WILLANDRA 57
MUNGO 58
MALLEE CLIFFS 59
KINCHEGA 60
MOOTWINGEE 61
STURT 62
MARRAMARRA 63
BUNDJALUNG 64
YURRAYGIR 65

NEW SOUTH WALES

In New South Wales, national parks are managed and protected by the State's National Parks and Wildlife Service (NPWS) who took over from the Crown Office in 1980.

National parks are defined as areas of predominantly natural landscape, flora and fauna permanently dedicated for public enjoyment and education. Historic sites, state recreation areas, large regional parks which provide a variety of outdoor recreational opportunities, Aboriginal areas and places, archaeological areas, wildlife refuges and declared game reserves are also managed by the NPWS. These last two may be publicly or privately owned and declared as parks with the consent of the owners.

New South Wales national parks and reserves total 3 368 447 ha, or 4.21% of the state's area.

Information about these areas, and addresses of regional offices, may be obtained from the NPWS headquarters, 189-193 Kent Street, Sydney, NSW 2000.

* Apsley Gorge
Armidale District, 500 km north of Sydney, 18 km east of Walcha off the Oxley Highway.
6670 ha of spectacular gorges and waterfalls, including Tia Falls, accessible by foot or water only, Apsley Falls, and waterfalls up to 600 m. Gully rainforest and grassy flood plains.
Contact: Senior Ranger, NPWS, Armidale.

* Bald Rock
Glen Innes District, 713 km north of Sydney, accessible by side road off Mt Lindesay Highway, 29 km north of Tenterfield.
2776 ha. Named after 200 m high solid granite dome (1277 m above sea-level). Mainly dry sclerophyll forest with other, varied vegetation and fauna.
Contact: Senior Ranger, NPWS, Glen Innes.

* Barrington Tops
Hunter Valley, 321 km north of Sydney, 38 km from Gloucester, accessible by side road off Gloucester Tops Road, 12 km south of Gloucester.
39 114 ha. Includes Antartic beech rainforest stands, grasslands and subalpine woodlands on plateau. Shy fauna but plentiful birdlife.
Contact: Superintendent, Raymond Terrace.

* Ben Boyd
Eden District, 490 km south of Sydney. 2 sections north and south of Eden. North access off Princes Highway; south via Princes Highway then Edrom Road and forestry roads.
9437 ha of rugged caves, beaches and cliffs with heath, sclerophyll forests and tall stands of coastal banksia.
Contact: Senior Ranger, NPWS, Eden.

Bents Basin

Situated in Sydney's outer western suburbs, 391 ha on the Nepean River, 8 km south of Wallacia. Bushcamping permitted, but booking required. Hawkesbury sandstone, carved by river, dominates. Picnicking and swimming.
Contact: The Manager, Bents Basin, State Recreation Area, Wallacia.

*Blue Mountains

Blue Mountains District, 80 km west of Sydney. 2 sections, north and south of the Great Western Highway.
215 955 ha of immense valleys, rolling plateaux and ridges. Mainly dry sclerophyll forest.
Also wet sclerophyll rainforest, swamp and heathland.
Contact: Park Superintendent, Blackheath.

Boonoo Boonoo

Glen Innes district, 720 km north of Sydney and 35 km north of Tenterfield, covers 2442 ha.
Approach road is gravel-based and fairly rough. Steep rainforested gorge and striking granite plateau. Accommodation in Glen Innes or bush camping in park.
Contact: Senior Ranger, NPWS, Glen Innes.

Border Ranges

Lismore District, 900 km north of Sydney, 12 km east of Tyalgum via Wiangeree Forest Drive.
31 229 ha in McPherson ranges. Steep terrain includes remnant stands of subtropical, warm and cool temperate and dry rainforest.

*Bouddi

Hawkesbury District, 70 km north of Sydney, accessible 19 km southeast of Gosford on scenic road through Kincumber, or via the Rip Bridge, Woy Woy.
1160 ha of marine national park. Coastal scenery and varied coastal heaths and forests.
Contact: Superintendent, Bouddi National Park, Gosford.

*Brisbane Water

Hawkesbury District, 60 km north of Sydney, 9 km southwest of Gosford on the Pacific Highway.
11 317 ha of sandstone country, eucalypt woods, hanging swamps and rainforest pockets. Many Aboriginal rock engravings.
Contact: Superintendent, NPWS, Gosford.

*Broadwater

Lismore District, 759 km north of Sydney, 3 km north of Evans Head on the Pacific Highway at Woodburn or Broadwater.
3691 ha of wet heath and swamp, spectacular wildflower displays and lengthy ocean beach.
Contact: Ranger-in-Charge, NPWS, Lismore.

*Budawang

Morton District, 297 km south of Sydney. Difficult access 15 km northeast of Braidwood via Moongarlowe.
16 102 ha including the rugged wilderness of Budawang Range and eastern scarp of the southern tablelands.
Contact: Superintendent, NPWS, Fitzroy Falls.

*Bundjalung

Lismore District, 725 km north of Sydney. Access from Pacific Highway, 8 km south of Woodburn along Gap Road to Jerusalem Creek.
17 544 ha. Includes the north coast's longest natural river environment, the Esk River, freshwater lagoons, rock platforms, mangrove mudflats and sandbars.

*Cathedral Rock

Armidale District, 565 km north of Sydney, 69 km from Armidale along the Armidale–Ebor Road or the Guyra–Ebor Road.
5194 ha of tableland forests, woodlands and swamps falling away from Round Mountain. Notable rock formations.
Contact: Senior Ranger, NPWS, Armidale.

Cattai

North-western suburbs of Sydney, on the Wisemans Ferry Road. Covers 223 ha with extensive frontages on Hawkesbury River. Basic camping facilities; good access. Includes Caddie homestead, built by convicts in 1821.
Contact: The Manager, Cattai State Recreation Area, Cattai.

*Cocoparra

Griffith District, 603 km west of Sydney, 25 km northeast of Griffith, accessible from Griffith, 25 km northeast through Yenda then along the Barry Scenic Drive or Whitton Stock Route.
8358 ha with varied trees and wildflowers.
Contact: NPWS, Griffith.

Conimbla

Bathurst district, 334 km west of Sydney, 18 km west of Cowra. Difficult access to this 7590 ha park. Turn-off from the Cowra-Grenfell Road. Open forest and steep western escarpment. Bush camping; motel and caravan facilities in Cowra.
Contact: Senior Ranger, NPWS, Bathurst.

*Crowdy Bay

Taree District, 392 km north of Sydney, 45 km northeast of Taree. Access from the Pacific Highway at Moorlands then via Coralville, or from Laurieton.
7237 ha of coastal dunes, sandy beach and headland, heath, swamp and small forest areas.
Contact: Senior Ranger, NPWS, Taree.

Sandstone formations in Bouddi National Park (Brett Gregory)

*Deua
Narooma District, 312 km north of Sydney, west of Moruya, accessible on western side from Braidwood–Kybeyan–Nimmitabel Road.
81 298 ha of wilderness with karst areas, caves, wild rivers after rain, open forest, heath, swamp and rainforest.
Contact: NPWS, Narooma.

Dharug
Hawkesbury District, 75 km northwest of Sydney via Wisemans Ferry across the Hawkesbury River, or from Gosford through Central Mangrove.
14 785 ha of sandstone ridges, deep gullies, and typical coastal forest. Notable convict road remains and Aboriginal rock engravings.
Contact: Ranger-in-Charge, Dharug National Park, Wisemans Ferry.

*Dorrigo
Armidale District, 590 km north of Sydney, 3 km east of Dorrigo via the Bellingen–Dorrigo Road and the Dome Road to picnic area.
7819 ha of wet schlerophyll and subtropical rainforest with ferns, orchids, mosses, lichens and fungi. Diverse birdlife and nocturnal mammals.
Contact: Ranger-in-Charge, Dorrigo National Park, Dorrigo.

*Gibraltar Range
Glen Innes District, 672 km north of Sydney, 79 km from Grafton–Glen Innes off Gwydir Highway.
17 273 ha of swamps, heaths, woodlands, forests and rainforests with abundant wildlife. Deep gorges, spectacular waterfalls and unusual rock formations.
Contact: Ranger-in-Charge, Gibraltar National Park, Glen Innes.

Goulburn River
Upper Hunter District, 57 038 ha, 300 km north-west of Sydney, 35 km south of Merriwa. Only a relatively new park, facilities are not yet developed here. Bushcamping is permitted. Semi-arid and basalt capped ridges. All drinking water should be boiled.
Contact: Superintendent, NPWS, Muswellbrook.

*Guy Fawkes River
Armidale District, 650 km north of Sydney, 60 km west of Grafton. Access to southern end from Marengo Road or from Hermani Drive via forest road to Chaelundi. Foot access from the old Glen Innes Road.
33 854 ha of rugged wilderness includes deep gorges, scree slopes, woodland to rainforest vegetation and abundant wildlife.
Contact: Ranger-in-Charge, NPWS, Armidale.

*Hat Head
Taree District, 478 km north of Sydney, 20 km east of Kempsey, accessible from Pacific Highway, from Kempsey towards South West Rocks.
6194 ha of coastal dunes, dune lakes, beaches and headlands, heath, swamp, and limited forest areas.
Contact: Senior Ranger, NPWS, Taree.

Heathcote
South Metropolitan District, 32 km south of Sydney, west of Heathcote. Access off Princes Highway, 3½ km south of Waterfall, along Woronora Dam Road.
2251 ha of spring wildflower displays, woodland vegetation such as eucalypts, blackbutt, bloodwood and many shrubs.
Contact: Superintendent, Royal National Park, Sutherland.

Illawarra
Five sections, totalling 1168 ha, south of Sydney from Bulli Pass to Bong Bong Pass. Beautiful backdrop to Wollongong. No camping facilities; picnic sites and barbeques provided.
Contact: The Manager, Illawarra State Recreation Area, Wollongong East.

*Kanangra–Boyd
Blue Mountains District, 180 km west of Sydney, 16 km from Jenolan Caves. Access via Great Western Highway and Jenolan, turning 5 km south of caves on the Kanangra Walls Road or south from Oberon via Shooters Hill and Mount Werong.
68 276 ha of wilderness with spectacular waterfalls, limestone caves and rugged forest areas.
Contact: Superintendent, Blue Mountains National Park, Blackheath.

*Kinchega

Kinchega District, 111 km southeast of Broken Hill, 2 km west of Menindee. Access via Barrier Highway to Broken Hill or via Ivanhoe; or from Mildura via the Silver City Highway.
44 182 ha of arid landscape comprising black soil flood plains, red soil plains and ridges and a system of saucer-shaped overflow lakes near the Darling River.
Contact: Superintendent, Kinchega National Park, Menindee.

*Kosciusko

Kosciusko District, 487 km southwest of Sydney, 60 km south of Cooma. Access from Cooma and Jindabyne then the Alpine Way to Thredbo, Geehi and Khancoban, from the Kosciusko Road via Sawpit Creek or via Tumut and Talbingo, turning off to Yarrangobilly Caves.
690 000 ha of alpine highlands up to 2228 m. Varied vegetation and seasonal snow and ice above 1850 metres.
Contact: Superintendent, Kosciusko National Park, Sawpit Creek.

*Ku-ring-gai Chase

North Metropolitan District, 30 km north of Sydney, via Pacific Highway, turning off for Bobbin Head at Pymble or Mount Colah; via Mona Vale Road, turning off at Terrey Hills for West Head.
14 717 ha of coastal and estuarine scenery, open forests, scrub, heath and limited rainforest.
Contact: Superintendent, Ku-ring-gai Chase National Park, Bobbin Head, via Turramurra.

*Macquarie Pass

Nowra District, 130 km south of Sydney, access off the Illawarra Highway, 9 km from Albion Park.
1064 ha. Rainforest and ferny eucalypt forest in the Macquarie Rivulet Gorge. Diverse bird and mammal life.
Contact: Superintendent, NPWS, Fitzroy Falls.

*Mallee Cliffs

Lower Darling District, 30 km east of Mildura near the junction of the Darling and Murray Rivers. Reached via the Stuart Highway and Murray Vale Highway through Mildura and Gol Gol.
57 969 ha. Semi-arid country and mallee vegetation, home of the endangered mallee fowl. Bushwalking.
Contact: Ranger, NPWS, Mildura.

Marramarra

North Metropolitan District, 40 km north of Sydney, accessible from Old Northern Road along Canoelands Ridge, or from Wisemans Ferry along Laughtondale Gully Road and Singleton Mill Road.
11539 ha. Mangroves, diverse flora and fauna. Marramarra Creek and Hawkesbury River views

*Mimosa Rocks

Narooma District, 413 km south of Sydney, 22 km north of Eega. Access in dry weather by forestry roads through Mumbulla State Forest otherwise 23 km south of Bermagui, thence gravel track turning off at Wapengo.
5181 ha of rocky headlands, caves and beaches.
Contact: Senior Ranger, NPWS, Narooma.

*Mootwingee Historic Site

A 68 912 ha park in the north-west of the State, 132 km north-east of Broken Hill. Access by dirt road from Broken Hill, Tibooburra or White Cliffs. Semi-arid environment, sandstone gorges, Aboriginal engravings and relics of pastoral era.
Contact: Senior Ranger, NPWS, Mootwingee District, Broken Hill.

*Morton

Nowra District, 155 km southwest of Sydney, 17 km south of Moss Vale. Access from Nowra and Moss Vale to Fitzroy Falls and Bundanoon. Access to southern section from Nerriga, Braidwood or 16 km south of Ulladulla off Princes Highway.
152 948 ha of sandstone cliffs, deep gorges, waterfalls and subtropical rainforest.
Contact: Superintendent Morton National Park, Fitzroy Falls.

*Mount Imlay

Eden District, 496 km south of Sydney, 32 km southwest of Eden. Difficult foot access from Burrawong Forest Road, south of Kiah, west of Princes Highway. 3764 ha of heavily forested area dominated by Mount Imlay (886 m).
Contact: Senior Ranger, NPWS, Eden.

*Mount Kaputar
Narrabri District, 570 km northwest of Sydney, 53 km east of Narrabri. Access at Narrabri, turn east towards Dawson Springs.
36 817 ha featuring Mount Kaputar (1509 m), volcanic remnants, varied vegetation and wildlife.
Contact: Officer-in-Charge, NPWS, Narrabri.

*Mount Warning
Lismore District, 883 km north of Sydney, 16 km southwest of Murwillumbah. Access via the Murwillumbah–Kyogle road through Dum Dum.
2210 ha of rugged rainforest-covered hills including Mount Warning (1156 m) and varied birds and reptiles.
Contact: Ranger-in-Charge, NPWS, Lismore.

*Mungo
Lower Darling District, 980 km west of Sydney, 110 km northeast of Mildura. Access in dry weather from Mildura or Balranald.
14 047 ha. Includes Lake Mungo and white sand dunes called the 'Walls of China' on lake's former edge.
Contact: Ranger, Lower Darling District.

*Murramarang
Nowra District, 275 km south of Sydney, 10 km north of Batemans Bay. Access from Princes Highway, south of Milton. Beach access by dirt track.
1608 ha of coastal park, ocean beaches, lake foreshores and eucalypt forest. Diverse bird life.
Contact: Superintendent, NPWS, Fitzroy Falls.

*Myall Lakes
Hunter District, 236 km north of Sydney, 16 km east of Bulahdelah. Access from Princes Highway, through Bulahdelah, Tea Gardens, or Seal Rocks Road.
31 055 ha. Includes series of fresh to brackish water lakes, spectacular headlands, and long beach expanses.
Contact: Ranger-in-Charge, Taree.

*Nalbaugh
Eden District, 515 km south of Sydney, 26 km southeast of Bombala. Difficult foot access from Cann River Road, or Wog Wog. No vehicle access.
3764 ha of rugged mountainous area dominated by Wog Wog and White Rock Peaks.
Contact: Senior Ranger, NPWS, Eden.

Nangar
Cleared plains surround this mountain range of forested hills in the Bathurst-Forbes district. Situated 59 km west of Orange, and covering 1550 ha. No facilities at present in this new park. Access is difficult, and bushwalking is rough.
Contact: Senior Ranger, NPWS, Bathurst.

*New England
Armidale District, 576 km northwest of Sydney, 67 km east of Armidale, or 14 km west of Ebor. Access via the Armidale–Ebor–Grafton road.
29 823 ha of rainforest, heath and snowgums on the cliff tops. Diverse plants and animals.
Contact: Ranger-in-Charge, New England National Park, Armidale.

Nightcap
Rainforest area, 35 km north of Lismore, covering 4945 ha. Cascading waterfalls and impressive lookouts. Picnic areas and basic camping facilities are provided.
Contact: Senior Ranger, NPWS, Lismore.

*Nungatta
Eden District, 525 km south of Sydney, 35 km southeast of Bombala. Access from the Bombala–Cann River road along the Genoa River's west bank, or from the Princes Highway turning west near Eden and through Towamba.
6100 ha of mountainous terrain and Genoa River flats.
Contact: Senior Ranger, NPWS, Eden.

Cascading waterfall in the lush New England National Park (Barry Slade)

Warm-temperate rainforest occurs in pockets of Royal National Park, such as here along Polona Creek (Brett Gregory)

Nymboida
White water area near Grafton, covering 1368 ha at the junction of Nymboida and Mann Rivers. Popular with canoeists and rafters. No facilities. Access difficult enter either on foot or canoe. Road to southern boundary of park from Grafton–Glen Innes Road.
Contact: Senior Ranger, NPWS, Grafton.

*Royal
South Metropolitan District, 36 km south of Sydney via the Princes Highway, turning off past Sutherland for Audley or at Waterfall; from Wollongong, via Stanwell Park.
15 014 ha of rugged sea cliffs, quiet inlets, rainforest pockets, waterfalls, swamps, heaths, woodlands, diverse bird life.
Contact: Superintendent, Royal National Park, Sutherland.

*Seven Mile Beach
Nowra District, 137 km south of Sydney, 6 km south of Gerringong. Access via Princes Highway through Gerringong.
730 ha of coast land with beaches, sand dunes and dune vegetation.
Contact: Superintendent, NPWS, Fitzroy Falls.

*Sturt
Tibooburra District, 353 km north of Broken Hill.
Access through Broken Hill and Silver City Highway or via Bourke and Wanaaring to Tibooburra. Impossible during and after heavy rain.
380 000 ha of vast open gibber plains and flat-topped mesas creating a semi-desert environment.
Contact: Ranger, Sturt National Park, Tibooburra.

*Sydney Harbour
Sydney District, located on Sydney harbour foreshores. Access from surrounding suburbs to Nielsen Park, Shark, Rodd and Clark Islands, Bradleys Head, Ashton Park and Dobroyd Head.
388 ha of sandstone headlands, sandy beaches, mixed coastal shrub and heath.
Contact: Superintendent, Vaucluse.

Tarlo River
Currently 5728 ha, 30 km north-east of Goulburn. New park that will eventually be expanded to about 12 000 ha. No access at present, as park is surrounded by private property.
Contact: Superintendent, NPWS, Nowra.

Thirlmere Lakes

South Metropolitan District, 105 km south of Sydney, 10 km from Picton, turning off Hume Highway 4 km south of Picton or 4 km north of Bargo.
630 ha featuring 5 interconnecting freshwater lakes, with extensive reed beds and floating islands.
Contact: Superintendent, Royal National Park, Sutherland.

Tomaree

A narrow coastal strip of 800 ha, just south of Port Stephens. Good access, but no facilities; close to towns of Shoal Bay, Fingal Bay and Boat Harbour. Swimming, surfing and bushwalking.
Contact: Superintendent, NPWS, Raymond Terrace.

* Wadbilliga

Narooma District, 354 km south of Sydney, 40 km west of Bermagui. Access from Princes Highway, through Narooma and Cobargo past Murrabine State Forest, or from Kybeyan. Foot access to the Brogo River.
75 767 ha of undisturbed river catchment including Tuross Falls and Gorge.
Contact: Senior Ranger, NPWS, Narooma.

* Wallaga Lake

Narooma District, 354 km south of Sydney, 18 km north of Cobargo. Access 2 km south of Dignam's Creek off Princes Highway, can be difficult.
1141 ha dominated by lake, inlets and shallow bays.
Contact: Senior Ranger, NPWS, Narooma.

Warrabah

Eighty kilometres from Tamworth, via Manilla and along the Namoi River Road. On the western slopes of the Namoi River, covering 2635 ha. Bushwalking and rockclimbing. Basic camping facilities provided. Access good, but unsuitable for caravans.
Contact: Senior Ranger, NPWS, Armidale.

* Warrumbungle

Coonabarabran District, 491 km northwest of Sydney, 37 km west of Coonabarabran. Access from New England Highway, turning west at Tamworth to Coonabarabran; from the Great Western Highway turning north at Lithgow, through Mudgee, Gulgong, Dunedoo and Coonabarabran.
19 651 ha of towering spires and domes rising among forested ridges and gorges, spectacular wildflowers and abundant birdlife.
Contact: Officer-in-Charge, NPWS, Coonabarabran.

Washpool

Rainforest wilderness covering 30 000 ha, 80 km from Grafton off the Gwydir Highway. Wild river gorges, good walking tracks and picnic areas. Easy access. One of the state's most important stands of north coast rainforest.
Contact: Senior Ranger, NPWS, Glen Innes.

* Weddin Mountains

Bathurst District, 390 km southwest of Sydney, 19 km southwest of Grenfell. Difficult access from Grenfell along the Bimbi or Barmedman roads, turning off the Holy Camp road.
8296 ha of wilderness with a crescent-shaped mountain range rising to over 333 m.
Contact: Officer-in-Charge, Griffith.

* Werrikimbe

Armidale District, 480 km north of Sydney, 87 km northwest of Wauchope. Access from Oxley Highway between Wauchope and Walcha, turning north at Seaview Road for 1 km then 21 km along Fenwicks Road, then follow Mooraback Road to camping area.
34 753 ha of wilderness park, featuring magnificent deep gorge and Mount Werrikimbe (915 m).
Contact: Senior Ranger, NPWS, Armidale.

*Willandra
Griffith District, 726 km west of Sydney, 64 km northwest of Hillston. Access via Mid-Western Highway and along the Mossgiel Road.
19 386 ha of flat terrain with occasional sand ridges; grass and saltbush plains broken by black box and lignum lined watercourses.
Contact: Manager, Willandra National Park, via Hillston.

Woko
In the Hunter district, 318 km from Sydney and 30 km from Gloucester. Varied vegetation, including 3 types of rainforest in this 8724 ha park. Good access; road leads right to camping area on Manning River. No marked walking trails, and terrain may be rough in parts. Swimming and bushwalking.
Contact: Superintendent, NPWS, Raymond Terrace.

*Wollemi
Upper Hunter District (northern section), Blue Mountains District (southern section). 100 km northwest of Sydney. Check with NPWS District Office or Central Regional Office for entry points and access routes.
480 130 ha of wilderness feature basalt capped sandstone peaks, gorges, tree-lined peaks, diverse vegetation and abundant fauna.
Contact: Officer-in-Charge, Blue Mountains National Park.

Yarrowitch Gorge
At junction of Yarrowitch and Warnes Rivers, covering 2965 ha, in the Armidale district. Vehicle access, best suited to 4-wheel drive, is from the Oxley Highway. Good campsites at 'Sunnyside', but walking may be a bit rough at times; river cascades make the effort worthwhile.
Contact: Senior Ranger, NPWS, Armidale.

*Yuraygir
Grafton District, 660 km north of Sydney, accessible from Pacific Highway to several points in the Park.
15 503 ha of coastal terrain featuring secluded beaches separated by rocky headlands, wet and dry heath, woodland, dune and paperbark / reed swamp and varied wildlife. Includes former Angourie and Red Rock National Parks.
Contact: Senior Ranger, NPWS, Grafton.

Wave-swept rocks in Yuragir National Park
(Brett Gregory)

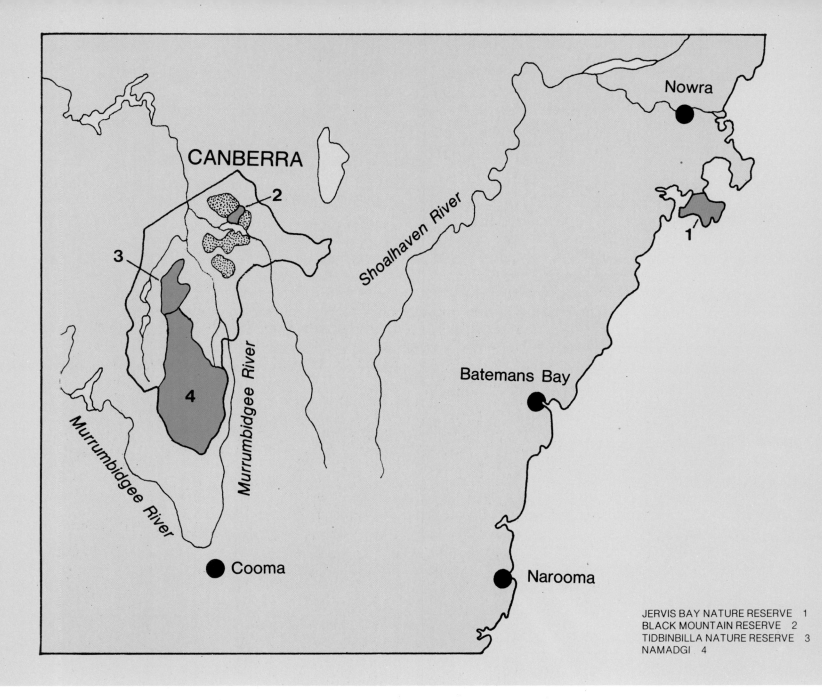

JERVIS BAY NATURE RESERVE 1
BLACK MOUNTAIN RESERVE 2
TIDBINBILLA NATURE RESERVE 3
NAMADGI 4

Floral extravaganza in Namadgi National Park (J–P Ferrero/Auscape)

THE AUSTRALIAN
CAPITAL TERRITORY

The ACT has only one national park,
Namadgi National Park, which is
administered by the Australian National
Parks and Wildlife Service, Woden, ACT.
Also under the control of this body are
Kakadu and Uluru. The latter two are
listed in the Northern Territory section.
Nature reserves in the ACT and Jervis
Bay are administered by the Australian
Capital Territory Conservation Service.

Namadgi
Declared in October 1984, Namadgi
covers some 940 000 ha, taking in what
was formerly Gudgenby Nature Reserve,
and joining up with Tidbinbilla Nature
Reserve in the north and Scabby Range
and Bimberri Nature Reserves in the
south. These nature reserves in turn join
up with the giant Kosciusko National
Park, providing in effect one huge
expanse of protected land covering well
in excess of 1.5 million hectares.
The park contains a wide diversity of
landforms, from rocky outcrops to
swamps; this diversity is reflected in the
impressive range of flora and fauna
species. There are also relics of old
stockmen's huts.
A visitors information centre is located in
the Gudgenby section of the park.
Contact: Senior Ranger, ANPWS,
Namadgi NP.

Black Mountain Reserve
Between the suburbs of O'Connor and
Aranda on the shores of Lake Burley
Griffin and part of Canberra Nature Park.
In the approximate centre is Black
Mountain (813 m) surrounded by Botanic
Gardens. Includes a number of walking
trails of varying degrees of difficulty.
Contact: The Manager Canberra Nature
Park, or the Director. Conservation and
Agriculture, Department of the Capital
Territory.

Jervis Bay Nature Reserve
198 km from Canberra and 203 km from
Sydney, accessible off the Princes
Highway, and Jervis Bay road.
4470 ha with a further 1450 ha managed
by the ACT in conjunction with the
Reserve. Undulating sandstone country,
considerable sand cover and precipitous
cliffs along the east and southeast coasts.
Varied flora including eucalypt forests,
relic rainforest, woodland, and dry heath,
coastal scrub, swampland and
mangroves. Diverse wildlife includes
numerous sea and land birds.
Contact: Department of the Capital
Territory headquarters, Jervis Bay
Village.

Tidbinbilla Nature Reserve
South of Canberra between the Cotter
and Murrumbidgee Rivers.
5515 ha. Includes 56 km of walking trails.
Large natural enclosures of kangaroo,
koala and waterfowl. Landscape varies
from wet eucalypt forests on Tidbinbilla
Range's lower western slopes and open
forest on the eastern side to ferny gullies,
mountain streams, lightly wooded valleys
and clusters of huge granite boulders.
Snow-capped in winter.
Contact: Manager, Tidbinbilla Nature
Reserve, or the Director, Conservation
and Agriculture, Department of the
Capital Territory.

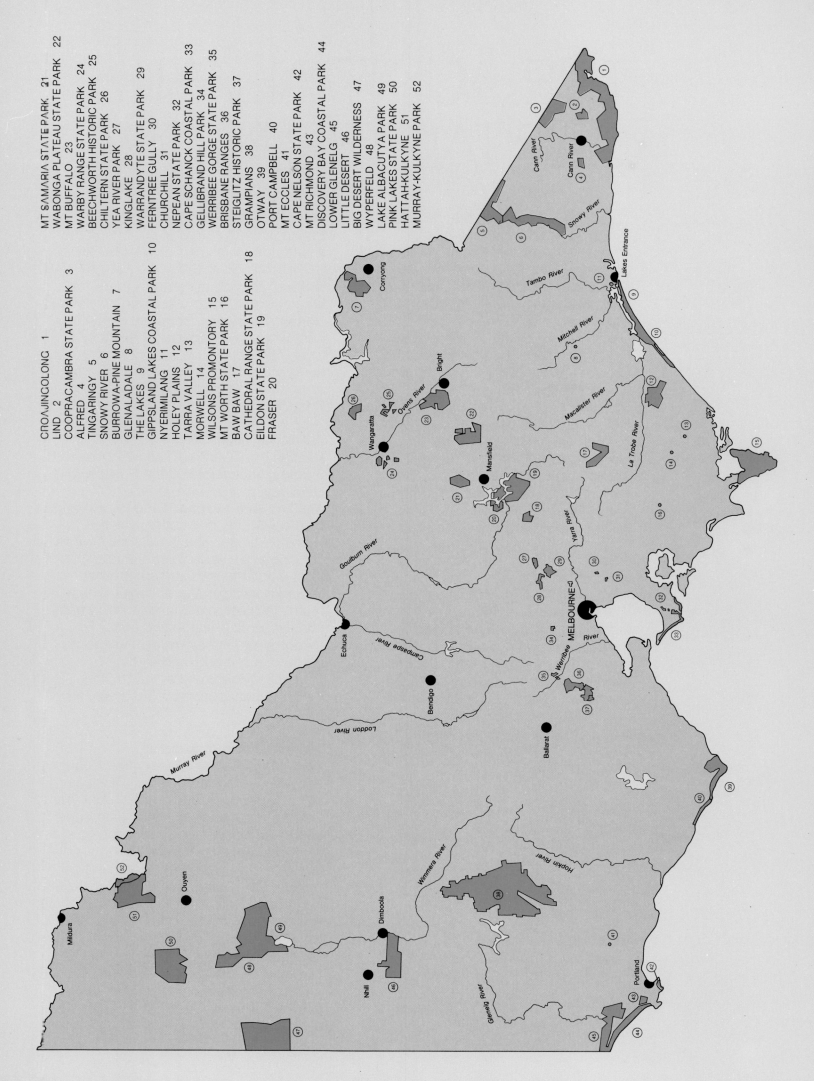

VICTORIA

In March 1986, Victoria's 54 national parks and state parks had a combined area of just over 1.5 million hectares. This huge area had been bolstered in late 1985 by the proclamation of the Grampians National Park. In late 1986–early 1987, it is expected the Victorian government will announce a new alpine park, increasing the state's already impressive list of parks.

As well as national and state parks, Victoria also has important historic sites, such as those at Steiglitz, Chiltern and Beechworth. They are open to the public; more information can be obtained from the NPS Head Office, 240 Victoria Parade, East Melbourne, 3002.

Alfred

500 km east of Melbourne between Mount Drummer and Karlo Creek flats on the Princes Highway between Cann River and Genoa.

2300 ha, largely undeveloped with warm temperate rainforest vegetation.

Contact: Ranger-in-Charge, Cann River.

*Baw Baw

About 200 km east of Melbourne; approach via Yarra Junction, Moe or Erica.

13 300 ha includes the Baw Baw plateau and parts of Thomson and Aberfeldy valleys, but not the village and downhill skiing areas.

Contact: NPS Head Office, Melbourne.

Beechworth Historic Park

Surrounds the town of Beechworth.

1130 ha of separate bushland areas featuring Inghams Rock, the Gorge Drive, Woolshed Falls and an area of bushland near Lake Kerferd.

Contact: NPS Office, Melbourne.

*Big Desert Wilderness

West of Hopetoun, on the Victoria–SA border. Access west of Murrayville–Yanac Road.

113 500 ha of prime wilderness with vast sand dunes, plains and heath.

Contact: North West District Office, NPS, Horsham.

Bogong National Park

Approximately 100 km from Wangaratta, in Victoria's north-east, Bogong covers 81 000 ha of high country, popular with cross-country skiers and bushwalkers alike. Falls Creek and Mt Hotham ski resorts adjoin the park. Large areas of forest, heathland and moss beds, important refuges for the mountain pygmy possum.

Contact: NPS District Office, Wangaratta.

Brisbane Ranges

80 km west of Melbourne with access off Anakie-Ballan or Anakie-Bacchus Marsh roads.
7470 ha. Includes 400 species of flowering plants, at their peak between August and November, and the scenic Anakie Gorge.
Contact: NPS Head Office, Melbourne, or Park Ranger.

Bulga National Park

About 30 km from Morwell, in the Gippsland district; 80 ha of giant mountain ash and myrtle beech, plus some particularly large tree ferns. Picnic areas and self-guided walks. Set close to Tara Valley National Park.
Contact: NPS District Office, Foster.

Burrowa-Pine Mountain

430 km northeast of Melbourne, northwest of Corryong with access from Cudgewa or Walwa.
17 300 ha with massive outcrops of granite and rhyolite, waterfalls and some rare plant species.
Contact: NPS Head Office, Melbourne.

Cape Nelson State Park

370 km from Melbourne, 12 km south of Portland.
210 ha with unusual vegetation, particularly the soap mallee unique to this area. Cape Nelson Lighthouse reached by sealed road through park.
Contact: NPS South West District Office, Portland.

Cape Schanck Coastal Park

90 km from Melbourne, accessible from the southern ocean beaches of Mornington Peninsula between Cape Schanck and Portsea.
1075 ha. Includes surf beaches between London Bridge and Cape Schanck, rugged cliffs, sand dunes and unusual rock formations sculptured by the surf.
Contact: NPS, Arthurs Seat.

Cathedral Range State Park

100 km north of Melbourne, accessible from Healesville or Alexandra, turning at Cathedral Lane between Buxton and Taggerty.
3570 ha includes the rocky razorback ridge of the Cathedral Range and the Little River gorge below the Cerberean Plateau.
Contact: NPS Head Office, Melbourne.

Chiltern State Park

Located north and south of the Hume Highway at Chiltern, 270 km from Melbourne.
4250 ha of box and ironbark forest, many wildflowers and unusual fauna, and several historic sites.

Churchill

32 km east of Melbourne, accessible via Churchill Park Drive which runs off Wellington Road, north of Dandenong.
193 ha of the vegetation once found between Dandenong and Ferntree Gully. A bird and possum habitat.
Contact: Ranger, Churchill National Park, Rowville.

Coopracambra State Park

On the NSW–Victoria border between Cape Howe and the source of the Murray River.
14 500 ha of wilderness along the steep sandstone gorge of the Genoa River.
Contact: NPS, Bairnsdale.

*Croajingolong

550 km from Melbourne, and south of the Princes Highway between Cann River and Genoa. It incorporates the former Wingan Inlet, Captain James Cook and Mallacoota Inlet parks.
86 000 ha, covering almost 100 km of East Gippsland coast with diverse vegetation and rare animals.
Contact: NPS Head Office, Melbourne.

Discovery Bay Coastal Park

400 km from Melbourne, extending from west of Portland to the South Australian border. Access is by sealed roads to Nelson Beach and Bridgewater Lakes or by gravel road to Swan Lake.
8530 ha of bare sand dunes, lakes and swamps, coastal heathland and a long ocean beach.
Contact: Ranger-in-Charge, Discovery Bay Coastal Park, Nelson.

Eildon State Park

160 km from Melbourne, south and east of Lake Eildon. Access by the scenic Eildon–Jamieson road along the south boundary of the park.
24 000 ha featuring the steeply dissected and forested Enterprise Range and Rocky Spur.

Ferntree Gully

36 km east of Melbourne, just north of Upper Ferntree Gully in the nearer Dandenong Range. Accessible by road through Oakley or Burwood, or by train, via Upper Ferntree Station.
459 ha with over 150 species of native plants.
Contact: NPS Head Office, Melbourne.

* Fraser

145 km north of Melbourne, 17 km northeast of Alexandra.
3750 ha of natural regrowth containing kangaroos and birdlife on the western shores of Lake Eildon.
Contact: Ranger-in-Charge, Fraser National Park, Alexandra.

Gellibrand Hill Park

25 km north of Melbourne, accessible off Somerton Road near Oaklands Junction.
266 ha including remnants of the area's original vegetation.
Contact: NPS Head Office, Melbourne.

* Gippsland Lakes Coastal Park

280 km east of Melbourne, with the eastern section at Ninety Mile Beach. Approaches at Seaspray and Golden Beach or by boat through the Lakes.
15 500 ha of sand dunes and sparse coastal vegetation.
Contact: NPS offices in Melbourne or Bairnsdale.

Glenaladale

300 km east of Melbourne, accessible by gravel road from Fernbank, 30 km north of Princes Highway.
183 ha notable for its dry forest covering and the Den of Nargun, a cave, curtained by a waterfall, which is important in Aboriginal mythology.
Contact: Ranger-in-Charge, Glenaladale National Park, Iguana Creek, via Bairnscale.

Soft tree ferns carpet the ground in sections of Bulga National Park (J–M la Roque/Auscape)

* Grampians National Park

Victoria's largest national park, the Grampians covers 167 000 ha, typified by rugged mountain ranges. The park is easily accessible, situated 260 km from Melbourne and 460 km from Adelaide. Spectacular wildflower display in Spring; camping, bushwalking and fishing also. Accommodation available in Halls Gap.
Contact: NPS Park Office, Halls Gap.

* Hattah-Kulkyne

470 km northwest of Melbourne, 36 km north of Ouyen, east of Hattah township. Accessible off the Calder Highway at Hattah, along the Murray Valley Highway 48 000 ha. Includes the Kulkyne forest and lake system.
Contact: Ranger-in-Charge, Hattah–Kulkyne NP, Roadside Delivery, Hattah, via Mildura.

Holey Plains

190 km southeast of Melbourne, 5 km southeast of Rosedale.
10 450 ha of low sandy hills, varied tree and shrub species and spectacular spring wildflower displays.
Contact: NPS Head Office, Melbourne.

Kinglake

65 km north of Melbourne, west of Kinglake and accessible from Whittlesea or Yarra Glen directions.
11 270 ha on the slopes of the Great Dividing Range with timbered ridges, wooded valleys, fern gullies, excellent views, native animals and birdlife.
Contact: Ranger-in-Charge, National Park Road, Pheasants Creek.

* Lake Albacutya Park

430 km from Melbourne, west of Rainbow.
10 700 ha containing the Lake and its shores, tall red gum woodlands and section of Big Desert dunes.

* Lakes, The

330 km from Melbourne, south of Sale and east of Loch Sport which is 42 km east of Longford. 5 km by boat from Paynesville.
2380 ha of diverse flora and fauna, with prolific birdlife on a peninsula projecting into the Gippsland Lakes.
Contact: NPS Head Office, Melbourne, or Park Ranger.

Lind

480 km east of Melbourne, off the Princes Highway between Orbost and Cann River.
1166 ha of typical East Gippsland forest featuring tall eucalypt stands. Best seen from the Euchre Creek road, north of the Princes Highway.
Contact: District Superintendent, NPS, Bairnsdale.

* Little Desert

375 km west of Melbourne, 8 km south of Kiata on the Western Highway.
35 300 ha of heathland broom and mallee eucalypt with over 200 bird species recorded.
Contact: Ranger-in-Charge, Little Desert National Park, RMB 389, Nhill.

Lower Glenelg

400 km from Melbourne in the southwest corner of Victoria, accessible from the north of Portland–Nelson road, along the Glenelg River.
27 300 ha. Contains the Glenelg gorges, Kentbruck Heath and an abundance of animals, birds and fish.
Contact: Ranger-in-Charge, Glenelg NP, Nelson.

Morwell

170 km southeast of Melbourne, 16 km south of Morwell. Approach via Jeeralong Junction and Junction Road.
283 ha containing steep sloping ridges and gullies, over 100 plant species and many native animals.
Contact: Ranger on site or NPS Head Office, Melbourne.

* Mount Buffalo

330 km northeast of Melbourne, 30 km from Porepunkah on the Wangaratta–Bright road.
31 000 ha of superb scenery, diverse wildlife and flora. Cross country and downhill skiing in winter.
Contact: Ranger-in-Charge, Mt Buffalo NP, Mt Buffalo.

*MacKenzie Falls
are compulsive viewing for
visitors to the Grampians
(H&J Beste/Auscape)*

Mount Eccles

33 km west of Melbourne, 42 km south of
Hamilton.
400 ha including the extinct volcano, Mt
Eccles, whose craters now contain Lake
Surprise; also a lava canal, lava cave and
the Stony Rises formed by lava flows
10 000 years ago.
Contact: Ranger-in-Charge, Mt Eccles
NP, Macarthur.

Mount Richmond

32 km west of Portland, 400 km from
Melbourne via the Princes Highway.
Access is from the Portland–Nelson–
Mount Gambier Road near Gorae West.
1707 ha. Contains 450 species of native
plants, over 100 species of birds and Mt
Richmond, a sand-covered volcano
commanding fine views.
Contact: NPS Office, Portland.

Mount Samaria State Park

210 km north of Melbourne with rough access 15 km north of Mansfield off Tolmie Road.
7600 ha of rocky outcrops with diverse flora and fauna and scenic views. Largely undeveloped.
Contact: Ranger-in-Charge, Mt Samaria SP.

Mount Worth State Park

130 km from Melbourne at the western end of the Grand Ridge Road. Access south of Warragul or Darnum and along Grand Ridge Road to Seaview.
1000 ha. Contains forested areas and a bird and animal refuge.
Contact: NPS Head Office, Melbourne.

* Murray–Kulkyne Park

Adjoins the Hattah–Kulkyne National Park, 500 km from Melbourne. Approach via the Murray Valley Highway or from Colignan.
1550 ha. Features long Murray River frontage and stands of river red gums.
Contact: Ranger-in-Charge or NPS Head Office, Melbourne.

Nepean State Park

75 km south of Melbourne, off the Peninsula Freeway through Arthurs Seat on to Purves Road.
1050 ha including 'Seawinds' garden on Arthurs Seat, Mornington Peninsula, a former grazing property and the largest area of uncleared land remaining on the Peninsula.
Contact: NPS, Arthurs Seat.

Nyerimilang Park

A new park overlooking the Gippsland Lakes, covering 176 ha. About 10 km from Lakes Entrance. Bushland, old farm buildings and ornamental gardens.
Contact: NPS District Office, Bairnsdale.

Otway National Park

Encompassing the coastline between Apollo Bay and Princetown is the 12 750 ha Otway National Park. Landscape varies from rugged cliffs fronting the Southern Ocean to fern gullies and tall forests. Camping, walking, fishing and surfing are all popular here.
Contact: NPS District Office, Colac.

* Pink Lakes State Park

490 km northwest of Melbourne, accessible from Underbool west of Ouyen.
50 700 ha with picturesque saltpans, saltbush flats and copi rises of the Raak land system. Two of the lakes yield salt harvests.
Contact: NPS North West District Office, Horsham.

* Port Campbell

250 km from Melbourne, south of Great Ocean Road between Princetown and Port Campbell, facing the Southern Ocean.
1750 ha of rugged coastal scenery and famous sea-sculptured landforms such as London Bridge and The Twelve Apostles. Contains penguins, mutton birds and other seabirds.
Contact: Ranger-in-Charge, Port Campbell NP, Port Campbell.

* Snowy River

450 km from Melbourne, south of Mackillop Bridge.
26 000 ha. Includes Snowy River with its gorge and rapids, and the rare brush-tailed wallaby.
Contact: Ranger-in-Charge, or NPS Head Office, Melbourne.

Steiglitz Historic Park

85 km west of Melbourne, adjoins Brisbane Ranges National Park. Access is off Anakie–Meredith road at Steiglitz.
655 ha centred on the old gold mining town of Steiglitz with its relics and display in the Old Court House. Spring wildflowers.
Contact: Park staff or NPS Head Office, Melbourne.

Tarra Valley

220 km southeast of Melbourne. Access on Tarra Valley Road, 30 km from Yarram, or turn off Princes Highway at Traralgon then via Gormendale and Carrajung.
140 ha. Includes Tarra River waterfall, and lush vegetation fostered by high rainfall.
Contact: Park Ranger or NPS Head Office, Melbourne.

*The Southern Ocean pounds into the coast at Port Campbell
(J–P Ferrero/Auscape)*

*Tingaringy

450 km from Melbourne, north of Mackillop Bridge on the Bucham–Delegate Road. Adjoins Kosciusko National Park.
18 000 ha of rocky peaks, cypress pine and white box forest.

Wabonga Plateau State Park

230 km from Melbourne, south of Whitfield or east of Tolmie via Mansfield, 21 200 ha.
A sloping plateau of sedimentary rock with cliffs, waterfalls and a steep razorback ridge to the east.
Contact: NPS Head Office, Melbourne.

Warby Range State Park

235 km north of Melbourne, 10 km west of Wangaratta. Access by turning left off the Hume Highway before Glenrowan.
3320 ha. Includes Mt Warby, Mt Bruno and Salisbury Falls, with dry rocky hills, granite ranges and diverse vegetation.
Contact: NPS Head Office, Melbourne.

Warrandyte State Park

30 km east of Melbourne along the Yarra River near Warrandyte, accessible from Warrandyte Road, Research–Warrandyte Road or Ringwood–Warrandyte Road.
218 ha with traces of gold-mining activity, moist dense river growth and dry open forest on the valley slopes.
Contact: Ranger, Warrandyte.

Werribee Gorge State Park

65 km west of Melbourne, west of Bacchus Marsh then north of Ironbark Road.
375 ha. Includes Werribee Gorge, spectacular scenery, varied plants and animals.
Contact: NPS Head Office, Melbourne.

*Wilsons Promontory

Victoria's oldest, best known national park. 230 km southeast of Melbourne. Turn south at Meeniyan or Foster on the South Gippsland Highway.
49 000 ha of diverse, scenic landscape, varied plants, animals, and birds.
Contact: Park Office, Wilsons Promontory NP, Tidal River, via Foster.

Wonnangatta — Moroka National Park

The 107 000 ha of this park, situated about 70 km from Mansfield, are not easily accessible, but certainly magnificent. The park takes in high peaks, snow-covered in winter, sub-alpine plains and deep valleys. Activities include skiing, camping and horse riding.
Contact: NPS Regional Office, Alexandra.

*Wyperfeld

450 km northwest of Melbourne, along the Henty Highway via Hopetoun, or from the Western Highway via Dimboola and Rainbow.
100 000 ha. Includes sandy mallee, dry lake beds fringed with red gums and heathland, and abundant wildlife including the rare mallee fowl.
Contact: Ranger-in-Charge, Wyperfeld NP, Post Office, Yaapeet.

Yea River Park

70 km from Melbourne, adjoining the Yea-Yarra Glen Road south of Glenburn.
220 ha featuring the Yea River, forested river flats and slopes.
Contact: NPS Head Office, Melbourne.

Tree ferns in Tarra Valley National Park, Gippsland

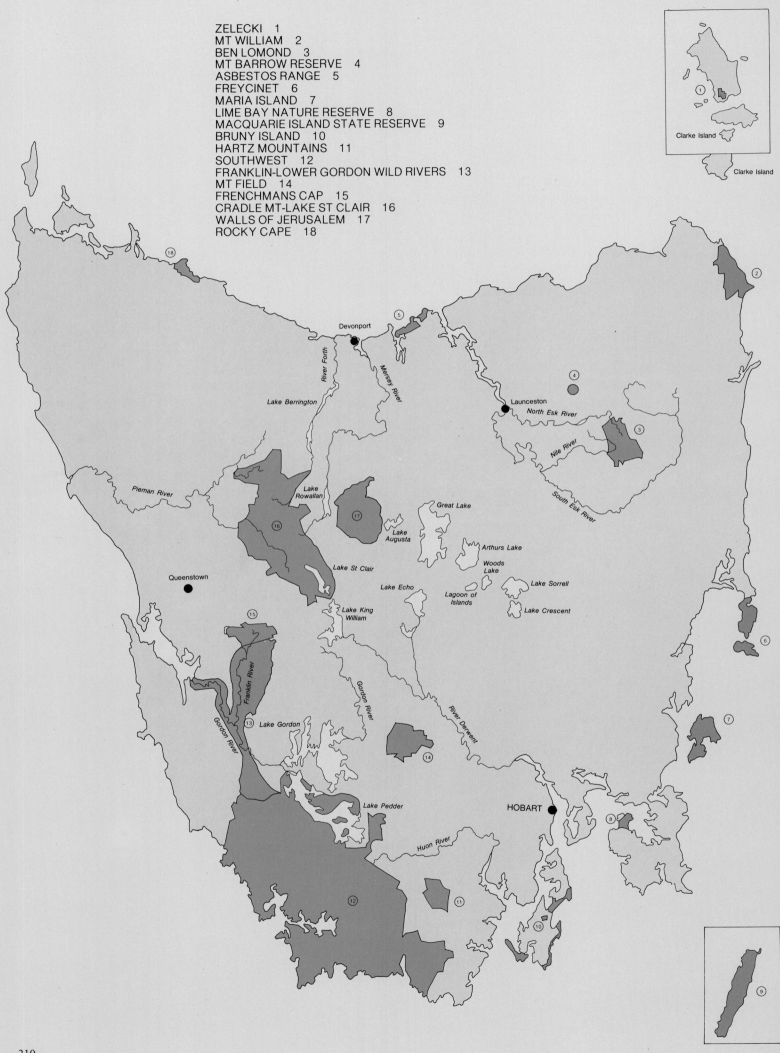

ZELECKI   1
MT WILLIAM   2
BEN LOMOND   3
MT BARROW RESERVE   4
ASBESTOS RANGE   5
FREYCINET   6
MARIA ISLAND   7
LIME BAY NATURE RESERVE   8
MACQUARIE ISLAND STATE RESERVE   9
BRUNY ISLAND   10
HARTZ MOUNTAINS   11
SOUTHWEST   12
FRANKLIN-LOWER GORDON WILD RIVERS   13
MT FIELD   14
FRENCHMANS CAP   15
CRADLE MT-LAKE ST CLAIR   16
WALLS OF JERUSALEM   17
ROCKY CAPE   18

TASMANIA

Tasmania has the largest percentage of its total area set aside as national parks and reserves in Australia. The state's Scenery Conservation Act of 1915 was the oldest legislation of its kind in this part of the world. The present-day National Parks and Wildlife Service, established in 1971, combines the functions of the former Scenery Preservation Board and the Animals and Birds Protection Board and has similar aims to these bodies in other states.

In excess of 800 000 hectares of reserves, including national parks, state reserves, historic sites and Aboriginal sites, exist. The NPWS also manages wildlife on Macquarie Island and in other remote areas.

Information about these areas can be obtained from The Director at PO Box 210, Sandy Bay, Tas. 7002.

* Asbestos Range
On the north coast east of Devonport. 4281 ha of coastal heathland.

* Ben Lomond
50 km east of Launceston in the state's northeast.
16 526 ha of mountainous terrain including Legge's Tor (1 572 m) favoured by naturalists, walkers and mountaineers. A popular winter sports ground.

Bruny Island
South of Hobart, accessible by car ferry from Kettering. A number of important reserves dot the island, including Fluted Cape State Reserve, Labillardiere State Reserve and Bruny Island Neck Game Reserve. Fairy penguins may be observed in certain areas.
Contact: Ranger, Bruny Island.

* Cradle Mountain-Lake St Clair
North access via Devonport, Sheffield and Wilmot to Waldheim south through Derwent Bridge on the Lyell Highway about 160 km from Hobart.
131 915 ha of spectacular mountain scenery including the serrated peak of Cradle Mountain (1600 m) and several peaks over 1200 m. Lake St Clair, on the southern boundary, at an altitude of 665 m, exceeds 5000 ha. Most Tasmanian animal life and immensely varied flora.

* Franklin-Lower Gordon Wild Rivers
Forming the central link in Tasmania's World Heritage Area, the park covers some 181 075 ha of genuine wilderness area. Borders Cradle Mountain–Lake St Clair in the north and South-west in the south. Includes the area at the heart of the Franklin Dam controversy, now protected by World Heritage listing.
Contact: The Director, Sandy Bay.

*Frenchmans Cap
On the west coast, 200 km from Hobart, between Derwent Bridge and Queenstown off Lyell Highway.
10 214 ha of rugged wilderness with Frenchmans Cap featuring its 1443 m jutting white quartzite formation.

*Freycinet
39 km south of Bicheno on a secondary road off the Tasman Highway via Coles Bay. With Mt Field, the first national park gazetted in Tasmania.
10 010 ha including the Peninsula and Schouten Island to the south, featuring unspoiled bushland dominated by spectacular red granite landforms known as The Hazards.
Contact: Park Ranger at Tasmanian NPWS.

Furneaux Islands
Located off the north-east tip of Tasmania, this group of islands is well-covered by reserves, including Strzelecki and Cape Barren Island. Many of the smaller reserves are vital seabird nesting areas, and should only be visited outside the breeding season to minimise disturbance.
Contact: Head Ranger, Strzelecki National Park, Flinders Island.

Hartz Mountains
Southwest of Hobart via the Huon Highway through Huonville and Geeveston.
6470 ha of rugged bushland ranging from alpine vegetation to rainforest, fern gullies and eucalypt stands, with snowcapped peaks, notably Hartz Mountain (1300 m), and several scenic high altitude lakes.

Ice-covered Lake Dobson, Mt Field National Park

Royal penguins cluster along the beach on Macquarie Island

Lime Bay Nature Reserve
On the northwestern tip of the Tasman Peninsula, 90 km from Hobart. Access by sealed road to Saltwater River, then on gravel to Coal Mines Historic Site and finally bush track to Lime Bay Beach.
1310 ha with coastal scenery featuring low cliffs, open woodland and coastal heath with varied waterfowl in seasonal sloping lagoon.

Macquarie Island State Reserve
1500 km southeast of Tasmania. Managed by the Tasmanian NPWS. Internationally recognised as an important widlife reserve used by seals, penguins and sea birds for resting and breeding. Proclaimed in 1933.

* Maria Island
Off the east coast.
9672 ha historic site and fauna sanctuary established as a national park in 1972. Formerly a convict settlement, grazing and industrial site. Features include convict buildings at Darlington, scenic limestone fossil cliffs, many native animals and several recently established bird species.

Mount Barrow Reserve
East of Launceston in the state's northeast.
459 ha of mountain terrain forming part of the North-Eastern Massif along with Mt Arthur, Mt Victoria and Ben Lomond.

Mount Field
80 km west of Hobart and about 40 km north and slightly west of New Norfolk in the Derwent Valley.
16 257 ha dominated by Mt Field West (1420 m). A high rainfall area notable for the winter ski resorts of Mt Mawson and Mt Field and the scenic Russell Falls (40 m) falling into a rainforest gorge. Abundant Tasmanian marsupial and birdlife including the nocturnal Tasmanian devil. One of the state's first national parks.

*Mount William
In the northeast between Ansons Bay and Musselroe Bay and accessible by a gravel road from Gladstone or St Helens. 13 806 ha of coastal forest, flat coastal plains, sweeping bays, white sandy beaches and granite headlands used as a sanctuary for the forester kangaroo and other wildlife and for unique plant life. Contains Mt William (216 m).

*Rocky Cape
Near Wynyard on the northwest coast. 3070 ha of coastal heath banksia and rugged coastline including a number of caves, one of which is an important archaeological site.

*Southwest
Tasmania's largest national park comprising almost the whole southwest corner of the state. 442 240 ha. Includes several river systems and major mountain groups, about 50 lakes (notably Lake Pedder, formed by the damming of the Serpentine River in 1972) and considerable fauna and endemic flora. Formerly inhabited by Aboriginal tribes.

*Strzelecki
In the south of Flinders Island in the Bass Strait Group. 4215 ha of mountain reserve with wet sclerophyll forests and abundant birdlife and wildlife, including the Flinders Island wombat.

The Walls of Jerusalem
Access to this park is restricted to walkers; there is no vehicular access. Detailed maps are essential, as track markers are not always clear, especially during winter when snow covers much of the area. Enter only with sufficient preparation, and enjoy scenery that is beyond compare. Large stands of pencil pine, great diversity of wildlife and many lakes and tarns.
Contact: Head Ranger, Cradle Mountain.

Cushion plants in the Walls of Jerusalem National Park (J–P Ferrero/Auscape)

Unparalleled lushness in south-west Tasmania (J–P Ferrero/Auscape)

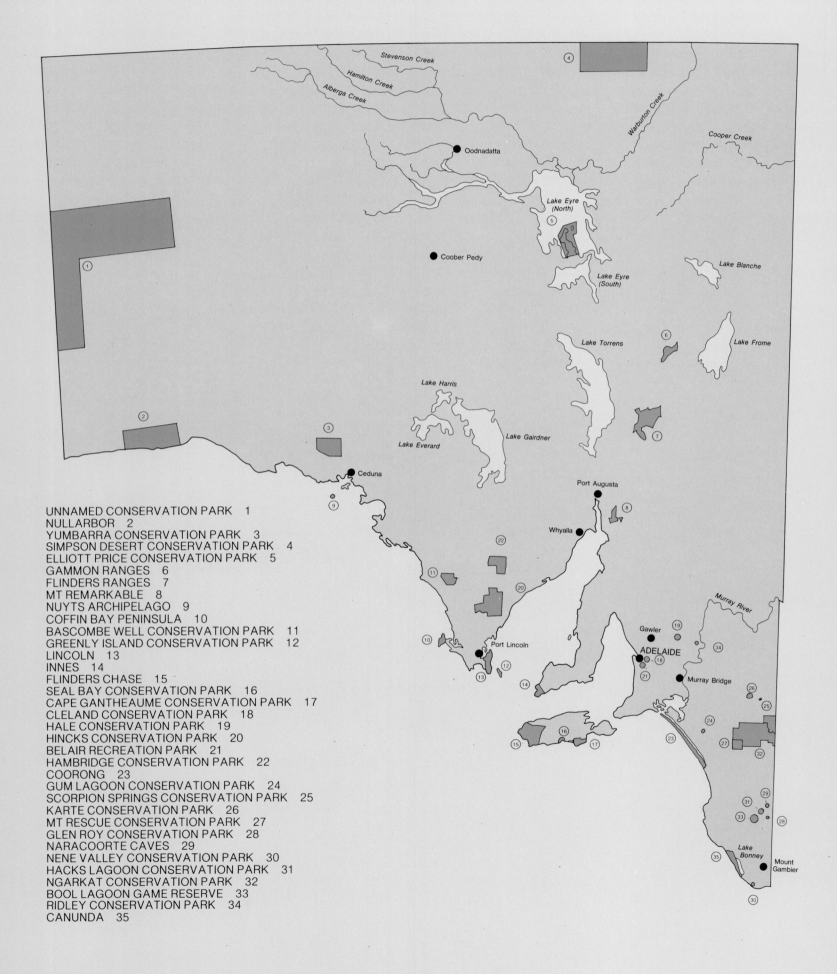

UNNAMED CONSERVATION PARK   1
NULLARBOR   2
YUMBARRA CONSERVATION PARK   3
SIMPSON DESERT CONSERVATION PARK   4
ELLIOTT PRICE CONSERVATION PARK   5
GAMMON RANGES   6
FLINDERS RANGES   7
MT REMARKABLE   8
NUYTS ARCHIPELAGO   9
COFFIN BAY PENINSULA   10
BASCOMBE WELL CONSERVATION PARK   11
GREENLY ISLAND CONSERVATION PARK   12
LINCOLN   13
INNES   14
FLINDERS CHASE   15
SEAL BAY CONSERVATION PARK   16
CAPE GANTHEAUME CONSERVATION PARK   17
CLELAND CONSERVATION PARK   18
HALE CONSERVATION PARK   19
HINCKS CONSERVATION PARK   20
BELAIR RECREATION PARK   21
HAMBRIDGE CONSERVATION PARK   22
COORONG   23
GUM LAGOON CONSERVATION PARK   24
SCORPION SPRINGS CONSERVATION PARK   25
KARTE CONSERVATION PARK   26
MT RESCUE CONSERVATION PARK   27
GLEN ROY CONSERVATION PARK   28
NARACOORTE CAVES   29
NENE VALLEY CONSERVATION PARK   30
HACKS LAGOON CONSERVATION PARK   31
NGARKAT CONSERVATION PARK   32
BOOL LAGOON GAME RESERVE   33
RIDLEY CONSERVATION PARK   34
CANUNDA   35

216

SOUTH AUSTRALIA

Includes some 6 699 808 ha of parks and recreation areas occupying 6.8% of the state. Examples of most of the state's natural environments, containing varied plant and animal habitats and landscapes, are featured. Four categories of reserves, under the South Australian National Parks and Wildlife Act, exist. These are:

National Parks
Twelve areas of national significance due to wildlife or natural land features.

Conservation Parks
Feature valuable wildlife or interesting natural features representing varied South Australian habitats and landscapes.

Game Reserves
For the management of native game species.

Recreation Parks
Include sporting, picnic, barbecue and other public facilities.

Information on all reserves is obtainable from the National Parks and Wildlife Service (NPWS) Department of the Environment, 129 Greenhill Road, Unley, SA 5061, or from ranger headquarters throughout the State.

Bangham Conservation Park
13 km north of Frances, accessible by road from Beachport along the western side of Lake George.
738 ha of stringybarks, heath and gum flats and some cleared land.
Contact: Senior Ranger (Southern), NPWS, Adelaide.

Beachport Conservation Park
2 km north of Beachport by road from Beachport along the western side of Lake George.
710 ha of sand dunes, coastal vegetation and a little mallee around Lake George.
Contact: Senior Ranger (Southern), NPWS, Adelaide

Bascombe Well Conservation Park
70 km east of Elliston, Bascombe features beautiful stands of red gums, sheoaks and native pines. Plentiful mammals and 75 species of birds. Park covers 31 135 ha.
4WD access only, especially difficult in wet weather.
Contact: District Office, Coffin Bay.

*Belair Recreation Park
13 km south of Adelaide one of the world's oldest national parks.
835 ha containing flora reserve, recreation facilities and Old Government House.
Contact: Information Centre in the Park or NPWS Head Office, Unley.

Big Heath Conservation Park
32 km southeast of Lucindale Reached by metal road along northern boundary, 4 km west of Struan.
2351 ha of sandplain and swamp with limestone rises, pink gum, heath and mallee vegetation. Contains red-necked wallabies and various swamp-birds.
Contact: Senior Ranger (Southern), NPWS, Adelaide.

Billiatt Conservation Park
37 km north of Lameroo. Access via the Lameroo-Alawoon road which bisects the park.
36 815 ha of sandplain and sandhill with dense vegetation and several species of mallee. Wide variety of birdlife.
Contact: Senior Ranger (Southern), NPWS, Adelaide.

*Bool Lagoon Game Reserve
17 km south of Naracoorte, accessible from main Naracoorte-Penola Road by sealed road to Lagoon.
2689 ha of wetland supporting numerous waterbirds, including the state's largest breeding colony of ibis. Excellent seasonal duck shooting.
Contact: Senior Ranger (Southern), NPWS, Adelaide.

Brookfield Conservation Park
Home of the southern hairy-nosed wombat, Brookfield was a gift to the people of South Australia from the Chicago Zoological Society. 11 km west of Blanchetown, it features red mallee and native boxthorn. Access to some areas is prohibited, due to research on wombats. Picnic areas provided; camping prohibited.
Contact: Western Murray District Office, Blanchetown.

Bucks Lake Game Reserve
30 km west of Mt Gambier along the Mt Gambier-Carpenters Rocks Road.
1387 ha on the southern end of Lake Bonney.
Contact: Senior Ranger (Southern), NPWS, Adelaide.

*Canunda
On the coast 13 km west of Millicent and about 420 km southeast of Adelaide, accessible via Southend township.
9207 ha of coastal sand dunes, limestone cliffs, drifting live sand dunes and Aboriginal campsites (artefacts have been found). Many species of birds and few native mammals.
Contact: Ranger-in-Charge, Canunda National Park, Post Office, Southend.

*Cape Gantheaume Conservation Park
On the south coast of Kangaroo Island 50 km south of Kingscote. Access by road, except for the southern two-thirds of wilderness, accessible on foot only.
20 805 ha of low undulating limestone plateau, the outcrops forming sea cliffs, mallee scrub and coastal heath. Abundant animal and bird life.
Contact: NPWS, Unley, or the Murray's Lagoon Ranger.

Carcuma Conservation Park
18 km northeast of Coonalpyn. No access for standard vehicles.
2881 ha of steep sand dunes with mallee and heathlands on interdune flats.
Contact: Senior Ranger (Southern), NPWS, Adelaide.

*Cleland Conservation Park
In the Mt Lofty Ranges between Greenhill Road (north), Mt Lofty Summit Road (east), the South Eastern Freeway (south) and Waterfall Gully Road (west), close to Adelaide.
710 ha of woodland and forest formations with high ridges to the north and east and rolling ridges and valleys to the west. A few peat bogs support king ferns and 26 ha native fauna zone features native animals.
Contact: Ranger-in-Charge at the Park or NPWS, Unley.

Coffin Bay Peninsula
On the western coast of Eyre Peninsula about 60 km northwest of Port Lincoln.
30 000 ha. Includes coastal scenery with mallee scrub and sand dunes.
Contact: Ranger, Coffin Bay, or NPWS, Unley.

*Coorong
Includes Younghusband Peninsula across Coorong Lake to Princes Highway, bisected by Coorong Game Reserve. Access from Princes Highway south of Salt Creek.
38 987 ha of unique geology, typical maritime sand dune vegetation and wildlife sanctuary. Vehicles probibited on Peninsula.
Contact: Ranger-in-Charge at the park or NPWS, Adelaide.

Danggali Conservation Park

Covering 253 230 ha, Danggali is accessible from either Burra or Morgan. Large populations of red and grey kangaroos, and plentiful bird life. All supplies should be carried in, as this is a fairly remote area. Cabin-type accommodation is available for restricted numbers.
Contact: Canopus Homestead, Renmark.

*Elliot Price Conservation Park

Formerly Lake Eyre Wilderness National Park.
64 500 ha of arid area including most of Hunt Peninsula, Brooks Island and part of the bed of Lake Eyre.
Contact: NPWS, Adelaide.

Fairview Conservation Park

17 km north of Lucindale, accessible from metal road along western boundary. 1089 ha of stabilised dune system featuring forest heathland and wetland areas supporting mallee fowl and varied water birds and native animals.
Contact: Senior Ranger (Southern), NPWS, Adelaide.

The Coorong, setting for the movie Stormboy, *is a vital area in waterbird conservation (G. Deichmann/Weldon Trannies)*

Ferries-McDonald Conservation Park
17 km southwest of Murray Bridge, accessible by metal roads along the southern boundary and through the park.
845 ha, mostly flat with mallee-broombrush, a wattle stand and features mallee fowl and many other birds.
Contact: Senior Ranger (Southern), NPWS, Adelaide.

* Flinders Chase
At rugged western end of Kangaroo Island.
59 003 ha of heavy forest and mallee vegetation. The Chase contains several distinct untouched habitats, supporting about a dozen native mammals and about 200 species of birds.
Contact: Ranger-in-Charge, Park Headquarters, or NPWS, Unley.

* Flinders Ranges
North of Adelaide in the Flinders Ranges, accessible by road via Wilmington, Quorn and Hawker then on to Wilpena.
78 426 ha containing Wilpena Pound, a huge rock-rimmed amphitheatre, covering about 10 000 ha of the park's southern section. Semi-arid climate but higher rainfall within the Pound supports varied vegetation. Scenic mountains and varied wildlife found north of Wilpena.
Contact: Ranger-in-Charge, Park Headquarters at Oraparinna (Telephone Wilpena 48 0001, or NPWS, Unley.

* Gammon Ranges
In the northern Flinders Ranges, east of Copely.
15 538 ha of wilderness area similar to Flinders Ranges National Park.
Contact: NPWS, Unley.

Glen Roy Conservation Park
32 km north of Naracoorte. Access 3.2 km east of Penola-Naracoorte Road but not suitable for standard vehicles.
540 ha of regrown red gum woodland with stringybark forest on sandy areas.
Contact: Senior Ranger (Southern), NPWS, Adelaide, or Naracoorte Conservation Park, Naracoorte.

Greenly Island Conservation Park
Off Point Whidbey; stunted sheoaks and ti-tree, tammar wallabies (introduced) and bush rats. Breeding area for Cape Barren geese and fur seals. Few landing sites, and dangerous seas.
Contact: District Office, Coffin Bay.

Gum Lagoon Conservation Park
33 km southeast of Salt Creek, accessible by good road along northern boundary.
5862 ha of undulating sandy country, limestone rises with forest and heath, and some lagoons surrounded by red gums.
Contact: Senior Ranger (Southern), NPWS, Adelaide, or Ranger, Coorong National Park, Salt Creek.

* Hacks Lagoon Conservation Park
16 km south of Naracoorte, accessible by sealed road to Bool Lagoon from main Naracoorte-Penola Road, then all-weather track through Game Reserve to boundary (not accessible to public).
193 ha. Has shallow lagoon and marsh which constitute Bool Lagoon Game Reserve, providing a protected area for waterfowl.
Contact: Senior Ranger (Southern), NPWS, Adelaide, or Resident Ranger, Bool Lagoon Game Reserve.

Hale Conservation Park
Northeast of Adelaide.
191 ha of steep, hilly reserve overlooking the South Para Reservoir. Contains western grey kangaroos and other mammals.
Contact: NPWS, Unley.

Hambidge Conservation Park
Inland from the Eyre Peninsula.
37 991 ha of sand ridge and plain. Varied small native mammals, including the dormouse possum and the little bettong, and numerous reptiles.
Contact: NPWS, Adelaide.

Hincks Conservation Park
In the upper Eyre Peninsula south of Hambidge Conservation Park.
66 285 ha of typical sand plain country. Stabilised dunes to the north and rocky ridges to the south. Varied plant life, notably mallee and broombrush, and many small mammals and mallee birds.
Contact: NPWS, Adelaide.

Clearly definable salt deposits in Lake Eyre South (A Fox/Auscape)

*Innes

At the southwestern tip of Yorke Peninsula, about 300 km from Adelaide. 9131 ha of undulating mallee landscape, spectacular coastal scenery with limestone cliffs, historic mining areas at Inneston and Stenhouse Bay, and varied birdlife including the western whipbird.
Contact: Ranger-in-Charge at the Park or NPWS, Unley.

Isles of Anxious Bay

These limestone islands, and their narrow sandy beaches, once used for grazing and guano mining, are important nesting areas for sea birds, pelicans and rock parrots. Also included in the area are the islands of Baird Bay and Venus Bay. As with all the South Australian islands, full details should be sought from the NPWS, as tides, currents and landing areas may prove difficult.
Contact: Far Western District Office, Streaky Bay.

Isles of Coffin Bay Peninsula

Located at the extreme south-west tip of Eyre Peninsula, a series of islands composed of limestone and sand, and covered with varied vegetation. Favoured nesting sites for shearwaters and petrels; home to white-breasted sea eagles. Egrets and oyster catchers on beaches.
Contact: District Office, Coffin Bay.

Karte Conservation Park

30 km northwest of Pinnaroo, access from Pinnaroo-Karte siding road which runs along east boundary.
3565 ha of fairly steep sand dunes with mallee and tea tree, mallee birds and western grey kangaroo.
Contact: Senior Ranger (Southern), NPWS, Adelaide, or Resident Ranger, Loxton.

Kelly Hill Conservation Park
100 km southwest of Kingscote on the South Coast Road of Kangaroo Island.
6307 ha of consolidated coastal dunes and limestone ridges, featuring the Kelly Hill Caves, rugged coastal scenery and a beach at the Southwest River mouth.
Contact: Ranger-in-Charge at the Park or NPWS, Unley.

Kyeema Conservation Park
South of Adelaide and east of McLaren Vale.
349 ha of mainly eucalypt forest with varied animal and birdlife.
Contact: NPWS, Adelaide.

*Lake Gilles Conservation Park
On eastern shore of Lake Gilles, 100 km southwest of Port Augusta. Access via Eyre Highway.
45 114 ha of sand dunes, sparsely covered by myall, black oak woodland and some mallee.

*Lincoln
Just south of Port Lincoln.
17 226 ha of spectacular coastal scenery backed by flat country covered with dune limestone, and moonah, mallee wattle, sheoak and dense underbrush.
Contact: NPWS, Adelaide.

Little Dip Conservation Park
3 km south of Robe, access from the Robe-Nora-Creina Road.
1956 ha of coastal dunes with dense vegetation and small lakes, notably Lake Saint Clair and Lake Robe.
Contact: Senior Ranger (Southern), NPWS, Adelaide, or Resident Ranger, Canunda National Park.

Lowan Conservation Park
13 km southeast of Bow Hill. The Bow Hill-Karoonda Road runs along the eastern boundary.
673 ha of mallee scrub containing mallee fowl, wedge-tailed eagles, kangaroos, echidnas and fat-tailed marsupial mice.
Contact: Senior Ranger (Southern), NPWS, Adelaide, or Resident Ranger at Loxton.

Martins Washpool Conservation Park
11 km southeast of Salt Creek.
Inaccessible to conventional vehicles. Access 7 km southeast of Salt Creek on Highway 1 approximately 3 km from park boundary.
563 ha of open floor flats surrounded by tea-tree with red and pink gums on rises.
Contact: Senior Ranger (Southern), NPWS, Adelaide, or Resident Ranger, Coorong National Park.

Messent Conservation Park
6 km northeast of Salt Creek, accessible by sandy track from Salt Creek (impassable in wet conditions).
12 246 ha of sand plain and mallee on stabilised dunes, sedge flats, swamp and lake. Contains common wombats and echidnas.
Contact: Senior Ranger (Southern), NPWS, Adelaide, or Resident Ranger, Coorong National Park.

Morgan Conservation Park
At North-West Bend opposite Morgan on the River Murray, accessible by ferry from Morgan.
362 ha of red gump swamp on a River Murray billabong.
Contact: Senior Ranger (Southern), NPWS, Adelaide, or Resident Ranger, Loxton.

*Morialta Conservation Park
North of Adelaide and reached by the Norton Summit Road or Morialta Road from Tranmere, or Stradbroke Road from Rostrevor.
373 ha largely natural with many walking trails, ornamental gardens and waterfalls, two with a drop of 33 m each.
Spectacular cliff-top views, abundant bird life and spring wildflower displays.
Contact: NPWS, Adelaide, or Ranger-in-Charge at the park.

Mount Boothby Conservation Park
20 km west of Tintinara, accessible by all-weather approach roads from Culburra.
4045 ha. Features flats supporting considerable heath and mallee, some pink gum open forest and granite outcrops at Mt Boothby.
Contact: Senior Ranger (Southern), NPWS, Adelaide, or Resident Ranger, Coorong National Park.

Mount Remarkable, in the Flinders Ranges (Douglass Baglin)

*Mount Remarkable
In the lower Flinders Ranges.
8648 ha of rugged rocky country with spectacular rock formations, narrow gorges and varied rock-dwelling marsupials inhabiting the caves and crevices.
Contact: NPWS, Adelaide.

Mount Rescue Conservation Park
16 km north of Keith with a generally passable sand approach from Tintara.
28 385 ha of sand plains, stabilised dunes, heath, mallee-heath and broombrush with pink gum on the rises. Features Aboriginal camp sites and burial grounds and grey kangaroos, echidnas, emus and mallee fowl.
Contact: Senior Ranger (Southern), NPWS, Adelaide, or Resident Ranger, Coorong National Park.

Mount Shaugh Conservation Park
60 km northeast of Keith near the Victorian border. No access for standard vehicles.
3460 ha of irregular sand dunes with mallee and heathland vegetation.
Contact: Senior Ranger (Southern), NPWS, Adelaide, or Resident Ranger, Coorong National Park.

Mud Islands Game Reserve
10 small islands in Lake Alexandrina, accessible by boat from Clayton or Point Sturt.
138 ha. Supports water-birds on reed-bed fringes.
Contact: Senior Ranger (Southern), NPWS, Adelaide, or Resident Ranger, Strathalbyn.

Munyaroo Conservation Park
Access to 12 384 ha Munyaroo park is through private property, so directions must be gained from the District Office, Port Augusta. It is, however, well worth the effort. White coastal sand dunes, backed by mangroves, with extensive clay pans and open woodland on the undulating northern plain. Bird life is plentiful, with mulga parrots, Port Lincoln parrots, galahs, emus, mallee fowl and collared sparrowhawks.
Contact: District Office, Port Augusta.

*Naracoorte Caves Conservation Park
11 km southeast of Naracoorte, accessible by sealed road to park from main Naracoorte-Penola Road.
272 ha of gently undulating limestone country on top of Cave Range ridge with red gum river flat along Mosquito Creek. Limestone caves containing a fossil chamber and bent-winged bats open to the public.
Contact: Senior Ranger (Southern), NPWS, Adelaide, or Resident Ranger in the park.

Nene Valley Conservation Park
29 km southwest of Mount Gambier accessible by all-weather road.
373 ha of low coastal dunes, swampy areas and heath.
Contact: Senior Ranger (Southern), NPWS, Adelaide, or Resident Ranger, Mt Gambier.

Ngarkat Conservation Park
Ngarkat takes in 262 700 ha of wild rolling heaths and mallee. Animals include pigmy possums, dunnarts and echidnas; over 120 species of birds have been recorded. This is fairly remote country, 20 km to the north of Keith, and full directions should be gained from the NPWS before entering, as signposting is sparse.
Contact: Murraylands Regional Office, Berri.

Nuyts Archipelago
The 18 islands of this group are covered by two conservation parks, Nuyts Archipelago CP and Isles of St Francis CP. Possibly the inspiration behind Swift's 'Lilliput', they were charted by Pieter Nuyts. Low vegetation, sand beaches and many rock areas. Surprisingly varied wildlife.
Contact: Far West District Office, Streaky Bay.

Nuyts Reef
Treacherous rocks off Cape Adieu, west of Fowlers Bay. Sea lions bask above water mark; resting place for crested terns. Extreme care should be exercised.
Contact: Far West District Office, Streaky Bay.

*Nullarbor
On the Great Australian Bight on edge of the Nullarbor Plain, bisected by the Eyre Highway.
231 900 ha of typical coastal vegetation.
Contact: NPWS, Adelaide.

Padthaway Conservation Park
1.5 km east of Padthaway, accessible by metal roads along the northern and southern boundaries.
984 ha of blue gum forest, some stringybark heather understorey, tall banksias, grey kangaroos, red-necked wallabies and echidnas.
Contact: Senior Ranger (Southern), NPWS, Adelaide, or Resident Ranger, Bool Lagoon Game Reserve.

Peebinga Conservation Park
30 km east of Pinnaroo, from the Pinnaroo-Loxton Road along the eastern boundary.
3371 ha of sand plain with low stabilised dunes supporting mallee and tea-tree, orchids and mallee birds.
Contact: Senior Ranger (Southern), NPWS, Adelaide, or Resident Ranger, Loxton.

Penola Conservation Park
11 km west of Penola accessible from the main Penola-Robe road.
226 ha of stringybark forest, heath and bracken understorey, swamp, numerous marsupials and a variety of reptiles.
Contact: Senior Ranger (Southern), NPWS, Adelaide, or Resident Ranger, Canunda National Park.

Piccaninnie Ponds Conservation Park
On the south coast near the Victorian border, access by metal road from Mt Gambier-Nelson road.
397 ha. Features permanent lakes and swamps fed by underground springs. Deep limestone caves attract divers (permit required).
Contact: Senior Ranger, Mt Gambier.

Pooginook Conservation Park
12 km northeast of Waikerie via the Morgan-Barmera Highway on the southern boundary.
2851 ha of low parallel sand ridges supporting mallee and porcupine grass with semi-arid shrub communities between the dunes.
Contact: Senior Ranger (Southern), NPWS, Adelaide, or Resident Ranger, Loxton.

Ridley Conservation Park
5 km south of Swan Reach, access along metal road running south between Swan Reach and Mannum.
414 ha. Contains disused stock route, remnant of false sandalwood community, some mallee and hairy-nosed wombats.
Contact: Senior Ranger (Southern), NPWS, Adelaide, or Resident Ranger, Loxton.

Scorpion Springs Conservation Park

18 km south of Pinnaroo. Metal road goes within 1 km of park then sandy track generally unsuitable for standard vehicles.

30 366 ha of tumbled dunes, irregular interdunes, freshwater springs and vegetation ranging from low open forest to heathland. Dingo habitat.

Contact: Senior Ranger (Southern), NPWS, Adelaide, or Resident Ranger, Loxton.

* Seal Bay Conservation Park

On the southern coast of Kangaroo Island, 50 km south of Kingscote.

700 ha of spectacular coastal scenery, and very accessible sea-lion colony.

Contact: NPWS, Unley, or the Murray's Lagoon Ranger.

* Simpson Desert Conservation Park

In the state's arid north.

692 680 ha of live sand dune desert with long parallel dunes running in the direction of prevailing winds, and varied animals including dingoes and camels. Varied plant life after good rainfalls.

Contact: NPWS, Unley.

Sir Joseph Banks Group Conservation Park

Situated at southern end of Spencer Gulf, an important breeding area for Cape Barren geese. Permission for entry must be gained before visiting these islands.

Contact: District Office, Port Lincoln.

Spring Gully Conservation Park

Near the centre of Adelaide, just east of Cleland Conservation Park.

405 ha. Contains unique red stringybarks, grey kangaroos and euros.

Contact: NPWS, Unley.

Swan Reach Conservation Park

11 km west of Swan Reach. The northern corner abuts the Swan Reach-Sedan Road.

2016 ha of false sandalwood open woodland with a grassy understorey, areas of dense mallee and bullock bush. Home of emus, western grey kangaroos and hairy-nosed wombats.

Contact: Senior Ranger (Southern), NPWS, Adelaide, or Resident Ranger, Loxton.

* Unnamed Conservation Park

A huge boomerang-shaped reserve in the northwest of the state on the border with Western Australia.

2 132 600 ha mulga, myall, spinifex, black oak, bluebush and marble gum stands.

Contact: NPWS, Adelaide.

Warren Conservation Park

Northeast of Adelaide close to Hale Conservation Park.

363 ha of steep, rugged country with lush undergrowth and tall timbers.

Contact: NPWS, Unley.

Whites Dam Conservation Park

6 km northwest of Morgan. The Morgan-Burra road abuts the Park.

911 ha of black oak woodland dominating an arid bluebush and herb community. Includes part of the Old Morgan-Burra travelling-stock route.

Contact: Senior Ranger (Southern), NPWS, Adelaide, or Resident Ranger, Loxton.

* Yumbarra Conservation Park

In the state's northwest, north of Koonibba Hill and Koonibba Mission.

106 190 ha of arid desert country with mallee and dune vegetation and waterholes occurring in granite outcrops.

Contact: NPWS, Unley.

WESTERN AUSTRALIA

Western Australia has the greatest area of parks and reserves in Australia and eventually up to 20 million hectares or almost 8 per cent of the state could become national park land. The National Parks Authority of WA, created 1976, is quite separate from the Wildlife Service, although they work in co-operation. Four broad categories of park exist. These are:
Natural areas
Generally in their natural state but with limited public access.
Wilderness areas
Completely unspoilt with foot access only.
Special areas
To protect plants, animals or other distinctive features.
Facilities areas
Provide amenities for visitors.
Reserves are classified as A, B or C, giving the park varying degrees of security against future legislative tampering. For example, Class A reserves cannot have their purpose changed except by Act of Parliament. Information about these areas is available from the NPA head office at Hackett Drive, Nedlands, WA 6009, or from rangers at individual parks.

Abrolhos Islands
Island group 60 km north west of Geraldton. Class A reserve controlled by the Minister for Fisheries and Wildlife. Noted for seabird life, the tammar wallaby and a non-venomous python and visited by turtles and hair seals. Humpback whales and dolphins sighted off the reefs.

Alexander Morrison
Class A reserve located north of Perth, northwest of Jurien Bay.
8501 ha comprising three smaller reserves and containing typical coastal plants and animals.
Contact: Ranger-in-Charge, Nambung National Park.

Avon Valley
Class A reserve located in the Darling Scarp river valleys. Limited access.
4377 ha containing magnificent scenery representative of the transition zone between forest block and wheat belt country.
Contact: Ranger-in-Charge.

*Badgingarra
Northeast of Cervantes township and Nambung National Park.
13 121 ha containing the black kangaroo paw and numerous rare and restricted plant species.

Boorabbin
Class A reserve adjacent to the Great Eastern Highway west of Boorabbin.
26 000 ha of sand-plain shrubland.

*Cape Arid
Class A reserve on the coast between Cape le Grand and Israelite Bay.
279 415 ha of magnificent scenery and views from the Lookout, plus the Belinup Hill Nature Trail, the first of its kind to be developed in a WA national park.

* Cape Le Grand
Class A reserve on the south coast 32 km east of Esperance, facing the Recherche islands.
31 390 ha of magnificent coastal scenery with granite peaks, swamps rich in birdlife, and a sandy beach.

* Cape Range
Class A reserve on the northwest coast near Exmouth; includes part of former Yardie Creek Station.
50 581 ha. Includes rugged limestone hills, deeply eroded gorges and picturesque coastline where many unique birds and creatures live.
Contact: Ranger, Exmouth.

* Chichester Range
Class A reserve in the Pilbara area south of Roebourne.
150 609 ha of great scenic beauty with popular Python Pool.
Contact: Ranger, Hamersley Range National Park, or Mobile Ranger based at Millstream during winter months.

* Collier Range
Class A reserve between the upper reaches of the Ashburton and Gascoyne Rivers.
277 841 ha of ungrazed spinifex and soft grass country.

D'Entrecasteaux
Series of Class A reserves along the southwest coast between Lake Jasper and the Walpole-Nornalup National Park.
36 599 ha sand dune, heathland, scrubland and woodland with smaller areas of karri, marri and jarrah forest.

Drovers Cove
North of Jurien Bay.
2681 ha of typical coastal plants and animals.
Contact: Ranger-in-Charge, Nambung National Park.

* Drysdale River
North Kimberley region; includes the Ashton Range and Carson Escarpment.
435 591 ha of diverse scenery with gorges, cliffs, broad rivers, including the Drysdale, plains, spectacular waterfalls, low, open forest, low woodland and small vine thickets with fringing communities along creeks and around swamps.
Contact: National Parks Authority before entering area.

Eucla
Class A reserve on the south coast at the WA-South Australian border.
3342 ha of arid to semi-arid sand hills, mallee country and coastal limestone cliffs.

* Fitzgerald River
On the South Coast between the Gairdner, Fitzgerald and Phillips Rivers, west of Culham Inlet and Hopetoun.
242 739 ha. Features magnificent coastal and mountain scenery, the Fitzgerald and Hamersley River gorges, and unique flora and fauna.
Contact: Ranger at Jerramungup.

Frank Hann
Two 1.5 km strips of land located either side of the Lake King-Norseman Road.
49 877 ha. Features cross-section of the wheat belt's heath flora.

* Geikie Gorge
16 km from Fitzroy Crossing in the Oscar Range
3136 ha. Contains scenic gorge in an ancient limestone barrier reef and sea creatures now adapted to freshwater. River trips available in dry season.

* Hamersely Range
State's second-largest park in the Pilbara Region.
617 606 ha of spectacular mountains, gorges, water courses and plateaux; notable for the Fortescue Falls, Circular Pool, Dales Gorge, Joffre Falls and Red Gorge.
Contact: Ranger-in-Charge, Park Headquarters.

Hassell
Class A reserve along the main Albany-Bremer Bay Road southeast of Perth.
1269 ha of flora and fauna.

* John Forrest
Class A reserve in the Darling Ranges about 27 km from Perth. Access by three entrances off Great Eastern Highway.
1578 ha of open forest and woodland, spring wildflower displays and a natural swimming pool.
Contact: Ranger-in-Charge, Park Headquarters.

Kalamunda
Class A reserve east of Perth and north of Armidale.
375 ha, mainly undeveloped, rich in wildflowers, particularly blue leschenaultia.

*Kalbarri
Class A reserve 644 km north of Perth near the mouth of the Murchison River.
186 096 ha with outstanding gorge scenery along the river, historic Wittecarra Gully, magnificent limestone and sandstone cliffs and numerous wildflowers.

Kings Park
Class A reserve located in the heart of Perth.
400 ha with botanic garden and areas of largely undisturbed or regenerated bushland.

*Leeuwin-Naturaliste
Series of Class A reserves along the coast between Cape Naturaliste and Cape Leeuwin.
15 493 ha of spectacular coastal scenery with heathland and forest, and many limestone caves, some, like Mammoth Cave and Devils Lair, containing fossils.

Millstream
Class A reserve at Millstream on the Fortescue River.
441 ha with 'staircase' series of pools providing an oasis in one of Australia's driest parts.

Moore River
113 km north of Perth.
17 453 ha left undeveloped. Swan coastal plain notable for outstanding wildflowers.

The limestone cliffs of Geikie Gorge
(Lee Pearce)

*Nambung

200 km north of Perth off the Geraldton Highway, south of Jurien Bay.
17 491 ha, including the picturesque 400 ha Pinnacles Desert containing thousands of limestone pillars, low sand plain heaths with wildflower displays, and a cave system along the Nambung River. Caves often sealed to prevent vandalism.
Contact: Ranger, Cervantes.

Neerabup

Class A reserve on the Perth-Yanchep Road just north of Wanneroo.
1078 ha. Notable for its spearwood formation limestone.

Peak Charles

Class C reserve.
39 959 ha with spectacular granite outcrops, panoramic scenery and representative southwest flora.

*Reefs and rocks, Rottnest Island
(H&J Beste/Auscape)*

Pemberton

Along Old Vasse Road near Pemberton.
Includes Warren (1356 ha), Beedalup (1531 ha), Brockman (48 ha), Pemberton (122 ha) and 206 ha of miscellaneous reserves.
All feature outstanding karri forest.

*Porongurup

Class A reserve between the Stirling Range National Park and Albany.
2401 ha with granite peaks of the karri-covered Porongurup Ranges and many wildflowers, native animals and abundant birdlife.
Contact: Park Ranger.

Rottnest Island

16 km from the mainland by air or launch from Fremantle.
2000 ha including extensive salt lakes edged with freshwater seepages which attract birds. Known for the quokkas or small wallabies.

Nature's Window, a miracle of erosion, Kalbarri National Park

* Rudall River
Near the Rudall River, east from Roy Hill and Nullagine.
1 569 459 ha sand dune and salt lake systems of the Northeast Pilbara.

Scott
Class A reserve 6.4 km northeast of August townsite at Scott and Blackwood river junction.
3273 ha of jarrah, marri and karri forests.

Serpentine
Class A reserve southeast of Perth and east of Kwinana.
635 ha with scenic river and waterfall and interesting rock formations.
Contact: Resident Ranger.

Sir James Mitchell
Class A reserve of 100 metre wide strips stretching each side of the South West Highway for 64 km north of Walpole to Northcliffe turn-off, covering 1087 ha.

* Stirling Range
Class A reserve 322 km southeast of Perth and 80 km north of Albany, accessible by sealed Chester Pass road from Albany.
115 671 ha enclosing the entire Stirling Range mountain system. Wildflowers, mountain peaks (1073 m), dense scrub with forests of jarrah, yate and wandoo and abundant local plant species.
Contact: Resident Ranger.

* Stokes
On the south coast of WA adjoining Stokes Inlet and Lake Gobinup reserve, west of Esperance.
9493 ha of waterway foreshores.
Contact: Ranger-in-Charge, Stokes National Park.

Tathra
Class A reserve southeast of Geraldton and east of the Geraldton Highway.
4323 ha of natural moorland, scrub and heathland; noted for wildflowers.

* Torndirrup
Southwest of Albany on King George Sound
3868 ha. Includes flora, fauna and rugged coastal scenery, particularly the rock formations known as The Gap and Natural Bridge.
Contact: Resident Ranger.

* Tunnel Creek
184 km east of Derby and 29 km southeast of Windjana Gorge National Park.
91 ha featuring Tunnel Creek, which penetrates the Napier Range through a large limestone tunnel.

* Walpole-Nornalup
On the south coast of WA, 418 km southeast of Perth, reached via South Western Highway, National Route 1 and South Coast Highway.
18 116 ha, with Frankland and Deep Rivers surrounded by karri and tingle high forest, and fine coastal scenery, including the Walpole and Nornalup Inlets, for 40 km from Irwin Inlet to Cliffy Head.
Contact: Resident Ranger.

Walyunga
37 km northeast of Perth.
1790 ha with scenic views, woodland, flora and Aboriginal history. Good picnic spots.
Contact: Resident Ranger.

Watheroo
Class A reserve north of Perth and west of the Great Northern Highway.
44 324 ha of native flora and fauna.
Contact: Ranger, Cervantes.

* William Bay
Small park on the south coast, west of Albany.
1902 ha of flora, fauna and coastal scenery, backed by scrubland and heath.

* Windjana Gorge
Situated in the Kimberleys.
2134 ha. Contains the winding Lennard River canyon 4 km long and up to 76 m high, through the Napier Range. Its pools harbour fish, waterbirds and fringing vegetation with native figs clinging to the rock faces.

* Wolf Creek Crater
104 km south of Halls Creek.
1460 ha containing a meteorite crater 800 m wide, 49 m deep with an area of 1296 ha.

* Yalgorup
Class A reserve on the coastal plain south of Mandurah.
11 545 ha. Contains a parallel lakes system noted for birdlife. Wood and heathland, interesting geological features and flora and animal life.
Contact: Resident Ranger.

* Yanchep
Class A reserve 53 km north of Perth on the Wanneroo Road.
2799 ha mostly in its natural state. It contains caves, tourist facilities, fauna exhibits, bushland and Loch McNess, home for waterfowl and other birds.
Contact: Resident Ranger.

MAJOR RESERVES

Charles Gardner Flora Reserve
Class A reserve south of Tammin.
792 ha of outstanding botanical interest.

Haddleton Flora Reserve
South of the Wellington Dam catchment area in the south-west of the state.
1325 ha reserved for the protection of boronia and other flora.

Penguin Island Sanctuary
Class A reserve 48 km south of Perth and 1.6 km offshore near Safety Bay.
13 ha. Contains protected penguin rookery. Part of the island leased as a holiday centre.

Stockyard Gully
Near the west coast north of Yanchep.
1406 ha conserving local flora, water and caves.

Yanchep Flora Reserve
Class A reserve 48 km north of Perth.
113 ha preserving local flora.

The view from Bluff Knoll,
Stirling Ranges National Park
(J–P Ferrero/Auscape)

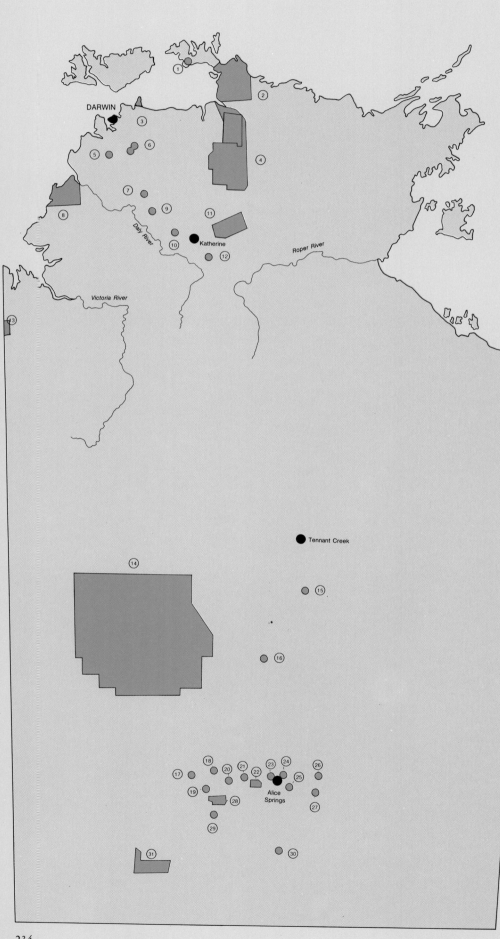

GURIG NATIONAL PARK   1
MURGENELLA WILDLIFE SANCTUARY   2
FOGG DAM   3
KAKADU NATIONAL PARK   4
BERRY SPRINGS NATURE PARK   5
HOWARD SPRINGS NATURE PARK   6
DOUGLAS HOT SPRINGS NATURE PARK   7
DALY RIVER WILDLIFE SANCTUARY   8
UMBRAWARRA GORGE NATURE PARK   9
KINTORE CAVES NATURE PARK   10
KATHERINE GORGE   11
CUTTA CUTTA CAVES   12
KEEP RIVER   13
TANAMI DESERT WILDLIFE SANCTUARY   14
DEVILS MARBLES CONSERVATION RESERVE   15
CENTRAL MOUNT STUART   16
REDBANK NATURE RESERVE   17
ORMISTON GORGE AND POUND   18
GLEN HELEN GORGE NATURE PARK   19
SERPENTINE GORGE NATURE PARK   20
ELLERY CREEK BIG HOLE NATURE PARK   21
SIMPSONS GAP   22
JOHN FLYNN'S GRAVE   23
ALICE SPRINGS TELEGRAPH STATION   24
EMILY AND JESSE GAPS NATURE PARK   25
TREPHINA GORGE NATURE PARK   26
N'DHALA GORGE NATURE PARK   27
FINKE GORGE   28
ILLAMURTA SPRINGS CONSERVATION RESERVE   29
CHAMBERS PILLAR   30
ULURU   31

NORTHERN TERRITORY

The Conservation Commission of the Northern Territory (CC of NT) was created in April 1980 and replaces both the former Northern Territory Reserves Board and the Territory Parks and Wildlife Commission.

Two national parks in the Northern Territory, Kakadu and Uluru, are managed by the Australian National Parks and Wildlife Service in Canberra. Five categories of land exist to preserve the state's natural and cultural features. These are:

National Parks
Large unspoilt natural conservation areas managed with minimal interference and available for public enjoyment and education.

Nature Parks
Smaller nature areas, usually offering more amenities for visitors.

Conservation Reserves
To protect features of particular scientific value.

Historical Reserves
Preserving sites of significant historical value.

Wildlife Sanctuaries
No longer controlled by CC of NT, but by traditional owners. Check entry details thoroughly before entering.

Game Reserves
For game management; some shooting under permit.

Information on these areas can be obtained from the Commission's Northern Region office, PO Box 38496, Winnellie, NT 5789.

Alice Springs Telegraph Station Historical Reserve
4 km north of Alice Springs. Turn right off the Stuart Highway to the car park. 445 ha commemorating the Overland Telegraph line constructors. Includes historic Telegraph Station, marked walking tracks and ranger-guided tours May to September.
Contact: Ranger, CC of NT, Alice Springs.

Arltunga Historical Reserve
111 km east of Alice Springs, in the eastern end of the MacDonnell Ranges. Access by Ross Highway or east off Stuart Highway 48 km north of Alice Springs through Garden and Ambalindum cattle stations.
Ruins of 1800s goldmining town.
Contact: Ranger, CC of NT, Alice Springs.

Berry Springs Nature Park
64 km south of Darwin, turning right off the Stuart Highway, on to Bynoe Road. 247 ha including natural spring and creek with pleasant, safe swimming. Abundant birdlife.
Contact: Ranger, Berry Springs, or CC of NT, Darwin.

Central Mount Stuart Historical Reserve
222 km north of Alice Springs. 2592 square metres. Contains cairn commemorating John McDouall Stuart, discoverer of Australia's geographical centre.
Contact: Ranger, Tennant Creek.

*Chambers Pillar Historical Reserve
161 km south of Alice Springs. 340 ha containing sheer sandstone pillar 33 m high and 6 m wide, rising from remote semi-desert terrain and inscribed with names of pioneers and early travellers.
Contact: Ranger, Alice Springs.

Cobourg Marine Park
Situated off the coast of Gurig National Park, a marine reserve of 229 000 ha. Includes reefs, seagrass beds and tropical marine animals.
Contact: Ranger, Black Point or CC of NT.

Cutta Cutta Caves Nature Park
West of the Stuart Highway, 26 km south of Katherine.
1499 ha featuring disctinctive karst landscape associated with Tindall limestone, a cavernous rock formed 500 million years ago. Abundant wildlife and some rare species. Walks and underground tours during dry season.
Contact: Ranger, CC of NT, Katherine.

Daly River Wildlife Sanctuary
On Daly River in north.
258 933 ha of coastal wetland formerly part of Daly River Aboriginal Reserve and now Aboriginal-owned.

Devils Marbles Conservation Reserve
418 km north of Alice Springs, traversed by the Stuart Highway.
1828 ha featuring the unusual 'balancing rocks' geological formation.
Contact: Ranger, Tennant Creek.

Douglas Hot Springs Nature Park
117 km south of Darwin.
3107 ha now offering improved access and car parking.
Contact: Ranger, Pine Creek.

*Ellery Creek Big Hole Nature Park
93 km west of Alice Springs.
1766 ha. Features a large permanent waterhole, popular for swimming and picnicking, formed by the Ellery Creek as it flows through a break in the MacDonnell Ranges.
Contact: CC of NT, Alice Springs.

*Emily and Jessie Gaps Nature Park
East of Alice Springs on the Ross River Road.
695 ha. Contains section of range broken by two attactive gaps and semi-permanent waterholes.
Contact: Ranger, Alice Springs.

*Finke Gorge National Park
138 km west of Alice Springs just south of Hermannsburg Mission along unsealed road 4WD vehicles.
46 000 ha of wilderness including the Finke River Gorge and Palm Valley (north) and sand dunes (south). Comprehensive Australian plant collections. Walking tours marked by natural landmarks, and commercial tours available.
Contact: Ranger, CC of NT, Alice Springs.

Fogg Dam Reserve
60 km south-west of Darwin off the Arnhem Highway. Possibly the finest bird habitat close to Darwin. Waterbirds in their thousands. Part of the failed Humpty Doo rice project.
Contact: CC of NT, Darwin.

*Glen Helen Gorge Nature Park
135 km west of Alice Springs.
386 ha. Contains a permanent waterhole where the Finke River flows through the ranges.
Contact: Ranger, Alice Springs.

*Gurig National Park
A remote coastal reserve covering 191 659 ha, jointly managed by the traditional owners and CC of NT. Includes the historical reserves of Fort Wellington and Victoria Settlement.
Contact: Ranger, Black Point or CC of NT.

Howard Springs Nature Park
30 km south of Darwin, 283 ha, access by side-road turning left off Stuart Highway.
Features natural spring swimming pool and rainforest pocket.
Contact: Ranger, Howard Springs.

Illamurta Springs Conservation Reserve
East of Alice Springs.
129 ha scenic reserve, permanent water, limited development and minimal visitors.

John Flynn's Grave Historical Reserve
5 km west of Alice Springs on Larapinta Drive.
3363 square metres. Contains memorial and grave of Rev. John Flynn (Flynn of the Inland).

*Black Point Lagoon, in Gurig
National Park, Cobourg
Peninsula
(F Woerle/Auscape)*

* Kakadu National Park

A vast area between the East and South
Alligator Rivers, and stretching from the
escarpment to the sea.
Kakadu includes 100 km of 250 metre
sandstone cliffs, thousands of Aboriginal
rock paintings at sites such as Nouriangie
Rocks, and the 200 metre high Jim Jim
Falls.
Contact: Australian National Parks and
Wildlife Service, Woden, ACT.

*Katherine Gorge

30 km west of Katherine.
180 352 ha. Contains sandstone plateau
and escarpment dissected by streams
and the 13 km Katherine River gorge.
Incorporates Edith Falls Nature Park.
Contact: Ranger, or CC of NT, Darwin.

Keep River National Park

Close to the WA border, north of the
Victoria Highway, 26 200 ha of
sandstone escarpment. Contains
examples of Aboriginal rock art.
Contact: Ranger, Keep River or CC of
NT, Katherine.

Kintore Caves Nature Park

North of Katherine.
423 ha. Possesses Tindall limestone
formation. Not open to the public; cave
viewing provided at Cutta Cutta Caves.

Murgenella Wildlife Sanctuary

Aboriginal-owned reserve on the
Murgenella Creek, Mini Mini Creek and
Malay Bay black soil plains.
310 719 ha.

237

N'Dhala Gorge Nature Park
88 km east of Alice Springs.
501 ha featuring rock drawings of sacred ritual head-dress said to prove that such decorations date back 10 000 years.
Contact: Ranger, Alice Springs.

*Ormiston Gorge and Pound
132 km west of Alice Springs via Larapinta drive and the Glen Helen Road. 4655 ha of scenic MacDonnell Ranges wilderness, containing Ormiston Gorge, a deep passage carved through quartzite by Ormiston Creek and ending in a permanent waterhole, and Ormiston Pound, a rugged natural enclosure 10 km across and surrounded by high ridges.
Contact: Ranger or CC of NT, Alice Springs.

*Redbank Nature Reserve
161 km west of Alice Springs in the MacDonnell Ranges.
1295 ha of outstanding scenery with one vehicular track terminating some distance from Ormiston Gorge.
Contact: Ranger, Ormiston Gorge.

Ruby Gorge Nature Park
90 km east of Alice Springs, 9257 ha containing water holes, steep rocky ridges and typical Central Australian vegetation.
Contact: CC of NT, Alice Springs.

*Serpentine Gorge Nature Park
101 km west of Alice Springs.
518 ha with permanent water encouraging fauna, and beautiful scenery.

*Simpsons Gap
8 km west of Alice Springs, accessible via Larapinta Drive. Rocky Gap, Bond Gap and Wallaby Gap provide foot access to the northern wilderness area. 30 950 ha of typical MacDonnell Range country and wildlife.
Contact: Ranger, CC of NT, Alice Springs.

Tanami Desert Wildlife Sanctuary
East of Tennant Creek.
3 752 900 ha. Aboriginal-owned.

*Trephina Gorge Nature Park
80 km east of Alice Springs.
1771 ha scenic reserve popular with tour operators.

*Uluru (Ayers Rock-Mt Olga) National Park
470 km southwest of Alice Springs.
126 132 ha of arid central Australia. Open landscape of sandplains, dunes and mulga wood dominated by Ayers Rock and the Olgas.
Contact: Ranger or Australian National Parks and Wildlife Service, Woden, ACT.

Umbrawarra Gorge Nature Park
25 km southwest of Pine Creek.
972 ha of unspoiled scenic gorges.
Contact: Ranger, Pine Creek.

A rare sight indeed: water lying deep on the ground in the Tanami Desert (G. Robertson/Auscape)

Index of Parks

This index covers National Parks and other parks and reserves listed in the Reference section. Names of National Parks are listed in **bold** type. References to illustrations are in *italic* type.